Jesus!
May I lick the bowl?

Jesus!
May I lick the bowl?

Willie Jewel Tabb

authorHOUSE®

AuthorHouse™ LLC
1663 Liberty Drive
Bloomington, IN 47403
www.authorhouse.com
Phone: 1-800-839-8640

Published by AuthorHouse 05/31/2014

ISBN: 978-1-4969-0710-3 (sc)
ISBN: 978-1-4969-0637-3 (e)

Library of Congress Control Number: 2014907788

Any people depicted in stock imagery provided by Thinkstock are models, and such images are being used for illustrative purposes only. Certain stock imagery © Thinkstock.

This book is printed on acid-free paper.

Because of the dynamic nature of the Internet, any web addresses or links contained in this book may have changed since publication and may no longer be valid. The views expressed in this work are solely those of the author and do not necessarily reflect the views of the publisher, and the publisher hereby disclaims any responsibility for them.

Acknowledgement

One of the marks of living a meaningful, spirit filled life is sharing it with others for the greatest good, and knowing that you have enriched the lives of others by sharing a part of yourself. I gratefully acknowledge the memory of the late, Selena Clemmons, a teacher and educator, who believed in me and made possible my very first poetry recital at Dunbar Elementary School as a student there during the early years of my childhood. Also, I honor the memory of the late Jim Collier, photographer, poet, artist, author, entrepreneur and multi-talented church member of mine who introduced me to a larger listening audience through the world of televised appearances. Having written poetry from a child into adulthood, there is no way I can begin to express my appreciation and heartfelt thanks to all who have encouraged me down through the years to become the author of published works, or those who supported me financially through purchases of poetry calendar fundraisers for my church home. If I have touched your life in some way poetically, thank you for allowing me to share my gift with you. And while I have acknowledged some who are no longer here, and sincerely attempted to thank all with whom I have shared a part of myself, I now shed light on a few who have impacted my world in an unforgettable way. Dr. Cloteal Morgan, Founder and Pastor of Redemption Ministries, Thank you! Having ministered through poetry as your co-host on KSTL, 690 A.M., was a dream come true. To a powerful Prayer Warrior, entrepreneur, scholar, teacher, Audio Technician, Visionary, and dear Sister in Christ, I express my sincere appreciation for your loyal support and prayers. Additionally, I am thankful to Dr. Delena King, who persistently prodded me into action whenever I tended to slack off short of reaching my goal. Prayer changes things! I express my gratefulness to Linda Tompkins, a Prayer Warrior, my church member, and dear friend, who faithfully prayed without ceasing for this devotional book to come forth, and to Linda's beautiful and talented mother, Poetess, Daisy Barnett, thank you, for your collection of inspirational poems included in this book.

This devotional book is lovingly dedicated to my husband, Bobby Tabb, our two children, Kevin Tabb and Eva Marie Kain and their families, and to all of my precious, eight grandchildren, Taylor, Ava Camille, Logan, Landon, Leila, Ella Faith, (my little angel), Danielle, Mariah, and my God son, George Nicholas Frazier III. Additionally, I honor the loving memories of my parents, Alton and Luella Phelps, grandfather, Albert Phelps, and my only sibling and big brother, Ordell Phelps. Also, I salute in loving memory, my friend in Christ, Dr. Leslie C. Chaney, an anointed and appointed man of God, who crossed over into glory on Good Friday, March 29, 2013.

Dedication

"JESUS! May I lick the bowl?" is dedicated to the following special people in my life who are all family: The late John (Nonnie) Jennings, known as the "Voice of Barry Field" and his surviving wife, (Mimi) Norma L. Jennings; grandparents of Taylor, Ava Camille, Logan, Landon, Leila, and angel, Ella Faith, all of whom are also the grandchildren of Bobby and Willie (Jewel) Tabb. Parents are Kevin and Jennifer Tabb.

Additionally, sharing the role of grandparents including Bob (Papa) and (Beba) Jewel Tabb, are Steven and Linda Kain, better known as (Gum PA) and (Granny Linda); and they are the grandparents of Danielle and Mariah Kain. Parents are Phillip and Eva Marie Kain.

All grandchildren are featured as follows:

Danielle Tene' front and back cover of book; also page 57 and page 318

Mariah Necole, page 57 and page 312

Leila Ruth, page 315

Left to right, Landon John and Logan Quinn, Page 320

Left to right, Ava Camille, Leila, Landon, Taylor, and Logan, page 376

Left to right, Ava Camille, and Taylor, and Center, from top to bottom, Logan, Leila, and Landon, page 390

Left to right, Landon, Leila, Logan, and representation of Ella Faith, personalized Angel Bear, page 392

Table of Contents

Introduction

Jesus! May I Lick the Bowl?

Oh taste and see that the Lord is good. And blessed are those who believe and put their trust in Him. (Ps 34:8).

Remember when you just couldn't wait to lick the bowl, the spoon, and the beaters clean immediately after mama had finally finished and poured the last of the batter into the cake pan in order to bake a mouth watering, sweet and tasty, butter pound cake?

Mama, may I lick the bowl? The batter is so sweet.
I can hardly wait to taste the cake we're gonna eat.
Mama, may I lick the spoon? Please hurry up! Get done!
Just let me have a little taste. I'm such an anxious one.

I love your homemade icing! Tell you what let's do.
Let me lick the beaters clean. I'll do it just for you.
Mama, may I lick the bowl? I'm your little cleanup crew.
You need not wash anything. I'll leave it spotless just for you.

Have you ever tasted Jesus? Desire to experience God, and savor the flavor of His sweetness with the same eagerness and anticipation, for He is good unlike anything you can ever experience or phantom on your own. God deserves to be tasted. So taste the variety of various flavors of this devotional guide which includes daily devotions for each day of the year, several Bible story-telling poems pertaining to men and women of Bible days, words of wisdom for married couples, children and youth poetry, Black History poetry, poems about mothers, memorial tributes, inspirational poetry of Poetess, Daisy L. Barnett and seven poetry devotional calendars. * Please note that the very first Poetry Devotional Calendar of 1995, "Time is Running Out, So Run That You May Obtain the Prize!" poetically spells out each month of the year in the book. The more you taste Jesus, the more you will crave for Him and His goodness. He is so indescribably delicious that once you taste of Him you will find yourself repeatedly asking, "Jesus! May I Lick The Bowl?"

January

This is a day that the Lord has made, so let us rejoice and be glad in it. (Ps 118:24)

> **J**esus is the only way.
> **A**lways take time to pray.
> **N**ever lay God's work aside.
> **U**nderneath His wings abide
> **A**nd walk with Him, side by side.
> **R**eclaim what Satan has taken away.
> **Y**ield unto the Potter. Today is your day!

It's January! Begin this day, to appreciate the goodness and mercy of our Heavenly Father. He gave His only son, Jesus, and He alone is the only way into salvation. Persist to avoid occasional lapses in spirit filled, daily devotions. Pray faithfully without ceasing. Of course, there are going to be days when busyness and distractions will surely happen, but never put God's work on the back burner. Always put Him first on your agenda and all else will work out accordingly. Stay closer than close to God and reside in His secret dwelling place, and you will endlessly abide underneath the shadow of His forever peaceful and protective wings. (Ps 91:1). Desire to walk with God! Can you think of a better walking buddy?

A Fixed Heart

Oh! My God! My heart is fixed. I will sing and give praise even with my glory. (Ps 108:1).

Recently at the 'Y', we were informed that music was banned from aquatic exercise classes due to safety regulations. This, of course, caused quite a stir among some; however, without the absence of music, the beat still goes on. Let me explain. No matter who we are, there are times when we must make our own music. How so? With a fixed heart, we can still pluck the harp, clash the cymbal, or strike a chord, and the music of the soul will joyfully resound. We are all melody makers because music resides in each soul.

> When life seems void of music,
> I will praise the Lord, and sing a song.
> My heart is fixed in Jesus Christ,
> To Him, I belong.

A Hungry Jack

Hell and destruction are never full; so the eyes of man are never satisfied. (Prov 27:20).

No matter what the gender, be it male or the weaker vessel, the eyes are never satisfied. I am only human, we say, and born with defects. True! But more often than not, eyes are bigger than bellies, and there is a tendency to bite off more than we can chew.

No wonder Jesus said that we should hunger and thirst after righteousness, and we will be filled. (Matt 5:6). Yet again, we are reminded in (John 6:35), that Jesus is the bread of life and whoever comes to Him shall never hunger, and whoever believes on Him shall never thirst. So then, in spite of our humanness, we can hunger righteously, and become perfect as He is perfect. (Matt 5:48).

The more we see, the more we want.
Stop feeding Hungry Jack.
Only God can help you
Resist Satan's hunger attack.

A Leaky Bucket

A talebearer reveals secrets, but a faithful spirit conceals the matter. (Prov 11:13).

Popular singer, Etta James, once sang, "Tell Mama all about It." If I may paraphrase, why not tell Jesus all about it? You can believe that folk with 'big ears, have big mouths' to go along with them.

There comes a time when it is needful to share what's weighing heavily on your mind with a trusted friend, or loyal confidant. That's fine. But make it a consistent practice to not think out loud. The world is always ready to listen, and your personal thoughts will be heard. What am I saying here? Do not reveal too much 'sworn to secrecy stuff.' Keep it under wrap. Some things are meant only for the ears of God. Got a secret? Tell Jesus all about it! Your secret is safe with Him.

Telling all your secrets
Is an open invitation
For busy bodies to disclose
Don't tell nobody information.

A Message

Pray without ceasing. (1 Thess 5:17).

Because our self-centered nature wants its own way, oftentimes, we tend to devote more time to self-pampering than spiritual renewal.

Take Jesus' example to heart. Pray without ceasing. Whisper a prayer. Sing a song of praise. Cast your cares unto the Lord. Share your thoughts with Him.

Renew your inner beauty each day. In manifold ways, it pays to stay prayed up.

> Whisper a prayer unto Jesus,
> Wherever you may be,
> Then rest assured contentedly.
> He will hear your plea.
>
> Sing a song unto Jesus.
> Praise Him with your voice.
> Spend some time with Jesus.
> Let all hearts rejoice.
>
> Take your burdens to Jesus.
> Give Him every care.
> There is not a cross to carry
> We are left alone to bear.
>
> Make known your thoughts to Jesus.
> Trust Him with all your heart.
> Less doubting, more believing.
> Feel your cares depart.

A Mind to Follow

Then Jesus said to His disciples," If anyone desires to come after me, let him deny himself and take up his cross and follow me." (Matt 16:24).

It may have been a Sunday School Teacher, a loved one, a cherished friend, or perhaps a chance encounter with a total stranger that prompted you to seek out your own personal salvation through Jesus Christ. But no matter how you were so richly blessed to hear and receive the Word of God, the crucial decision to deny yourself and pick up the cross, and follow Jesus, is the wisest choice you will ever have to make during your brief earthly experience on your way to your final destination.

Eternity! We will either spend it one way or the other; with God, or without Him. It is your choice; yours alone.

> God is a loving God,
> Whom we should honor and cherish
> And it is not His will at all
> That anyone should perish.

A Money Mouth Fish

And when they were come to Capernaum, they that received tribute money came to Peter, and said, does not your master pay tribute? (Matt 17: 24 &27).

When Peter and Jesus entered into Capernaum, apparently it was customary to pay tribute money, so Peter was approached by the tribute collectors, and his answer to their question was yes. Jesus who knows all things was ready to instruct Peter what to do relating to his response that the tribute would be paid.

It is important to point out; however, that Peter had no money, and nor did Jesus. Yet He commanded Peter with authority to go down to the sea, cast in a hook, take up the very first fish, open its mouth, remove the money, and then go pay the tribute for both of them. A Genie is an imaginary, supernatural being that pales in comparison to a real, supernatural, Supreme Being, such as Jesus Christ.

> No one can blow out candles
> To make a Genie wish,
> Or when in need of money,
> Extract it from a fish.
>
> Lord Jesus, on the other hand,
> He can do impossible things.
> Nothing is too difficult.
> He is the King of Kings.

A Ram in the Bush

And Abraham lifted up his eyes and looked, and behold behind him a ram caught in a thicket by his horns; and Abraham went and took the ram and offered him up for a burnt offering in the stead of his son. (Gen 22:13-14).

Abraham experienced more than ever before, a hands on, real life experience when God instructed him to sacrifice his only son, Isaac. And while not everyone can display unwavering trust in God as did Abraham, there are times when we are unable to pick and choose the outcome of unforeseeable, must act, or no win situations when trouble shows up unannounced and knocks upon the door with an element of surprise that knocks us down upon our knees.

When was the last time that happened to you, and amazingly, God provided a ram in the bush?

> Jehovah Jireh is the place
> Named by Abraham
> Where God rewarded his great faith,
> And He blessed him with a ram.

A Small Tree Limb Miracle

Now God worked unusual miracles by the hands of Paul. (Acts 19:11).

Speaking of unusual miracles, in the year of 2008, I saw the muddy face of an innocent, little boy, on the Channel Four News Broadcast. It was mentioned that a small tree limb was all that prevented seven year old Brendon, from being swept away in a rain swollen creek in Saint Peters, Missouri. That is, at least what the news media had to say about it.

I say, isn't God amazing? Some may call it luck, but the hand of God was all in that life threatening situation and due to divine intervention, the rescue team was able to save a child from harm's way.

> Someone's precious, little boy
> Could have been swept away,
> But a small tree limb miracle
> Suddenly came into play.

A Sure Win

Let everything that has breath praise the Lord! Praise ye the Lord! (Ps 150:6).

When you think about the goodness of God, there is always something to cheer about because you are on the winning team. God never fails, and so it is with God that He will always cause us to triumph and experience victory through Jesus Christ. So praise Him for His mighty acts, and His known fragrance will linger on with the sweet smell of victory. (2 Cor 2:14).

Chances are you have experienced defeat given certain circumstances, but when God's hand is in it, it is for certain, you will win it. God is an unbeatable foe. David rested assured in (Ps 25:2), that his complete trust in God would allow him to victoriously reign over his enemies, so he praised God all the more, and claimed a sure win. So celebrate the awesomeness of God, for He is indeed worthy of all praise. Want to experience God firsthand? Be a Cheerleader for the Lord. A sure win is guaranteed.

> Praise ye the Lord!
> There is always something to cheer about.
> Praise Him for His greatness.
> Lift up your voice and shout.
>
> Praise the Lord up high above.
> Do not miss the chance!
> Sing songs! Play instruments!
> Anointed feet! Praise dance!
>
> Jesus paid the price.
> Love chose to redeem.
> Victory is yours,
> So join the Praise Team.
>
> Be a Cheerleader for God.
> All praises be unto the Lord.
> The more you cheer for Jesus,
> Great will be your reward.

A Toad in the Road

As a bird that wanders from her nest, so is a man that wanders from his place. (Prov 27:8).

There is much to be said about the ultimate purpose. Think about it. A person without a vision is like a toad in the road aimlessly leaping around and getting nowhere at all. And why is that?

According to (Eccles 3:1), there is a time for every purpose under the heaven. Those who build in Jesus have a very secure nesting place in Him, and never leave home without a flight plan. But those who jump around without a purpose consistently play the game of Leap Frog and wander from their place over, and over again. If you don't know Him, the time is at hand. So stop leaping around like a toad in the road and become spirit driven and powerfully compelled to move forward and experience the blessing of the purpose for which you have been called.

One without a purpose
Plays Leap Frog like a toad,
But a man with a vision,
He sees clearly down the road.

A Whale of a Time

Arise! Go to Nineveh! Save the city from wickedness! (Jonah 1:2).

Jonah refused to go to Nineveh as God had commanded him to do so, but decided to flee to Tarshish, therefore, he went down to Joppa, and boarded a ship bound for Tarshish. But the Lord sent a mighty tempest upon the sea, and the crewmen aboard the ship grew fearful of the menacing storm, and asked Jonah what should they do? Jonah found himself in a very 'fishy' situation because he knew what he had to tell them to do, and so he did. He instructed them to throw him overboard, and the sea was calm once again.

As you get to know God better, as did Jonah, you will alarmingly discover that obedience, above all else, is a mandatory requirement strictly enforced by God Himself.

> Now Jonah heard every word
> The Lord had to say,
> But he was thrown overboard.
> He failed to obey.
>
> A great fish came after him.
> It swallowed Jonah whole.
> And it was then he realized
> That God was in control.
>
> Three days and nights Jonah prayed,
> And when finally vomited ashore,
> He did as God had told him to
> Not so long ago before.

Always Room

Do not think of yourself more highly than you should, but think soberly. (Rom 12:3).

I enjoyed a spirit inspired high praise service at the National Baptist Convention in Kentucky, 2008. I learned a great deal, as did those who attended with me. As I think back and recall some of the many teachable things we were taught, I remember one thing in particular that has remained with me even now unto this day. An officer at the convention repeatedly recited each day during the assembly, the following quotation. "The greatest room in the world is room for improvement."

No matter how we may attempt to do things a better way, and no matter how much we think we might know; there is always room for improvement.

> We will never know it all.
> There is something new, from day to day.
> So ask the Lord to humble you
> And then kneel down to pray.

An All Occasion God

In all thy ways acknowledge Him, and He shall direct your paths. (Prov 3:6).

As so often happens, some folk tend to feel as though God is unable to handle everything that happens to us in a lifetime, but that is the farthest thing from the truth. No matter how great, or insignificant circumstances may appear to be, God is an all occasion God with unlimited power. He alone can solve any problems we may have. All He needs for us to do is trust Him, and move out of the way.

We really do have a Friend in Jesus, and we can share anything with Him, no matter how challenging or hopeless the outlook may seem. There are no separate Gods to handle certain difficulties, but one all occasion God to handle everything.

> He is an all occasion God,
> So ask for what you need.
> Then count on Him to work it out.
> God is able! Yes indeed!

An Evening in Paris

And the Lord said unto Moses, take unto thee sweet spices, stacte, and onycha, and galbanum, these sweet spices with pure frankincense, of each shall there be a like weight. And thou shall make it a perfume, a confection after the art of the apothecary, tempered together, pure and holy. (Ex 30:34-35).

My mama loved Evening in Paris perfume. It was her favorite fragrance. As a child, I would open the dark blue bottle with its fancy hanging tassel, and dab a little behind both ears. Just like mama, it smelled heavenly to me.

During the days of Moses, an altar was built upon which to burn incense, and Moses' brother Aaron, was consecrated to burn sweet incense every morning when he dressed the lamps. We must also have a spirit of consecration when we kneel before the altar so that God will be pleased with a sweet smelling savor to honor Him in a most holy manner.

> Oh! Taste and see that God is good;
> An indescribably delicious flavor,
> And He is pleased when we impart
> To Him, sweet scented savor.

Abigail

And David said to Abigail, Blessed be the Lord God of Israel, which sent thee this day to meet me; and Blessed be thy advice, and blessed be thou, which has kept me this day from coming to shed blood, and from avenging myself with mine own hand. (I Sam 25:1-42).

There lived an upright woman. Her name was Abigail.
She was kind in spirit, and carried herself very well.
Abigail was a woman of God, blessed with good understanding.
She was very beautiful, meek and undemanding.

Her husband's name was Nabal. He was evil in his way.
Nabal was great and prosperous, but his soul had gone astray.
Now Nabal sheared his sheep with his own shepherds in Carmel.
David's servants tended with them, assisted and treated them very well.

So David sent his ten young men as Messengers from him.
That Nabal might find favor, but he simply railed on them.
Nabal being a greedy man, selfishly replied,
"Share my bread? My water? My flesh? Oh! No! Request denied!

Who is David, and who are his servants that he should ask? How dare!
I know not these people, and so, I will not share."
David's anger was kindled when Nabal requited him evil for good,
So he sought to kill him, and his men, like a revengeful leader would.

When Abigail heard the news that her husband would surely die,
She made haste with wisdom God gave her from on high.
She gathered together 200 loaves, 2 bottles of wine and 5 sheep ready dressed.
5 measures of corn, 100 clusters of raisins, 200 fig cakes, then forward she pressed.

She fell on her face before David, a humble handmaid with an offering
To intercede for her husband who had wrought such an evil thing.
David accepted the offering, and there was no bloodshed.
Because Abigail was wise, David knew no dread.

When Abigail told Nabal of all that had been done,
At that time he was stricken just like a frozen one.
God had moved His hand, and Nabal's body became as stone.
His heart died within him, and 10 days later, he was gone.

Nabal's heaped up evilness returned upon his own head.
David was spared from sin, and God's vengeance prevailed instead.
Abigail was a woman of wisdom who honored God in her life.
David came to seek her out, and then he claimed her as his wife.

About My Father's Business

And Jesus said at the age of twelve, "Why are you looking for me? Don't you know that I must be about my Father's business?" (Luke 2:49).

The time has come to work heartily unto the Lord, and not men. (Col 3:23). The time has come to work with all of your might to do whatever needs to be done for the advancement and the promotion of God's kingdom, for there is no work in the grave to which we are headed. (Eccl 9:10). The time has come to work the works of Him that sent you while it is day, for when night comes, no man can work. (John 9:4).

> Must be about my Father's business!
> There's no time to tarry.
> Night is swiftly closing in
> And I've a cross to carry.
>
> Must be about my Father's business!
> Lest suddenly, He should come
> Like a thief invades the night
> And find my work undone.

Afflicted Blessings

Though I have afflicted thee, I will afflict thee no more. (Nah 1:12)

Due to lack of rain, and famine in Bethlehem, Naomi migrated to the land of Moab with her husband Elimelech, and their two sons, Mahlon and Chilion. With the passage of time, however, life altering changes occurred when suddenly, her husband died, and that is not all. Following the death of her spouse, both sons passed away also, leaving Naomi, and her two Moabite daughters-in-law, Orpah, and Ruth, as three bewildered, widowed women with seemingly no end in sight to their affliction.

Eventually, having heard that the famine had ended in her homeland, sparked a glimmer of hope for survival in Naomi's grim corner of despair, so she kindly blessed Orpah and Ruth, and then urged them to return to their families since there were no longer any living heirs to sustain her family in Moab. So of course, she saw no future hope or prospective husbands for Moabite women in Israel.

Although Naomi was met with strong opposition by both parties, with a parting farewell kiss, Orpah finally obeyed and returned to her people as suggested, but relentless Ruth, however, adamantly refused Naomi's request, and stubbornly clung to Naomi with a persistence that commanded attention. Ruth vowed that she would worship her mother-in-law's God, and reside wherever she lived, and die wherever she died. Such loyalty could not be dismissed nor denied, so Naomi concurred, and Ruth accompanied Naomi to Bethlehem.

To make a long story short, there is an end to affliction. Consequently, Boaz married Ruth, and she and Naomi both prospered from hardship to kinship with a new family in the land of Israel. (Ruth 1 & 4).

> Lay hold to your blessing.
> Run and tell the story.
> Affliction born through suffering
> Will soon bear witness to God's glory.

Angels in Charge

For he shall give his angels charge over thee, to keep thee in all thy ways. (Ps 91:11).

Have you ever witnessed a miracle? More often than not, there is news one would rather not hear about at all, but as I watched the News channel one day, some time ago, a miracle happened in Apache Junction, Arizona in August of 2007.

For whatever reason, a woman was driving on a flooded road with her baby and the turbulence of the flood swiftly washed her car up the road, and then on downstream. Suddenly, she was faced with a life threatening, "Lord, what am I to do now situation?"

Has not a miracle driven some to the rediscovery of God's sovereign power? Look at the total picture in retrospect. Some may call it luck, but somehow and in some unexplainable, miraculous way, the car got stuck under a walkway. Got lucky? I think not! God commanded His angels to take charge of the entire circumstance. And was it by chance that someone just happened to be right there to rescue the woman and her baby from the trapped vehicle? Come on now! God sent a Good Samaritan to bail them out of harm's way just in the nick of time.

> Whenever some poor soul is saved
> From an impending doom,
> The devil has to back up,
> And give God all the room.

Artificial Insemination

But you shall receive power after that the Holy Ghost is come upon you, and you shall be witnesses unto me both in Jerusalem, Judea, Samaria, and unto the uttermost part of the earth. (Acts 1:8).

After Jesus spoke these words to His disciples, He was transported out of their sight into glory. Absolutely no one else could have paid a steeper price for our salvation, and the gift of the Holy Spirit, for the supreme sacrifice He made is incomparable and unlike any other known to humankind. But the story didn't end there. When the apostles in Jerusalem heard that Samaria had received the Word of God, they sent unto them Peter and John, who when they arrived, prayed for them that they might receive the Holy Ghost. (Acts 8:15-17). Pay close attention! Those who received the Word were baptized in the name of Jesus only. Only through the laying on of the apostles' hands could the Holy Ghost be given at that time. Anything else would have been artificial insemination.

The Bible speaks in (John 14:16), of a Comforter who will abide with us forever. Satan's main cross-purpose is to confuse our thoughts any way possible in order to draw attention unto him, but unless Jesus impregnates your soul, the growth inside of you is artificially inseminated.

> The false conception of Satan's seed
> Will abort and destroy the soul.
> But those reborn in Jesus Christ
> Have Holy Ghost control.

Away With Do It Yourself Kits

I can do all things through Christ which strengthens me. (Phil 4:13).

There is a saying that goes, "a donkey's lips will never fit on a horse's mouth." Problems will arise when we choose to work things out on our own. More than often, we resort to drastic measures and when all else fails, we attempt to force square pegs into round holes, and then we try to complete puzzles with missing pieces by playing the game of mix match.

Give it up! Ask for help from the only one who knows what to do, how to do it, and when to do it.

> Cancel out the order.
> Away with the do it yourself kit.
> Just call upon the Master.
> You cannot match His wit.

Away With the Blue

These things have I spoken unto you, that in me you might have peace. In the world you shall have trouble, but be of good cheer, I have overcome the world. (John 16:33).

Some things are not easily overcome, especially teetering on the brink of despair. When stretched beyond what you think you can handle, I find it helpful to change the channel of your mindset. Above everything else, Jesus has assured us of peace in the time of trouble. So why allow mishaps, and misfortunes to squelch your hope. So whenever Satan reminds you of all the reasons you should be sad, depressed, and color your world blue, fight back! Don't throw a pity party. Cry if you must, but turn down his invitation of despondency. Learn how to glorify the Lord in the fire until His reflection can be seen. He will be your song in the night, and joy will come in the morning.

> Sinking in troubled waters,
> The color is blue.
> I wonder why should I bother?
> What am I to do?
> Can't make the pieces fit,
> But I won't give up, or quit.
>
> My world is blue!
>
> Trying to hang around,
> The color is blue.
> See-saws go up and down
> And so does life too.
> Through valleys of despair,
> Does anybody care?
>
> My world is blue!

Crying releases sorrow,
The color is blue.
Maybe another tomorrow
The sun will shine on through.
I know that I can take it,
For only the strong can make it.

My world is blue!

Feeling a lucky notion,
The color is blue.
Just gotta stay in motion,
And to myself be true.
I know that Jesus loves me.
He picks me up, and hugs me.

So why am I blue? Away with the blue!

Beat the Clock

Whereas ye know not what shall be on the morrow. For what is your life? It is even a vapor that appears for a little time, and then vanishes away. (James 4:14).

None of us are really so different from each other. Before long, no matter how we may differ in nationality, creed, or color, we all have one thing in common that brings about equality. Death!

Early on in my lifetime, I recall a very popular T.V. Game Show, "Beat the Clock!" Only a limited amount of time was allowed for participating contestants to perform required feats successfully in order to beat the clock. It was extremely entertaining to watch people racing to beat the clock in a specified amount of time in order to win the big prize.

In the same way, it is of great importance that we beat the clock in our decision making. How so? Our stay on this earthly planet is indeed limited. It can never be too early to decide to accept Jesus as Lord, and Savior. But it can be too late if you don't beat the clock of your lifetime. Life is swiftly ticking away, so don't run out of time. Beat the clock! Decide right now! It's a matter of life, or death.

> Very soon the clock of life
> Will sound its final chime
> So hurry! Run to Jesus!
> Beat the Clock! Be on time!

Be Careful Who You Sleep With

Whoever digs a pit shall fall therein, and he that rolls a stone, it will return upon him. (Prov 26:27).

Are you sleeping with the enemy? Do you lie down with an unforgiving spirit, and entertain thoughts of wrathful vengeance in order to even the score with someone who yanked your chain? If the answer to this question is yes, you are dangerously sleeping with the enemy.

It was Pastor, Paul E. Sheppard, (One place.Com), who said that "the ground is even at the foot of the cross." All other ground; however, may be uneven for many reasons. When such is the case, and things are unequal, many lose an awful lot of sleep vowing, scheming, and attempting to somehow equalize the situation by seeking out revenge upon those whom they feel have engaged in unfair tactics directed toward them. Don't do it!

There is a trend employed throughout scripture that warns us to be angry and sin not. Let not the sun go down upon your wrath. Neither give place to the devil. (Eph 4:26 & 27). Try as you may to even the score in a lopsided attempt to pay someone back, tit for tat, and to exact revenge for some injustice, and sad but true, you may be the one who winds up paying an even greater price on down the line. Let God mete out vengeance. His justice goes beyond the grave. It is very easy to fall into the habit of sleeping with the enemy. In one fell swoop, Satan can win you over with uncontrollable anger, and an unforgivable spirit. All these things give a mighty foothold to the Devil, but you can keep the enemy at arm's length if you simply be careful who you sleep with.

News Flash! An extremely, disgruntled employee spent many a sleepless night with the enemy prior to committing mass murders of innocent victims, and suicide at the job site. News Flash! A recently divorced and enraged spouse spent many a restless night with the enemy prior to killing his entire family, and also himself. Never has been known such repetitive, copycat violence than in today's society. Be careful who you sleep with! You may wake up to regret it.

> Think lovely thoughts, kind and pure,
> And sound sleep is yours for sure,
> Plotting all night angrily?
> Your bed mate is the enemy.
>
> And now before I fall asleep,
> I pray, Dear Lord, no anger to keep.
> Should evil have place before I wake.
> I pray, the Lord, the enemy take.

Beguilingly Yours

His own iniquities shall take the wicked himself, and he shall be bound with the cords of his own sins. (Prov 5:22).

We have all had our moments when we were fallible and susceptible to fall easy prey to the alluring, fascinating, and enticing temptations of the darker side. The truth be told, there are numerous connivers and tricksters who are artfully deceitful, crafty, and extremely treacherous in compelling innocent victims to join the forces of evil.

According to the Word of God, the art of deception is a very tricky thing indeed, and those who are fueled by such passion to engage in chicanery, or the use of clever devices to mislead others are, sadly enough, choosing their own fate of self-inflicted punishment as the end result.

> To those who are inclined to sport Satan's style,
> The noose you tie for others will hang you after a while.
> The wicked will be bound with his own sinful cord.
> Before you build a gallows, repent before the Lord.

Big Wigs Fall Off!

He that is of a proud heart stirs up strife, but whoever puts his trust in the Lord shall be made fat. (Prov 28:25).

Perhaps the hardest thing for those sitting in high places not to do is to avoid getting the fat head. The "I am large and in charge syndrome" is extremely difficult to shun especially when too many in leadership roles would rather march to the beat of their very own drums instead of trusting God to fatten them up from a prosperous standpoint of view. God's concern is with our limited view and self-centered pride. There comes a time when there is a need to search within and gradually begin to focus on what we are really all about. Are your fires of passion ignited by self, or does God supply the fuel for the fire? True enough, big wig people do experience abundant benefits. But those who do things their own way with a detached interest from God will never reap long lasting prosperity.

Biblical truths reveal that many kings and emperors were big wig people who were proud, powerful, well to do, and extremely wealthy and prosperous, but surprisingly, God knocked them to their knees. The big wigs fell off, and great was the fall. God dusted, and busted, and they were sore disgusted.

> Getting too big for one's own britches
> Can bust a loose a whole lot of stitches,
> Don't let Fat Head mentality
> Wipe out your prosperity.

Bishop's Dream

Unto Him, Be glory in the church by Christ Jesus throughout all ages, world without end. Amen! (Eph 3:21).

For years Bishop Willie J. Ellis Jr, Pastor of the New Northside Baptist Church had dreamed of building a Conference Center, and because of his determination, and faith, it finally happened. To God, Be the glory! The following poem was written and recited at the Grand Opening Celebration.

Impossible as though it may seem, never give up on your dream.
Hang in there, and see it through. Bishop Ellis, Hats off to you!
Our Leader and dreamer stepped up to the plate, and challenged New Northside to pull its weight;
To share a dream, and then follow it through unto completion until it comes true.

Daring to risk, and take a chance; Unstoppable! He stayed his stance,
And for every skeptical 'Nay Sayer' Bishop became a dragon slayer.
Some may have doubted and disbelieved, but a blessing of faith has been received.
His dream came true! To God, Be the glory! Years from now, they will tell the story.

Bishop's dream from the Lord has blessed Goodfellow Boulevard.
The sky is the limit! What a breakthrough for New Northside, and all of you.
Bishop Willie J. Ellis, Rest in peace! Your good works shall never cease.
The future will become the past, but all that's done for Christ will last.

With the passing of the years, New Northside is still shifting gears.
With a Grand Opening Celebration, we salute this blessed dedication.
The dream is now a reality, and so we have gathered joyfully
To fellowship, and dine at dinner in our New Northside Conference Center.

There's a modernized kitchen and banquet hall; a gym for sports, and basketball,
And New Nurseries added to the Day Care; a dream, come true, beyond compare.
There's a brand new stage and all of that. New Northside is where it's at.
"A church where everybody is somebody, and Christ is all!" Praise God now, one and all.

For pioneers who paved the way, a lasting tribute stands today.
A commemorative wall has been set in place. Names adorn each special space.
Future members will recall whenever they gather at the wall
To remember the golden legacy of how New Northside came to be.

Once a dream, but now a reality! We dedicate this facility.
It bears the name of its creator. We know that God showed him favor.
Wave the banner! Let the bells chime! A historical moment is written in time.
Let joy resound repeatedly! New Northside is making history.

Bring Down the House

His Lord said unto him. Well done good and faithful servant; thou has been faithful over a few things. I will make thee ruler over many things; enter thou into the joy of thy Lord. (Mat 25:23).

How do you bring down the house? Turn it out with a stellar performance—Of course! And God expects the same from all of us as Children of the Kingdom of God. You can tell a lot about committed Christians by the way they perform on the stage of life. Everything they do, and everywhere they go, their little lights are always shimmering, and shining.

Examine your life. Many areas in the Believer's way of life require constant maintenance in order to remain well polished. It is by no means enough to say that I am a Christian. You need to 'strut your stuff,' live the walk and talk the talk. All eyes are on you. If a dull finish does indeed exist, it is never too late to polish up your act and get it together. And it is also important to remember that you are not performing for a pat on the back, but a crown on your head.

> Bring down the house!
> Give the Lord your very best.
> Don't think that He will settle
> For anything that's less.

Buck Wheat

Another parable he put forth to them, saying, the kingdom of heaven is like a man which sowed good seed in his field. But while men slept, his enemy came and sowed tares among the wheat and went his way. (Matt 13:24-25).

Specifically, let's talk about the parable of the tares. First of all, wheat refers to those who are saved. Next, the tares are those who are unsaved. Thirdly, both are allowed to grow together until the harvest comes.

When you butt heads with the Devil, God had better be on your side. What is needed is some buck in your wheat. There are many definitions to define the word buck, but in this particular instance, buck means to summon one's courage or spirits, and it also means to stubbornly and obstinately resist, or to balk. It takes a courageous and high-spirited soldier to serve in God's army, and it takes a stubbornly persistent and obstinate warrior to balk against Satan, your archenemy, and all the tares among the wheat. But in the times of the harvest, God will instruct the reapers to gather the tares first, and bind them in bundles for burning, but the wheat will be gathered into His barn. (Matt 13:26-30).

> In active Christian Combat
> There are tares among the wheat.
> So summon daily courage,
> Don't give in to defeat.

Butter and Oil

The words of his mouth were smoother than butter, but war was in his heart; his words were softer than oil, yet were they drawn swords. (Ps 55:21).

We are reminded in (Ps 19:14) to let the words of our mouths and the meditation of our hearts, be acceptable in the sight of the Lord. We are also reminded in (Prov 25:11) that a word fitly spoken is like apples of gold in pictures of silver. Also (Prov 18:21) tells us that death and life are in the power of the tongue, and they that love it shall eat the fruit thereof.

Often words that some may utter
May spread across as smooth as butter,
And whispered words as soft as oil
Can hurt, discourage, rend, or foil.

Meditate at Jesus' feet.
Let your words be kind and sweet.
Dirty words will only soil,
So let God spread your butter and oil.

Can't Be What U Ain't

And I was afraid, and went and hid your talent in the ground; look, there you have what is yours. (Matt 25:25). Therefore take the talent from him, and give it to him who has ten talents. (Matt 25:28).

I was a member of the Junior Choir at Trinity Mount Carmel Baptist Church, where I learned an invaluable lesson from Mrs. June Martin, our anointed and gifted musician at that time. She had us recite the following words of wisdom before each choir rehearsal, and I committed it to memory even unto this day. "I am one, and only one. I cannot do everything, but I can do something. That I can do, I will do, if God Be my help."

If you can't be who you want to be,
Simply be who you are,
And the very best of you
Will outshine any star.

If you can't do all you want to do,
Then just do all you can,
Or your gift will be taken away
And another will finish your plan.

If there are places you can't go,
Be content wherever you are.
Life is for living, not merely existing,
Be it at home, abroad, or afar.

It's so wonderful to imagine,
But life is not a fairytale.
So keep it real in all you do,
And things are bound to work out well.

February

Run in such a way that you may obtain the prize. (1 Cor 9:24)

Freedom! Jesus has granted us liberty.
Every drop of blood shed at Calvary
Bought each ransomed soul with an enormous price.
Realize that Jesus sacrificed His life.
Understand that fallen man was doomed a dying nation.
After Adam sinned, Jesus altered the situation.
Redemption reigns! The battle is won.
Yahweh is the King, the Father and the Son.

We are never altogether the same once the hand of God touches the soul. Freedom and liberty are yours for the asking, and every precious drop of blood purifies the sin sick soul. So real to all Believers is the realization that Jesus bought us with a price. We shall grow stronger the longer we allow Christ to infiltrate us with the presence of the Holy Spirit. Continue to honor the supreme and ultimate sacrificial Lamb of God and praise Him for the gift of salvation. Redemption reigns! Salute the King of Kings, and the Lord of Lords.

Carry Your Corner

And whatsoever you do, do it heartily, as to the Lord, and not unto men. (Col 3:23).

As a youth, I was asked to speak on the topic of "Carry Your Corner." Once I fully understood what the subject matter really meant, I was blessed to deliver a very effective and thought provoking speech to the congregation at the youth assembly.

The big question to be asked, of course, is what does it mean to carry your corner? One good example of carrying your corner is found in Daniel, Chapter 6. Since Daniel was preferred above the presidents and princes because of his excellent spirit, no fault could be found in him. So the presidents and princes plotted against Daniel and devised a scheme concerning the law of his God to entrap him. A decree was signed that no one should petition any God or man for 30 days with the exception of King Darius. Daniel, however, ignored the decree as his enemies knew he would and continued to pray 3 times a day, giving thanks to God. Daniel was thrown into the lion's den and because he persisted in carrying his corner, God delivered him from the lion's den, and all ended well.

And while we may never end up in the lion's den, or be thrown into a fiery furnace like Shadrach, Meshach and Abednego who refused to serve or worship other Gods, recall that Jesus was with them in the furnace, and they all remained safe from harm's way. I rest my case. Whatever God has asked you to do, do unto the Lord and not unto man. No one else can do what God has planned for you to do, so carry your corner.

> Carry your corner!
> Believe me! It is true!
> No one else can carry
> The corner God gave you.

Cat Prayer

Evening, and morning, and at noon, will I pray, and cry aloud, and he shall hear my voice. (Ps 55:17).

Anything at all, no matter how insignificant it may seem, should be covered by prayer. There were, and still are, cat lovers, and my daughter is definitely one of them. Melvin was her adorable pet cat. There was one catch however, Melvin had no front claws, and regardless to how she attempted to protect Melvin and keep him indoors, it was of no use whatsoever. Melvin would always be a daring, outdoor cat.

Constantly concerned for such a well-loved pet, I wrote a Cat Prayer for Melvin, and asked my daughter to pray it faithfully before releasing Melvin into the outdoor world. Surprisingly, Melvin survived many fights and close encounters with would be attackers, and if I may so, had more than likely surpassed nine lives plus. The Cat Prayer not only made an impression on my daughter's husband who faithfully reminded her to recite the Cat Prayer for Melvin before letting him out, but my granddaughter, Danielle Tene' who was only six at the time, memorized the Cat Prayer, and never allowed Melvin to go outside until the prayer had been offered up to God on his behalf.

> Father God, Dear Lord, I pray,
> Keep me safe, both night and day.
> The others have four claws, I only have two,
> So thank you, Lord Jesus! You know what to do.

Meow anyhow! Melvin died of natural causes many years later.

Celebrate the Change

Therefore if any man be in Christ, he is a new creature, old things are passed away; behold all things are become new. (2 Cor 5:17).

No longer conformed to this world, a transformation has taken place by the renewal of the mind, and now you may prove, what is that good and acceptable, perfect will of God as a new creature in Christ. (Rom 12:2).

We celebrate promotions, birthdays, anniversaries, new homes, new babies, and so on. But everything pales in comparison to celebration of a new body in Christ.

A transformation has taken place.
A sinner has been saved by grace.
With a renewed, Holy Ghost mind,
Claim the reward of a lasting kind.

God removed all defected parts.
Behold His molded work of art.
Daily upon His Word, we thrive.
Jesus keeps us all alive.

Come and see a special feature!
A reborn, sanctified, new creature!
If God has made a change in you,
You need to celebrate Him too.

There is every reason to rejoice
What a sound, life changing choice.
Folks may jeer, and think you strange,
But honey, celebrate the change.

Centerpieces

We are His workmanship (Eph 2:10).

Just as a striking centerpiece eloquently adorns any décor, all Saints are eye-catching attractions when wholeheartedly centered in Jesus. The Creator designed us with that purpose in mind.

When the glory of the Lord shines upon us, the entire world will see the light. Everyone will stop to notice and admire the beautiful centerpieces of God's creations. The Spirit of God is much too awesome to ignore when exhibited, and displayed through the manifestation of the Holy Spirit. None of the centerpieces are alike. Each is known for its own unique style, and individual beauty. All centerpieces boldly displayed are easily recognized, and identified by the holy seal of approval. Rescued, reconciled, redeemed!

> When God is the center of your life,
> All eyes will focus on you;
> A priceless, centerpiece of art;
> God perfected through, and through.

Changeless God

For I am the Lord! I change not. (Mal 3:6).

The truth is, some people are downright unapproachable. You would never dream of asking them for a favor, nor to lend a helping hand even when it is needed. Additionally, some folks change like the weather, and we just never know how to take them, or where they are coming from. Thank heaven, God does not have to be psyched, duped, or buttered up at all in order to communicate with Him. He is readily approachable, always available and easily accessible at all times. God is absolutely, positively, completely unchangeable. Try Him and see.

I sure hope that God is in a real good mood.
I simply could not bear it if I should find Him rude.

Oh! Woe is me! What shall I do?
I need someone to pull me through.

I think I'll call up God today, and then check out His voice.
How He sounds will let me know if I made the right choice.

Good morning God! If I may ask, how are You today?
Hope You're not feeling moody. If so, I'll go away.

I trust I'm not too worrisome although I fear, I well might be.
Day and night, I'm calling You, and You don't even charge a fee.

Every time You turn around, I'm always on the other end.
Some folk don't even answer me, but on You Lord, I can depend.

So here I am again, Dear Lord. Trouble is my name.
I pray with all my human heart that You are still the same.

"Dear Child, need I remind you, apparently you forgot.
Yesterday, today, and forever," I am God! I change not!"

Changing Seasons

To everything there is a season and a time to every purpose under the heaven. (Eccles 3:1).

During the summer months, I look outside and all I can see from my backyard are tall, green, leafy trees, and thriving, heavy foliage, but when the seasons change and winter comes, all is stripped bare, and I can see all of the houses of the neighboring community behind me upon the hill.

As so often happens, life has its changing seasons, and due to the thickness and density of stormy trials, we are unable to see clearly all around us until once again, the seasons of the soul change, all is stripped bare, and we can see as has been so often stated that "God was right there all the time."

When summer is upon us,
We may not see God there,
But He is visible to view
When winter comes, and strips us bare.

Cleaning Out the Closet

So teach us to number our days, that we may apply our hearts unto wisdom. (Ps 90:12)

It was Mark Twain who said, "The secret of getting ahead is getting started." Since time is such a valuable commodity, while waste it by going through the motion of cleaning out closets that continue to remain cluttered because it may come in handy again someday, some year on down the line. If you can't wear it, someone else can. If you're not using it, someone else will. Getting started and never finishing is getting nowhere.

Like jam packed and cluttered closets, we continue to occupy the storage space of our mindset with discarded thoughts and memories of clinging skeletons that hog and clog up all the main frame spaces of the mind. To be unlike all is to learn how to clean out the closet. Get rid of it, shake it off, and unclog the drain pipe; doing so, will allow adequate space for room to grow into the present.

> I can't wear it anymore.
> I need to throw it away.
> If I could lose a pound, or two,
> It sure would make my day.
>
> I can't wear it anymore,
> But it might come back in style.
> I haven't gained that much weight.
> 'I think I'll keep it for a while.
>
> If only I could toss it away.
> My closet overflows.
> But some day, I'll wear it again.
> When? Only God knows.
>
> So, I'll just keep on dreaming.
> I'm sure, I'll wear it again.
> But the odds against that happening
> Are few and slim, girlfriend.

Clip and Use

And Abraham, the Father of Faith, was fully persuaded that what God had promised, He was able to deliver. (Rom 4:21).

Somehow I suspect that I am not the only one who has ever clipped out valuable coupons, tucked them neatly away, and then allowed them to expire without redeeming them at their face value. What a shame!

How many times we find this to be true with the promises of God. Faithfully, we read about His promises all the time, but so seldom do we come to appreciate the full extent of His goodness and blessings because we fail to clip, use and reap the abundant benefits of each daily special offered at our fingertips. What is significant is that His promises have no expiration dates, but all earthly vessels; however, will expire at the appointed time of departure.

> Clip and use God's promises
> Before it is too late!
> All earthly vessels
> Have an expiration date!

Close to Home

The troubles of my heart are enlarged. Oh bring me out of my distresses (Ps 25:17).

More than often, when things hit too close to home, the way we deal with circumstances each day will depend on how we choose to handle it all. Continuing to stew over uncontrollable factors is pointless and unhelpful. A wiser use of time should be invested in looking up instead of down. Unthinkingly, we focus on the magnitude of trials instead of the attitude needed in order to sustain us throughout it all, and in the midst of it all.

So then, when there is trouble brewing on the home front, seek out shelter in the hollow of His hands, and then praise God all the more in the fire until His reflection can be seen in us.

> Sometimes things hit too close to home.
> So short is our attention span.
> God must have all eyes on Him to focus on His will and plan.

Counting Sheep

Blessed shall you be when you come in, and blessed shall you be when you go out. (Deut 28:6).

How many times we find ourselves counting sheep instead of counting all of our blessings. Many a restless night is far spent musing and pondering over unresolved issues, and petty problems. Stop!

Need you be reminded that God is a problem solving and burden bearing God? Do not believe that we have begun to realize or even understand for that matter, how He works, just know that He does, and that is enough. Rather focus on what He has already done, continue to obey Him, and He will turn things around and allow you to view concerns from a totally different perspective. After all, have not some of life's seemingly worst scenario situations turned out for your good? Out of trials come triumphal victories, for all things work out good for those who love God, (Rom 8:28) and, of course, obey Him. (Deut 28:2).

> Counting imaginary sheep
> Will never bring contented sleep,
> But when upon blessings dwell,
> Fall asleep! All is well.

Crafted and Grafted

I am the vine, you are the branches. He that abides in me, and I in him, the same brings forth much fruit, for without me, you can do nothing. (John 15:5).

More than ever before, God, in ways few people ever experience, is teaching us life lessons unsparingly. What it boils down to is this. A variety of uncontrollable factors are happening because God wants us to grow to the extent that we will cling to the vine and abide therein as branches fully dependent on Him to sustain us spiritually. You will be powerfully compelled to maintain absolute and uncompromised obedience when you fully abide in Him. There is no other way.

Unthinkingly, and of a sinful and fallible nature, we are often tempted to detach ourselves from the vine, and unless we are crafted and grafted back into the vine, we will surely wither away and die a spiritual death.

> Like instruments of music
> Go flat without fine tuning,
> Branches clinging to the vine,
> Certainly need pruning.
>
> No demon in hell can block your blessings
> When connected to the True Vine.
> How deeply blessed are we to say,
> HE is a Friend of mine.

Copy Cats

Let this mind be in you, which was also in Christ Jesus. (Phil 2:5).

Of course, it is true that God's ways are not our ways, nor His thoughts, our thoughts. (Is 55:8).

So then, how do we become more like Him? When you fully understand what it takes to be like Jesus, only then will you become fully aware of the fact that insincere, halfhearted and hypocritical living will never allow you to role model Christ Jesus. You must be completely sincere, wholeheartedly committed, and totally God honoring in imitating His mannerisms, assuming Christ likeness, mimicking His behavior, and faithfully abiding in Him, and that is the only way. Let the same mind be in you which was also in Christ Jesus.

> Some folks call us copy cats
> And say "what's the matter with them?"
> But in order to be like Jesus,
> We Christians must act just like Him.

Dealing from the Bottom

Every work shall be judged. (Eccles 12:14).

It is so stated in (Prov 5:22), that all who are wise through Satan, and are educated by him will be taken in their own craftiness and bound with the cords of their own sins. Come to the realization that as long as Satan is controlling all the cards, you are working for him, and you cannot deal yourself out of the game. Satan guarantees that his strategy is a sure win, but what he fails to let you know is that you have been set up to be let down, fixed up to be broken, and bought out to be sold out to the forces of evil, and that every work, whether good or evil, will be judged. Only Jesus can beat the devil's highest winning cards, and deal you out of the game, for He always knows where Satan is coming from.

The devil's three unseen winning cards are S, I, & N, and only the three and one connection of the Father, Son, and Holy Ghost can out deal his hand. The good news is that Jesus has already beaten the devil against all odds when He purchased us through redemption upon the cross of Calvary, but the decision is yours to tell the devil that the game is over. Remember! You will never beat Satan at his own game when you go it alone because he secretly deals from the bottom of the deck. With so much at stake, why gamble with your own soul?

> Satan has been loosed,
> And he is free and on the prowl.
> He is all that is ugly.
> He is wicked, evil, and foul.
>
> Once you have opted
> To sit in on his game,
> Nothing in your life again
> Will ever be the same.
>
> Your winnings may increase at first,
> But very soon will drain.
> He will rob you poor in spirit
> And your soul attempt to gain.
>
> The devil deals from the bottom.
> A hidden card, you cannot see.
> Don't gamble with the devil.
> He will cheat to win your destiny.

Death By Way of Mouth

But the tongue can no man tame; it is an unruly evil, full of deadly poison. (James 3:8).

Death by way of mouth is an ongoing thing promoted by evilness, and death continues to happen to quick tongued, unsuspecting victims. Be mindful to be slow to speak because a soft answer turns away wrath, but abusive language stirs up anger. (Prov 15:1).

Be swift to hear the Word of God, for it is the only tongue tamer that can harness, and muzzle the lips of contention. Become open to the fact that many more will perish by way of mouth unless it is strongly emphasized that life, and death lie in the power of one of the body's little members, the tongue. (James 3:5). Now what does that mean? Simply stated, ask God to keep the door of your lips closed when it is unwise to speak, and then to open it when silence is NOT golden. There is a time to speak, and a time not to speak. (Eccles 3:7).

What is significant is that he who keeps his mouth, keeps his life, but he that opens wide his lips shall have destruction. (Prov 13:3).

> One of the body's tiniest members
> Will stir up anger, woe, and strife,
> Avoid a quick and ready tongue.
> It can swallow up your life.

Deceitfully Yours

Faithful are the wounds of a friend, but the kisses of an enemy are deceitful. (Prov 27:6).

How deceitful are the kisses of an enemy. The kiss of Judas was one of betrayal. (Matt 26:48).

Eve was deceived by the Serpent and disobeyed God. She plucked fruit from the forbidden tree of life in the middle of the Garden of Eden, and ate it, and then enticed Adam, who also disobeyed God and ate the forbidden fruit. Deception brought about disobedience, and disobedience brought about death. Read (Gen 3:1-6).

Have you been kissed by an enemy lately? Beware!

> The camouflaged endearment
> Of an enemy's kiss is far from sweet.
> Deception is no good at all.
> Neither is deceit.

Dividing the Spoils

Cast in your lot among us. Let us all have one purse. (Prov 1:14).

In the first chapter of Proverbs, wisdom warns us to beware of those who are greedy of gain. Chances are you may feel tempted by blood thirsty, evil doers who will promise you anything in order to entice you to leave the paths of righteousness and join them in the ways of darkness. Be not deceived! Bad company corrupts all that's good.

It is almost certain that those who are eager to commit the ultimate crime in order to obtain ill-gotten gain would certainly have no problem backstabbing members of the gang when the big payday finally arrives, and then it's no longer the more the merrier, but the lesser, the better.

> Careful! You may be counted out
> When dividing the spoils are due.
> Don't cast lots with the devil.
> It's an unwise thing to do.

Do you have His Autograph?

And the disciples went, and did as Jesus commanded them. They brought the donkey and the colt, laid their clothes on them and set Him on them. And a very great multitude spread their clothes on the road; others cut down branches from the trees, and spread them on the road. Then the multitude who went before and those who followed cried out saying: Hosanna to the son of David! Blessed is He who comes in the name of the Lord! Hosanna in the highest! (Matt 21:6-9).

The triumphal entry into Jerusalem is the only time Jesus was treated royally. At no other time was He given the Red Carpet Treatment. Christ healed the sick, fed the hungry, gave sight to the blind, and commanded demons to depart, but no one asked, "May I have your autograph, please?" He was despised, denied, mocked, beaten, tried, and convicted, tortured, and disfigured on a cross, and there is no one greater than Him, but no one asked, "May I have your autograph, please?"

Many of us have autographs of well known, renowned celebrities and famous people among our prized possessions, but Jesus signed His own autograph, not with a pen, but the shedding of His blood upon the cross of Calvary. Do you have His autograph? If so, you own a piece of the Rock because salvation is solid as a rock.

> No one else could pay the debt
> So Jesus bore the blame.
> Yes! He washed away our sins.
> With blood, He signed each name.

Don't Cherish What Will Perish

Naked came I into the world, and naked will I depart. (Job 1:21).

Be thankful! Appreciate! Enjoy! But know that hoarding earthly possessions are to no avail. There is absolutely nothing that we may place into storage for future use after our departure from planet earth, so get over it! No! Basking in affordable luxuries is not necessarily sinful at all, but the Word is, "where your heart is, also your treasure will be." Concerning such, we find that the Bible warns us not to lay up earthly treasures only to be stolen away by thieves, or invest far too much in costly garments that will eventually decay with the passage of time. There is a saying that goes like this; "I have never seen a hearse with a U-Haul It behind it.".

Don't be fooled! Death will rob you of your riches and leave you very poor in heaven if you have failed to store up your heavenly treasures up above. (Matt 6:19-21).

> We brought nothing with us,
> And we will take nothing away.
> Lord teach us not to idolize
> Earthly things, we pray.

Don't Rush Me! God

Hope deferred makes the heart sick, but when the desire comes, it is a tree of life. (Prov 13:12).

God does not deal with time constraints. No one can dictate the actions or understand the thoughts of God. Nothing can restrict Him. Nothing can limit Him. Nothing can regulate Him. He is in a league all by Himself, and absolutely no one can tell Him when to make His move. His time management is out of this world, and His response, and turnaround time is not of our choosing. Thank God!

We are living so fast that we tend to forget
That God does not hurry. His pace is set.
So if prayers aren't answered right away
Do not give in unto dismay.

Time invested in prayer is never a waste,
But don't expect God to haste.
Whatever be the weight, or trial,
Deferred hope is not denial.

Don't send an ASAP note to God.
He may not honor your rush job.
Your problems, He will solve all of them.
But deadlines are no good to Him.

God takes His own time,
But He's never too late.
So stay on the line,
Or hang up and wait.

There is no such thing as a faxed prayer.
Kneel at the altar, and tarry right there,
And when at long last, the answer does come,
You'll know why He rushed NOT to get it done.

Down Pat

Be diligent to present yourself approved to God, a worker who does not need to be ashamed, rightly dividing the word of truth. (2 Tim 2:15).

My granddaughter, Danielle, committed her Easter speech to memory and then, she continuously rehearsed it over and over, and over again, until finally she came over to me and said with a shout of assured victory, "Beba! I've got it down pat!" Surprisingly, her little sister, Mariah, who had also followed in her big sister's footsteps proudly echoed," Me too Beba! Me too!"

Begin today to take spiritual inventory, and be positively sure that you have everything you need, and that you are doing all that you can to better able yourself to work out Christian Discipleship by learning how to stay on top of things. This much I know, with a fixed purpose in mind, you cannot practice enough, or study too much when employed as a workman of God's Kingdom.

> Before anyone can say
> I have it all down pat.
> Daily discipline is required,
> So study, pray, and all of that.

Dry Brooks

And it came to pass after a while that the brook dried up because there had been no rain in the land. (1 Kings 17:7).

As Elijah had predicted, and according to his word, no dew nor rain fell on the earth.

Is anything too hard for God? Most of us are familiar with the saying "into each life some rain must fall." One of the advantages of trusting Christ when troubles are raining down upon us is that He has power with effortless ease to sustain us throughout dry brook seasons. You must look to God alone. The way you deal with circumstances each day depends on how you shoulder the load; alone or with Him.

> When troublesome, rainy day seasons in life
> Dry up all of the brooks.
> The sun will suddenly reappear.
> It is never as bad as it looks.
>
> Through each drought season in your life
> Lift your eyes unto the mountains.
> Almighty God has the power
> To rain down flowing fountains.

Dust Shaking Awakening

And whosoever shall not receive you, nor hear your words, when you depart out of that house or city, shake off the dust of your feet. (Matt 10:14).

It has long been recognized that in order to achieve the goal of winning souls, someone has to be willing to travel on foot, door to door, to deliver the word to the un-churched, and the unsaved. It is reasonable to expect that many will not receive you, and thus, turn a deaf ear to the gospel and refuse to accept the extended invitation. When that happens, depart peacefully, walk away, and shake the dust off your feet as did the disciples of long ago who wore sandals and walked on dusty roads to ring out the message of salvation.

> Each day Jesus is calling,
> So heed unto His voice.
> Harden not your heart.
> Make Christ Jesus your choice.
>
> When Saints of God shake the dust
> Off their gospel shoes,
> Think again! Sinner man,
> You stand your soul to lose.
>
> Please! Do not ignore
> The free gift of salvation,
> For doing so will surely bring
> Eternal doom and damnation.

Entrusted into My Care

For this child I prayed, and the Lord has given me my petition which I asked of him. (1 Samuel 1:27)

Hannah pleaded with God for a son, and then she vowed that she would in turn dedicate him to the Lord, all the days of his life, and that is not all there was to it. When Hannah was blessed and conceived in her womb, and her child was finally born, she named him Samuel because she had asked the Lord to bless her with a child. Consequently, after Hannah had weaned him, she took Samuel to Shiloh, and as she had promised, Hannah presented him unto the Lord in the house of God.

More women than not, will become first time moms sooner or later. Traditional blessings and christenings are done for most new comers, but do not fail to bring them to God's house constantly, so they will continue to grow in Him as time wears on. After all, children are entrusted into our care only for a limited period of time, so make the time count for the lives we have been given to nurture as mothers and also fathers as well.

I witnessed the miracle of childbirth when my very first child, Kevin Quinn Tabb was born into this world on February 2, 1970.

> It was not a fantasy, or dream. Kevin Quinn arrived on the scene.
> I held my baby in my arms, and how I marveled at his charms.
> Such small hands, and tiny feet! Clinging close, and smelling sweet.
> I bowed my head and said a prayer, and felt the presence of Jesus there.
> Dear Lord, you gave this child to me though only temporarily.
> I pray that when he leaves the nest, I will have done my very best
> To let him know he is YOUR child, and mine only for a while.

I am blessed to say that Kevin is an accomplished musician, Head Band Director, loving husband, caring father, great son, wonderful big brother, and most of all, a Child of the King.

I love you son! MOM

Expect Delays

Wait on the Lord! Be of good courage, and he shall strengthen your heart. (Ps 27:14).

While driving to work, my attention was drawn to signs posted along the highway. EXPECT DELAYS! More often than not, the same signs are visibly posted on the spiritual highway leading up to heaven. There is also a syllabus denoting all that is required for a personal and up close relationship with God, and waiting is at the top of the list. You cannot hurry God! His timetable is not of your choosing, yet he specializes in time management.

So expect delays when walking with God, but rest completely assured that you will gain renewed strength to soar like an eagle through it all. "Put this in your pipe and smoke it!" God is always on time!

> And if He should decide
> Not to answer right away,
> Learn how to wait on God.
> There will be some delay.

Expected Ends

For I know the thoughts that I think toward you, says the Lord, thoughts of peace and not of evil, to give you an expected end. (Jer 29:11).

I would have likely never written this had I not been in the process of changing channels, and my attention was drawn to a young woman sharing a personal testimony around the globe, on the 700 Club televised series. She mentioned that she had faithfully prayed for God to protect her husband, and safeguard him from all harm; however, September 11 happened, and her loved one was counted among the dead leaving her in a state of shock. Her grief seemed unbearable, and she felt totally forsaken and absolutely abandoned. Even more so, she constantly experienced the worst kind of pain.

911 is unforgettable for very understandable reasons to all Americans and of course, she along with many others, posed the very same question. Why God? One day on her way to wherever she was headed at that particular time, a strange thing happened. Someone walked up to her and placed a tract into her hand, and the scripture read (Jeremiah 29:11). It is not so strange, however, that God spoke to her, and instantaneously she experienced her expected end, and claimed peace from her grief and suffering. What a woman! What a testimony! What a God!

> All good and bad must pass through Him.
> God is unlike any friend.
> But all things work out good
> To give you an expected end.

Face of an Angel

And all that sat in the council, looking steadfastly at him, saw his face as it had been the face of an angel. (Acts 6:15).

In the greatest of difficulties, there comes a time when there is a need to grasp unseen strength. In Dr. Martin Luther King's quest for equality, we saw the face of an angel that stood out in a very prejudiced, non-peaceful, and unfriendly world. King saw the glory of God upon the mountaintop, and the heavens opened as he viewed the Promised Land shortly before his assassination happened in Memphis, Tennessee. The Holy Ghost accompanied him unto the very end of his earthly journey.

Stephen performed great wonders and miracles in the mighty name of Jesus, yet his enemies were unable to resist the wisdom of God and spirit of this godly Saint with the face of an angel. So they plotted, and Stephen was falsely accused, but before he was stoned to death, filled with the Holy Ghost, he looked up to heaven, and saw the glory of God, and Jesus standing on the right hand of God.

> Have you seen the face of an angel?
> God gives His own, a distinguishing mark.
> Even enemies can't help but notice,
> An angel's face outshines the dark.

Fact, or Fantasy?

The truth is God's word will never pass away. (Matt 24:35.)

Much too often, focus is centered on what is imagined, or unreal. We reach out to touch what we feel is tangible only to discover that it was only a mirage. Truthfully speaking, life is not a fairytale. It is the real thing. To believe that one will live happily ever after is true for all Saints of God, but false for the unsaved. Only authors of books can guarantee happy endings in this world, but not in the world to come, so grab hold to what is true, for it is the Word of God that will last forever, and that is a fact. Are jagged edges cutting you deep? Come to Jesus. Wake up to reality. Unlike Humpty Dumpty, only God can put us back together again. So come on! Absorb the Word like a sponge and receive salvation. It is the gift of new beginnings, and the ending of all fantasies. The truth will set you free.

> Your life is not a fantasy,
> So please, do not pretend.
> Prepare for eternity.
> Temporal things will surely end.

Favor Brings Promotion

And the king loved Esther above all the women, and she obtained grace and favor in his sight more than all the virgins; so that he set the royal crown upon her head, and made her queen instead of Vashti. (Esther 2:17).

The Story of Esther is, of course, found in the Book of Esther. Read all about it and witness that favor does indeed bring about promotion.

Esther was the niece of a Jew named Mordecai.
He was God's chosen, blessed with favor from on high.
Mordecai was very wise, and Esther, was beautiful and fair,
So he taught her all the ropes, especially how to beware.

Now Haman was an evil man, who plotted to kill the Jews,
But God held Jews in high regard, and so they could not lose.
Mordecai refused to bow to pagan royalty,
So Haman vowed to carry out his conspiracy.

Whenever God grants favor, there is no contest.
King Ahasuerus loved Esther better than all the rest.
Of all the lovely women who appeared upon the scene,
Esther won his heart and became the reigning queen.

The king himself was clueless because he never knew
Until the time was right that Esther was a Jew,
For God had set in motion that she would become a Savior
Of all the Jewish people, for He had given favor.

To save her native family, Esther fasted and prayed.
She feared not for her life, and so a way was made.
Esther obtained full favor from her husband the king,
So much so that when she asked he would grant her anything.

So Queen Esther took control of a troubled situation,
And extended to Haman, her enemy, a royal invitation,
But little did he know that he had sealed his own fate
And death was but a step away because he chose to hate.

Meanwhile the king discussed with Haman of a certain need
To honor someone special who had done a kindly deed.
Haman thinking of himself as the honoree
Suggested to the king; "Treat this person royally!"

"Let him ride the king's horse, said Haman, and sport the king's attire,
And then ride through town on horseback. What honor could be higher?"
So the king instructed Haman to array Mordecai,
And escort him through the city. King's orders, he could not defy!

At the eloquent banquet, Esther unleashed the news.
She pointed out Haman who planned to kill all Jews.
So when the king was made aware that Esther was a Jew,
Haman realized that he had met his waterloo.

The gallows that were waiting to hang Mordecai
Were the very same gallows that hung Haman high.
Speaking of favor that comes from the Lord,
Favor brings promotion! God will always reward.

March

But if we hope for that we see not, then do we with patience wait for it. (Rom 8:25).

> **Me**—is a word that labels individuality.
> **A**ll means unlimited possibilities that lie within me.
> **R**eservoirs are wellsprings of wisdom and resources.
> **C**hrist, in me, will conquer negative forces.
> **H**ope is the result of unseen, yet chartered courses.

Dear Heavenly Father, in you I am alive, I move and am human. No one else can be me, for I am me all by myself. Thank you for creating me in your image. As I seek to unearth and excavate the unlimited possibilities that are secretly hidden within, allow me to drink from the wellsprings of your wisdom, and prime the pump of resources overflowing with your holy Word. You make me so much more than a conqueror; therefore, I will not give in to defeat, or circumstance. Even when hope seems temporarily deferred, I trust the answer will come at the appointed time. When I must feel my way along with blind faith, Lord teach me, I pray, how to grope in hope. Amen

Flaming Hearts

When all the people saw it, they fell on their faces, and they said, the Lord, He is the God; The Lord, He is the God. (1 Kings 18:39).

When Elijah proposed spiritual warfare with the natural element of fire, I was reminded of a song I sang as a youngster many years ago. "I don't want to set the world on fire. I just want to start a flame in your heart."

The Israelites were prone to serving Pagan gods, as other nations, so there was a dire need to rekindle the flame of faithfulness to the one and only true God of Israel; therefore, Elijah boldly challenged King Ahab, and all of the pagan prophets with a fiery proposal as a solo representative of the God of Abraham, Isaac and Jacob. "He said call on your Gods, and I will call on the name of the Lord, and the God that answers by fire let Him be God," and it was so. The pagan god was lifeless, deaf, and unresponsive, but the God of Israel answered with fire and there was victory at Mount Carmel.

> The altar was completely broken down
> And was much in need of repair.
> The idol worshipers fell on it,
> Overcome by defeat and utter despair.
>
> The false priests cut themselves and bled;
> However to no avail.
> Elijah knew without a doubt
> The true God would prevail.
>
> God who answered with fire,
> Set ablaze the offering,
> And all who had disbelieved,
> They paid tribute to the King of Kings.

Follow ME

Trust in the Lord with all your heart, and lean not unto your own understanding. (Prov 3:5).

It is possible that up until this moment you have yet to experience a life changing encounter on a spiritual level. Open your heart and let Jesus fill it. Begin living a spirit filled life, and then trust God for every single detail of your life from now on. No more doubting. Trust the Good Shepherd, and then follow Him.

> The time has come. Have faith in ME.
> Believe, although you may not see,
> How I will bring a turnabout.
> Rely on ME! Never doubt.
>
> When the flood of the enemy
> Sets you out adrift at sea,
> Fear not dark seasons of the soul.
> Follow ME! I'm in control.

Foolish Folly

Answer not a fool in his folly. (Prov 26:4).

There is nothing of any lasting good to be gained from foolish folly. We know only too well that it is a waste of time to reason with those who are prone to foolishness because fools despise wisdom and mock sin. Foolish folly is wholeheartedly engaging in unpractical dealings, acting without remorse, and sinning without regret. It is thinking that one will escape having to give account of all unrighteous seeds so willingly sown of one's own accord. It is living a God fearless life without considering that tomorrow may not be yours to have. Foolish folly is never taking God seriously at His Word. A fool has no delight in understanding. (Prov 18:2).

Being foolish will lead to an unavoidable woe unless those who are foolish desire to become prudent and wise in heart, for understanding is a wellspring of life for the righteous, but the instruction of fools is folly. (Prov 16:22). So if you desire to be a fool, why not make it count for something and be a fool for Christ's sake. Read (1 Cor 4:10). Good! Now read (1 Cor 2:14). May the Word convict you to know that the natural man is a fool, and unless you decide to let him die, and be reborn of the spirit, you will never be able to discern foolishness through the wisdom of God. What am I saying here? You will remain a fool!

> Want to be wise? Then follow this rule.
> Avoid the presence of a fool.
> Dwell among the prudent and wise,
> And you will see things through God's eyes.

Four Little Wise Things

There be four things which are little upon the earth, but they are exceeding wise. (Prov 30:24).

A time honored practice of the ants, is to gather meat during summertime. Unlike the sluggard, and slothful, the ants are wise enough to "make hay while the sun is still shining." How wise! Next, are the conies. These little creatures build their homes in the hills as a source of protection from intruding wild animals. How wise! In addition to the ants, and the conies, the third small things are called locusts. Interesting to note, is the fact that they have no leader, yet so amazingly, they move forward in bands. How wise! Finally, the fourth tiny wise things are known as spiders, and what is so unique about creepy crawlers is that they are able to survive anywhere at all. Even in king's palaces! How wise!

> Ants, conies, locusts and spiders
> Seem insignificant due to their size,
> But yet if we consider their way,
> We too can learn how to be wise.

Frigid and Rigid

The fruit of the spirit is love, joy, peace, longsuffering, gentleness, goodness, faith, meekness and temperance. (Gal 5:22-23).

A gentle spirit in a loving way, can give joy, and peace through longsuffering to frigid and rigid folk, for we are told that we should overcome evil with goodness. When we persevere and strive to remain meek, and humble, we can defrost icy spirits when those icicles are protruding and heavily hanging out.

When a constant spirit of temperance is exhibited, Saints can instantly warm up cold blooded people, and quickly thaw them out as the temperature of the Holy Ghost continues to escalate to the point of a burning sensation. Remember, warmth is like a cozy fire on a cold wintry day. It is always welcomed, and warmly received.

> If there's a chill in your air,
> God did not put it there.
> Were it not for goodness, many would faint.
> Thank God above for a warmhearted Saint.

Garment or Torment

So he said to him, Friend, how did you come in here without a wedding garment? And he was speechless. (Matt 22:12).

Once upon a time, Jesus shared the parable of the great wedding feast wherein a certain king commanded his servants to invite guests to his son's great marriage, and wedding feast, but they were unwilling to accept the invitation and did not come. Again, he sent out other servants inviting more to come in and partake of the royally prepared wedding feast, but some were too busy, and some of the others not only refused the invitation, but also killed the messengers.

The king, of course, wielded his wrath and burned up their city, for they were unworthy, and then he instructed his servants to go unto the highways and gather both good and bad, so the wedding hall was filled with invited guests who accepted the extended invitation; however, the king discovered there was one uninvited guest. How so? This one particular guest was improperly dressed without a wedding garment. So when questioned by the king he remained speechless, so the servants bound him and cast him into outer darkness. The end!

> Invited to the wedding feast?
> Don't arrive without your garment,
> Or the King will cast you out.
> So be it; Garment, or torment.

Gehazi Greed

But he went in, and stood before his master, and Elisha said unto him, where are you coming from, and he said, thy servant went nowhere. (2 Kings 5:25).

Some things are not easily overcome. If you are like most, certainly you can understand what drove Gehazi to deceive Naaman, and then lie to his master, Elisha, in order to retrieve riches under false pretenses. Greed!

Naaman, Captain of the host of the King of Syria, was high on the totem pole. He was an honorable man respected by the King, but there was one major drawback. Naaman was a leper. Having heard that the prophet, Elisha, in Samaria could heal him of such a dreadful disease, he called on Elisha and awaited a response from him. But Elisha, as humbling as it may have been to Naaman, sent a messenger out to him who instructed him to go and wash in the muddy Jordan seven times, and be healed. And so it was!

Naaman was so appreciative that he desired to bless Elisha with a generous offering, but Elisha refused to accept the gift offered him. As you can guess, Gehazi, Elisha's servant, cleverly seized the opportunity to obtain wealth for himself, but his excessive, extreme desire for riches caused him to pay a far greater price than he had sought to gain through dishonesty.

> Satan has many deadly traps
> And one is known as greed.
> Gehazi was stricken with leprosy.
> God also cursed his seed.

Getting By Blessings

What wilt thou that I shall do unto thee? (Luke 18:35-43).

Even though some of the crowd rebuked the blind man by attempting to silence him, he persistently cried out to Jesus until Christ commanded that he be brought before him. Of course, Jesus already knew that the blind man desired to receive his sight. Still, He asked him, "What wilt thou that I shall do unto thee?"

Undoubtedly, that same question is also directed to us each time we approach the throne of grace in prayer. Surely, we can ask God to fulfill His promises by asking in the name of Jesus, and then claiming through faith, His will by His word, as we kneel before Him, and make our requests known unto Him. So don't just settle for every day blessings. Ask for the moon, and then you will walk among the stars.

> When the Lord shall ask of you,
> "What will you have me do?"
> Speak your request and then believe
> That He will follow through.

Give It A Rest!

Even God rested! (Gen 2:2).

As we sail across the flowing sea of life, so often we are swept away by strong moving currents that hurriedly carry us further along downstream. Twirling whirlpools encircle us, and with a sucking motion, we become entrapped as we begin to sink deeper and deeper into the depth of the bottomless sea of unrest.

Does not God give His beloved rest? There comes a time in life when we need to be washed ashore by the lazy, slow moving waves of ease unto the shores of calm, serenity, and the banks of quiet peacefulness.

Give it a rest! Refrain from the jet set, turbo charged, hustle bustle, and helter-skelter, fast paced lifestyle. Caution! Attempting to be everything to everybody all the time will eventually wipe you out, and shut you down. So pare down! Chill out! Unwind! Steal away!

> Nothing at all has changed.
> God still knows what is best.
> So do yourself a favor.
> Steal away and learn to rest.

Give It All You've Got

I must work the works of him that sent me, while it is day. The night will come when no man can work. (John 9:4).

In which way do we most honor our Lord and Savior, Jesus Christ? By giving Him all we've got.

It takes a fervent spirit
To reap heaven's reward.
A wise and faithful servant
Will labor long, and work hard.

Do not be sluggish, or slothful.
Tend the Master's field.
Be about God's business
And then the crop will yield.

Soon the roll will be called
When the day is done,
So work while it is day,
For very soon the night will come.

"Be steadfast and immovable."
Refuse to faint not.
Serve the Lord with gladness.
Give it all you've got.

The first will be last,
And oh, how hearts will envy
When God crowns all his servants
To rule over many.

A portion of the meat
Will be given in due season.
So give it all you've got.
There is no better reason.

God at His Best All the Time

Is anything too hard for the Lord? (Gen 18:14).

There is never a time when God is not at His best. Every day in myriad ways, we discover that there is never a time at all when God is not at His best. When we feel the weakest and most vulnerable, is certainly the time to lean on God, and not question His moves, but trust Him through it all.

As we remain anchored, steadfast and spiritually centered in Him, instead of attempting to handle our problems singlehandedly, our less than perfect drawbacks will become fewer in number as our self driven notions surrender unto divine assistance.

All we need to remember is that God doesn't need our help whenever we need help from Him because God is God at His best all of the time! He is in a class all by Himself! He is the Master! So trust Him!

> When life throws you a curve ball
> That you do not understand,
> Toss it up to Jesus,
> And leave it in His hand.

God Found Me

Likewise, I say unto you, there is joy in the presence of the angels of God over one sinner that repents. (Luke 15:10).

The topmost place of power is found when we are brought into situations which oblige us to exercise faith. It is then, we truly discover that God's saving grace and undying love, spans every gulf, and bears us over every abyss of trouble. What a blessing that someone always has us in mind, and sets aside the time to pray for us!

Like the prodigal son, an unwise one,
I was on my own.
Strung out, stripped bear, with no one to care.
The street was my home.

Made very bad choices, ignored angel's voices,
I did it my way.
There were unfamiliar faces, in strange, unwelcome places.
Hear what I say!

Throughout all my straying, I heard my mama praying
Lord! Save my child!
Satan held me fast, but now I'm saved at last,
And so, I smile.

God found me!
I was blind, confused and lost,
But the power of the cross
Set me free.

God found me!
He answered mama's prayer,
And lifted me up where
I longed to be.

God found me!
He said, "Child! Welcome home!"
No more will I roam.
I'm His alone.

Yes! God found me!

God Is Bad With the But(s)

And the Lord said, Simon, Simon! Indeed, Satan has asked for you, that he may sift you as wheat. But I have prayed for you that your faith should not fail; and when you have returned to me, strengthen your brethren. (Luke 22: 31 & 32).

I wrestled with this particular message a long time, but it kept coming back to me, over and over again. So here it is. If someone were to say to you, "go head on with your bad butt!" How would you feel about that? From a slang point of view, bad takes on a completely new meaning. It means you have it all together! You've got it going on!

We all know that the word butt means the rear end, or something we sit on. But the 'but' I'm talking about in relation to God is the 'but' that makes a vast difference in a situation and phenomenally changes the outcome to swing the odds in our favor when adversities appear to be hopeless and beyond our control as to a feasible solution. Satan would have sifted Simon as wheat. But Jesus prayed that his faith would not fail. Many are the afflictions of the righteous, but the Lord will deliver him out of them all. (Ps 34.19). Get the picture? Sure you do. God is big and bad! He reigns supreme, and He is God all by Himself. There is absolutely no one, and positively nothing that can equal or measure up to God. So bow down and salute His majesty because He is worthy of all praise. God is indeed bad with the 'but(s).'

> Thank God that when we find ourselves
> Entrapped and caught up in a rut,
> It is God who makes the difference.
> He is bad with the 'but(s).'

God Is My Backbone

The Lord is the strength of my life. (Ps 27:1).

According to Webster's dictionary, backbone is defined as the spinal column and main support. Additionally, from another point of view, backbone also means someone who is strong and courageous, and the main source and strength of one's life. Isn't God all of these things and more?

One of my mother's favorite hymns was "I know what He is to me." From her personal experience with the Master, she wholeheartedly, undoubtedly affirmed, that Jesus was her backbone; her all and all.

Is God your backbone? If not, without Him, you are headed for a backbreaking experience. After all, it is Satan's job to render you helplessly and spiritually inactive. Do not suffer mercilessly from spiritual paralysis. Do not allow Satan to crash your system and shut you down. Look up, and log into the main support system. Jesus Christ.

> Put your trust in Jesus.
> Don't try to go it alone.
> He is joy and strength in life.
> God is your backbone.

God Is My Therapist

In all thy ways acknowledge Him and He shall direct thy paths. (Prov 3:6.)

"How may I help you?"
Oh! God! I have some issues.
"To cry is human. Grab a tissue.
Weeping endures for only a while.
Joy will comfort you soon, dear child."

I'm upset and so angry!
"What's this all about?
I'm sure that I can bail you out!"
Well! Uh! God, I don't even remember.
"Then why are you still stirring the cinder?"

Life is like a puzzle.
Nothing seems to fit.
"Then stop relying on your own wit.
If you think that you can figure things out.
The time has come for me to bow out."

By the way,
I can't make our session tomorrow.
"Then you will borrow unbearable sorrow."
But God, I'm unable to pay the fee.
"You need not worry! My service is free!"

God Unlimited

He is able to do exceeding abundantly above and beyond our expectations. (Eph 3:20).

Stop limiting God! Oftentimes, we expect so little from such a great big God. His promises are extraordinarily large, but small thinking on a minor scale results in shrinkage and reduction in size of so many numerous and countless blessings because we fail to think outside of the box we have placed God inside of. Maximum faith! Great blessings!—Minimal faith, tiny blessings.

> Unlimited blessings will overflow
> If only you will just let go.
> Believe that God will abundantly bless.
> Then trust Him in His faithfulness.

Good While It Lasted

Surely goodness and mercy shall follow me all the days of my life, and I will dwell in the house of the Lord forever. (Ps 23:6).

There is a saying that goes, "It was good while it lasted." And while that is true in some instances, the goodness of God is an exception to the rule. He never reneges, or fails to carry out a promise, or commitment. So if or when a cheerful good morning greeting is exchanged with a gloomy, 'what's so good about it response,' don't be at a loss for words. In the words of a very popular old song, always "accentuate the positive and eliminate the negative," with the uplifting Word of God.

First of all, it is a day the Lord has made, so we should rejoice and be glad in it. (Ps 118:24). Also in (Lamentations 3:22 & 23), we are reminded that the Lord is a compassionate God whose mercy never fails, and because of His renewed compassion every morning, and His great faithfulness, we are not consumed.

In summation, although many earthly things are ephemeral, and only last a short time, we may rest assured that God's goodness and mercy will follow us all the days of our lives, and we will dwell in His house forevermore. Insofar as God is concerned, thank God, we will never have to say that His goodness was good while it lasted.

> Charlamane Ervin, a member of New Northside Baptist Church,
> Has always claimed and understood
> That "God is good all the time,
> And all the time, God is good."

Goody Two Shoes

Withhold not good from them to whom it is due when it is in the power of your hand to do so. (Prov 3:27).

Let me define what good really means. A good definition for goodness is defined as "having desirable qualities; not spoiled or ruined; able to be used." So then, God is looking for 'Goody Two shoes' people. Those who unselfishly choose to do good rather than be up to no good, and those who are willing to go above and beyond to give a refreshing cup of cold water to a thirsty neighbor in need. (Matt 10:42). These are they who will be remembered for their goodness long after they have passed on through this world and into the next one.

According to (Luke 11:5-7), any time at all is a time to do something good. No matter what the hour, when there arises an opportunity to do some good to someone, by all means, do it. Don't delay!

> Better a goody two shoes
> Than be a soulless heel.
> Have a mind to do some good.
> Then act out how you feel.

Gospel Wheel Meals

I am not ashamed of the Gospel of Christ. (Rom 1:16).

One of the special marks of a Christian is holy audacity. When God brings about a wonderful newness to our lives, it is our duty to share it with others. Think about where your heart really belongs and you will gain the spiritual fortitude to forge ahead and run the risk of approaching total strangers, and sharing the Word of God with them even though they may be unwilling to receive or accept it as such. Why? Because saving souls is a top priority thing. You have only begun to realize the life changing encounters that happen when holy boldness steps into play.

Everywhere we go someone is hungry for the Word, so we must feed God's sheep and continue to bring lost sheep into the heavenly fold. Sister Jeanne Anderson, a spiritually inspired, high praising Child of the King, makes it her business to feed the spiritually starved folk on her personal bus ministry by boldly witnessing for the Lord to people in transit aboard the Bi-State Bus in Saint Louis, Missouri. How bold is that?

> Serve Gospel meals on wheels
> So hungry souls may be fed.
> The Word of God can feed the world
> With everlasting, living bread.

Grasshoppers and Giants

And there we saw the giants, the sons of Anak, which come of the giants and we were in our own sight as grasshoppers and so we were in their sight. (Num 13:33).

Moses sent spies into Canaan to search the land, whether it be good or bad, tents or strongholds, and also if the inhabitants were weak or strong. There are all kinds of ways that we can view a situation. Let me explain. By anyone's standard, the fruit was plentiful, and the cities were walled. With this in mind, Canaan seemed an ideal place to be. But that wasn't the whole story. There were giants in Canaan. The harsh reality is that most of the spies passively resigned themselves to the fact that it would be impossible to overcome the giants that loomed ahead of them, so fear toyed with their minds. But Joshua, the son of Nun, and Caleb, the son of Jephunneh, stood their ground with differing opinions. They urged the Israelites to seize the opportunity to step forward and exercise faith, and slay giants victoriously in the Name of the Lord!

> Feeling like a grasshopper?
> So often, we all do.
> But when it comes to giants,
> God will fight for you.

Gun Happy Smoking Guns

The fear of man brings a snare, but whoever puts his trust in the Lord shall be safe. (Prov 29:25).

Although we live in a world that is quite often unsafe, we need not fear. Dangers do exist, but we are still safe in God's loving and protective arms.

Not long ago, I sorrowfully recall having read of a tragedy that happened because a man assumed that someone with evil intentions had broken into his home. Thinking that all of his loved ones were sound asleep in bed, he heard what he thought was an intruder. Immediately, he aimed his weapon, spontaneously released the trigger, and without even so much as a word of warning opened fire on whom he thought meant to cause him, or his family bodily harm. He discovered, however, as he recognized the limp and lifeless figure sprawled out before him, that he had mortally wounded his own daughter who had decided to arise early, and take out the trash. And while there is a growing concern for protection in our homes, it is sincerely hoped that such an ill twist of fate will not continue to happen again. Certainly, we want to feel safe in our homes, but the flip side of the coin is that Satan can seduce us into becoming too gun happy, and then, sadly regretful, later on. Too many loved ones, including innocent toddlers, are victims of guns. Beware of weapons in the home!

> Once you pull the trigger.
> Nothing can be undone.
> Be sure it's not your loved one,
> Before you aim and fire the gun.

Hand me down Religion

Heaven and earth shall pass away, but my words shall not pass away. (Matt 24:35).

It is reasonable to expect fads and trends to come in, and go out of style, but there is more than underlying evidence that 'Hand me down Religion' is here to stay.

It has long been recognized that the ancient landmarks of times past are still well known guideposts in our modern praise world of today, and we as recipients of that old fashioned religion should continue to play an increasingly important role in continuing to maintain, and heighten the awareness of the Old School Religion, and pass it on down the line to the future churches of tomorrow.

Undoubtedly, the soul stirring hymns, knee slapping and toe tapping quartets, church picnics, social gatherings, long miles of walking, and wagon rides to the little country church in the woods, still delivers the same soul saving message of our ancestors to our somewhat sophisticated and dignified manner of praising the Lord. It still takes that old 'Hand me down Religion" to keep us spiritually strong and fit in order to keep moving on in the name of the Lord. As is so often stated, "when praises go up, blessings come down" from generation unto generation, down throughout the coming years.

> Echoes from the past
> Still usher us up higher.
> Old Hand me down Religion!
> It will set your soul on fire.

Hanging By A Hinge

Now unto him that is able to keep you from falling. (Jude 1:24).

Holding fast to an unanchored foundation is not a good thing, for doing so will result unfavorably. It will cause you to dangerously hang by a hinge, and then dangle precariously in mid air. Believers may rest assured in knowing that there is nothing more solid than Jesus. But what if you have not claimed a piece of the rock? Then expect your foundation to crumble any day now. Jesus is the only true foundation there is.

Should you eventually find yourself clinging to the edge of life's cliff in a desperate attempt to hold on for your own life's sake, don't count on the devil to throw you a lifeline because he is the reason you are haphazardly holding on in the first place. His rope; however, is much too thin, and will not support you at all, and he is completely aware of that. Besides, isn't it his job, any way he can, to entice you to let go and take the plunge down below? Your only hope then is Jesus. He alone, is able to keep you from falling, and plummeting down into the cannon of destruction anxiously awaiting your arrival.

Hanging by a hinge on the brink of disaster? Have you invested in a piece of the Rock? If not, now would be a good time to do so. God's grace will catch you if you are willing to look up, cry out, and receive His outstretched almighty hand of grace and mercy. Want to be daring? Grab hold to a piece of the rock, and cling unto a rock solid foundation.

> Hanging by a hinge
> Is not at all divine
> Unless the net that catches you is the real True Vine.

Happy Death Day!

Precious in the sight of the Lord is the death of his Saints. (Ps 116:15).

Year after year, as time continues to roll around, from a child on, we have enjoyed the traditional Happy Birthday song, so cheerfully sung to us by our loved ones, and so many other well wishers.

So often it is stated, "Everybody wants to go to heaven, but nobody wants to die." Death, the grim reaper, is the uninvited guest in every home. And while no one can change the inevitable, we can spiritually prepare ourselves for the triumphant change over from mortality to immortality when our time journey on earth comes to its final close. How so? Accept Jesus as your personal Savior, and immediately your name will be written in the Book of Life, and you will pass from death unto life everlasting. How simple is that? According to (Matt 25:21), God's Sheep will inherit the kingdom prepared from the foundation of the world. So if you must die, and you surely will, die in Jesus Christ and have a Happy Death Day!

> Only the redeemed
> Will hear the angels sing
> Welcome home! Oh! Child of God!
> Behold the risen King.
>
> So it is all up to you.
> Decide! Do not delay.
> Let God receive you unto Him
> And have a Happy Transition Day.

Happy Rocking

Come apart to a desert place and rest a while. (Mark 6:31).

From an old spiritual hymn were penned the words, "Rock my soul in the bosom of Abraham. Lord! Rock my soul!" There were, still are, and will always be, those who have mastered the art of rocking. Like a gentle, soothing lullaby lulls a baby into a sweet, contented state of peacefulness, rocking is good for the soul. Try it! Steal away, meditate, and feel life's rhythm sway. Happy rocking!

Oh! How I love my rocking chair.
Gonna rock my cares away!
Hard times ain't forever,
And I'm not here to stay.

Oh! I love my rocking chair.
It soothes a tired soul.
I love to rock, relax and sing.
It makes me feel complete and whole.

Oh! I love my rocking chair.
Yes! You will find me there.
Tarrying with Jesus,
I greet Him with a prayer.

Oh! I love my rocking chair.
I keep time with my feet.
I sway to even rhythm
And rock steady to the beat.

Gonna rock away frustration!
Gonna rock the blues away!
Gonna rock away all sadness!
Rock me Lord! I pray.

Oh! I love my rocking chair!
Gonna rock my cares away!
Hard times ain't forever
And I'm not here to stay. No! I'm not here to stay.

Healing of the Mind, Body, and Soul

Who himself bore our sins in his own body on the tree, that we, having died to sins, might live for righteousness, by whose stripes we are healed. (1 Pet 2:24).

Search the scriptures, and you will find
That healing comes with a Christ like mind,
So let the same mind be in you,
And a brand new creature will spring anew.

Haven't you read? Haven't you heard?
There is healing in the Word.
Through His Word, the truth is revealed,
And with His stripes, we are healed.

God will keep you spiritually fit and able.
He is marrow to the bone, and strength to the navel.
So keep your body in Christ alive,
And watch your countenance flourish and thrive.

Let God have complete control.
Give Him your mind, your body, and soul.
Overweight? Want to be slim?
Cast every care you have on Him.

Trust God and put your mind at ease.
He is the healer of all disease.
Diligently seek Him, and He will reward
A sound mind, strong body, blessed soul in the Lord.

Healing Wounds

Faithful are the wounds of a friend, but the kisses of an enemy are deceitful. (Prov 27:6).

Have you ever experienced open rebuke voiced in earnest by a very dear and caring friend? Many there are who become defensive and tell their friends to butt out and mind their own business when they know deep down within their hearts, that true friends are only attempting to save them from the pit of self destruction.

If you have recently been approached by a friend who loves you, and desires to save you from a life threatening situation, read (Prov 27:5). Open honesty is far better than secret love. An enemy will wound to destroy, but a loyal friend will hurt in order to help. The inflicted wounds of a friend are deep, but faithful.

> Friends do not throw punches
> Like enemies to knock you out.
> They only fight to help you
> Make the right turnabout.

Healthy Happiness

A merry heart does good like medicine, but a broken spirit dries the bones. (Prov 17:22).

Indeed it is good to have a cheerful heart. Laughter works like medicine and gives the soul delight, but who can bear a broken spirit, for it causes the heart to sorrow.

What is significant is that if you do not have the joy of the Lord, it is impossible to be happy of your own strength. For joy without God is very short lived, but the joy of the Lord is everlasting strength unto life; and only He is the giver of such joy.

In the greatest of difficulties, only God can allow you to remain cheerful through it all. He can bring a troubled heart out of distress. (Ps 25:17). When life seems fragile and fragmented, talk to Jesus! Happy are the people whose God is their Lord. (Ps 144:15).

Invest in healthy happiness! "Smile, Jesus loves you!"

> Who can mend a broken heart?
> Wounds of life cut deep.
> Happy are those whose God is their Lord.
> God will a cheerful countenance keep.

Hey! Goodbye!

And he said unto them, this is my blood of the New Testament, which is shed for many. (Mark 14:24).

According to (1 Pet 1:18-19), we were not redeemed with corruptible things such as silver or gold, but with the precious blood of Christ, as of a lamb without blemish and without spot.

There is a television commercial that I just love to watch. A woman is so confident that the Tide stick will remove all stains from soiled clothing that she breaks out with a victory song while applying it to the stain, and then very excitedly watches it disappear from the spotted garment. The man with her is so embarrassed when she repeatedly and publicly sings the very popular "Na Na, Na Na! Hey! Goodbye song" that he inquires if it is necessary for her to sing that song every time the Tide stick removes a stain from his clothing. And her reply to him is always the same. "Yes!"

> Jesus Christ died for all
> He wiped all sin away.
> We too, can shout a victory cry.
> Thank God for Jesus! Hey! Hey!

Holding On To Daddy

After this manner therefore pray ye. Our Father which art in heaven! (Matt 6:9).

Some time ago, a true human interest story was televised. It immediately attracted my attention. A concerned mother alarmingly discovered that her little girl was missing. Frantically, she searched for her everywhere, and continuously called out her name, but there was no answer. Of course, fear gripped her heart as she pondered over everything imaginable that might have happened to her daughter. Thank God! The child was returned to her family safe, and unharmed.

Surprisingly, the little girl had decided to accompany her dad to work. Her father sped away in his truck unknowingly unaware that his child was clinging to the back of his truck as he zoomed down the highway, rounding dangerous curves. Thankfully, several drivers in close proximity on the road at that time, spotted the small form desperately holding on, and clinging to her daddy's truck in motion, and successfully managed to get the truck driver to pull over. Needless to say, dad was absolutely stunned, and completely blown away. She wanted to be with her daddy, and she wasn't at all afraid because she knew her Father was driving that truck.

    With childlike faith
    Learn how to cling.
    Don't let go of Jesus for anything.

April

Every good and perfect gift is from above. (James 1:17)

> **A**lways believe you are special in a God blessed way.
> **P**ositively claim your gifts and use them every day.
> **R**ealize your calling. Unto yourself be true.
> **I**nvolve yourself busily, for there is much to do.
> **L**ist your capabilities now, and then simply follow through.

Affirm and see yourself as God's special creation. Think positive thoughts. Share your talent with others along the way. Doing so will leave no room for vanity. With an unselfish spirit, answer the call to your purpose in life, and by all means, to yourself be true. Only then, will your gift make room for you, and you will engage in fruitful endeavors blessed by God, yielding a bountiful harvest worthy of a good and faithful laborer. There is so little time, and so much to do, and few are willing to work in the Master's Vineyard. Pray your gifts honor God's glory. Amen

Horoscope Hope

In all your ways acknowledge Him, and He shall direct your paths. (Prov 3:6).

Although it has been noted that horoscopes are not to be taken seriously, and are only meant for fun, a great number of people allow such to govern their lives. Faithfully, without fail, many anxiously read those daily horoscopes, and then consult the charts in order to determine just how the day will go, or end. If all appears to be astrologically safe, the day begins with great confidence in horoscope hope.

Are you aware that some people prefer to socialize only with those who are compatible to their zodiac signs, and carefully avoid contact with those who are not? At this point, it is safe to assume that 'horoscope hope' may be classified as 'horror'-scope, dope mentality.

Want accuracy? Allow Jesus to tell your fortune. Stop trusting the crystal ball to reveal all of the answers for you. Only God can!

> Horoscope hope will fail,
> For only God can foretell
> Man's future and his destiny.
> So count on Him for accuracy.

How Busy Is Your Body?

Be quiet, and mind your own business. (1 Thess 4:11).

It is good and acceptable in the sight of God to live as quietly, and peacefully as possible according to His holy word.

How busy is your body in matters that should be of no importance to you at all? Quit dipping into someone else's pot of soup, and stir your own porridge. Surprisingly, you may return only to discover that your own pot of soup is burnt, scorched, and bubbling over simply because you were not minding your own business.

Troubling your neighbor's water is not a good thing to do. And if you are one of those people who delight in doing so, the word of caution is—careful! the worst is yet to come. Your own dried up brook!

> Being a busy body
> Will keep things in a tizzy,
> So mind your own business
> And keep your body busy.

How Far away is Heaven?

The day of the Lord comes as a thief in the night. (1 Thess 5:2).

How far away is heaven?
We can't ask those who die,
But a glimpse of heaven's glory
Is like a sun-lit sky.

Heaven is as near
As Jesus is the open door.
Yet it is far beyond our reach.
No flesh and blood can explore.

How far away is heaven?
It is but a breath away.
The longer we exist,
It draws closer every day.

Earthly eyes have not seen,
Nor have human ears heard,
The unseen, untold, heavenly bliss
That is promised in the Word.

How far away is heaven?
Don't ask me? I don't know.
Just keep your house in order.
Stay packed, and ready to go.

Hurdle Jumping

Thanks to God who will always cause us to triumph. (2 Cor 2:14).

Jumping over life's hurdles will develop surefootedness. God compels His people to become champions; therefore, begin to see each hurdle, not as a stumbling block, but as just another reason to champion another cause in the name of the Lord. It is known as spiritual conditioning!

Every time there is an occasion to rise above seemingly insurmountable odds, and land on your feet, you will claim another victory. Be prepared to stagger, stumble, fall, limp, and even crawl if you must, but don't give up because the end is in sight, and "practice makes perfect."

So next time when trouble jumps up to meet you, back up! Get a running start! Gain momentum! Leap higher, higher, and up, and over with confidence. God is on your side, and He will not allow you to fail.

> Back up! Get a running start!
> Leap high, and land on your feet.
> Either way with God you win.
> There is no defeat.

I Don't Have the Money! Honey!

Be content with such things as you have. (Heb 13:5)

There is a wife whose husband's favorite saying is "I don't have the money, honey!" While it may be true that most of us may never sit in the queen's palace, sweet contentment with what we do have can still bring pleasure to those who are willing to improvise and enjoy royalty through simplicity.

It has been said that the best things in life are free. So if your dreams are bigger than your wallet, or purse, enjoy what you can. Nature is free. Bask in the sunlight! Dance in the moonlight! Enjoy the refreshing, summer breeze! Listen to the quiet! Play in the sand! And of course, whenever you can, save! Pay close attention to the following words of wisdom, and I quote, "Make more! Desire less!"

Don't waste time wishing for BIG money. Time will pass you by, dear honey!

> If we were all millionaires,
> We would not have financial cares,
> But being rich without having money
> Is the greatest wealth! Dear honey!

I Know Him

And to know the love of Christ, which passes knowledge, that you might be filled with all the fullness of God. (Eph 3:19).

God has known all along the kind of person you will become after making Him the object of your affection. When we meet God on a more intimate level, and share our innermost feeling with Him, through these experiences we come closer to God, and thus enjoy our lives more abundantly.

I hear Him in the quiet hush
As I walk along life's way.
He speaks above a whisper,
His holy will to obey.

I see Him in the fury
And tempest of a winter storm.
I marvel at His power.
He shelters me from harm.

I feel Him gently stirring
Way down deep within my soul.
I praise Him as almighty God.
What a blessing to behold.

I know Him as a Warrior
To whom the battle belongs.
Victory is mine!
Throughout the night, I hear songs.

I trust Him as a loyal friend
Even unto my last breath.
Nothing separates God's love.
No! Not even death!

I know Him as a Savior.
When all hope was lost.
I turned around and met Him.
He was standing at the cross.

If It Feels Right, Do It!

There is a way that seems right unto man, but its end is the way of death. (Prov 14:12).

If it feels right, do it? I think not! Everything that feels right to us, is not necessarily so! Today, I want you to become aware of the fact that feelings are hatched in the chamber of internal character, and only God knows exactly what we are thinking and feeling all of the time because He alone, knows where we are coming from.

Some folks believe that people who pray are weak, but actually the more we pray, the stronger and wiser we become. The sooner we begin to acknowledge the Lord, the sooner our shortsighted, terminal thinking becomes a thing of the past. With that in mind, how much more then do we need to depend on the Holy Spirit to thoroughly search and seek out with profound introspection, a foolproof system to avoid false and misleading misconceptions that tend to result in poor, and unwise choices when making crucial or life changing decisions.

> Do not trust your gut instinct,
> Or act out how you feel.
> Be led by Godly wisdom,
> And know the Master's will.

If You Let Go, God Will Catch You

What time I am afraid, I will trust in thee. (Ps 56:3).

As I caught the tail end of the evening news broadcast, a young mother shared some incredibly astounding news. Due to a life threatening situation, she was instructed to release her little girl, who was desperately clinging to her mom and allow her to fall to safety. How extremely difficult it must have been for that mother to pry her child's hands away from her and let her fall in order to save her life. But courageously, she followed through and obeyed the command.

What totally amazed me; however, was the end result of it all. Standing next to her mother, was her precious daughter, safe and unharmed.

How often do we helplessly cling from the edge of life's cliff anticipating the worst and expecting a crash landing only to discover that even if we have to let go, God will catch us!

> Sometimes God will shake us loose,
> And simply let us fall,
> Just to let us know
> That He can catch us after all.

I'm A Witness

And Joshua said unto the people, you are witnesses against yourselves in that you have chosen to serve the Lord. (Joshua 24:22).

Let me share a fundamental lesson on swearing yourself in as your own witness. One need only recall how Joshua refused to leave out one single detail of letting the truth be known about the seriousness of Covenant keeping. He left no stone unturned in warning the Israelites that violation of the Covenant would result unfavorably against them since they had so willingly reaffirmed to continue to serve the Lord at the Covenant renewal ceremony in Shechem. And since they confessed with their own mouths to remain true to the God of Moses, such a testimony could bring good, or on the other hand, not so good results based upon their own chosen actions. And the same applies to us today. When we vow to serve God, we must obey His word in order to be an effective witness for Him.

> When you pledge an oath,
> Do not walk astray.
> God's blessings will continue
> When we honor and obey.

It Pays To Be Scared

Fearing the Lord is the beginning of wisdom. A good understanding have all they that do His commandments. His praise endures forever. (Ps 111:10).

It is increasingly less likely that we will faithfully adhere to laws unless such ordinances are strictly enforced when we choose to ignore, or disobey cited rules and regulations. The Holy Bible specifically outlines do(s) and don't(s) in order to live godly, and to an even greater extent, points out the consequences of failure to abide by His commandments. Believers are those who fear God to the point of seriously taking Him at His word. They absolutely refuse to second guess wise counsel, and sound instruction from the Lord.

It is more than safe to assume then, that godly fear is indeed the very best kind of fear to experience, and if you are not afraid of God, you should be! Don't take this the wrong way. To fear the Lord is to reverence Him, and respect all that He is. To not fear God, on the other hand, is to disrespect Him, and to deny all that He is, and is it not indeed a fearful thing to fall into the hands of the living God? (Heb 10:31).

It pays to be scared,
So live holy, and fear the Lord.
Those who do not fear Him
Will reap a 'Sinner's reward.'

It Takes No Fool to Learn
that God Loves Everybody

Greater love has no man than to lay down his life for his friends. (John 15:13).

The inspirational hymn, "What a Friend We Have in Jesus" is a well-loved, all time classic. Jesus is our Friend, and we are His friends when we honor Him and love Him enough to obey His Word.

It takes 'no fool' to learn that (John 3:16) is a real eye opener that points us to the whole truth, so help us God. Only a fool will deny Jesus according to the Word of God, and only a fool will believe that love does not love anyone. God is love, and that is why Jesus died for the understandable reason of salvation. God loves everybody, but not everybody loves Him back. How sad!

> Do not remain a plumb fool,
> Or you will surely die.
> Fall in love with Jesus.
> Stake your claim on high.

It's all in the Face

A merry heart does good like a medicine, but a broken spirit dries the bones. (Prov 17:22).

The more we maintain a cheerful countenance, the better we understand how doing so affects how we look, and how we feel. No matter how we may attempt to fake it, or mask our feelings, it's all in the face. Anyone can be a sad sack. That's easy. But happiness, a continual feast, is a state of mind only for those who choose to claim it.

Countenance is defined as an appearance, or the expression of the face. What does your face say to those around you? What does your countenance reveal to a stranger in passing? What does your aura emanate to the world?

> Worry free trust in God
> Will press all wrinkles away,
> So put on a happy face,
> And let God make your day.

It's Your Move

Behold! He stands at the door and knocks! (Rev 3:20)

Quiet! Listen! He is knocking at the door. Answer, and receive the invitation of a lifetime, and then He will enter and fellowship with you, and you with Him also. To have a close, rewarding relationship with Jesus is the right thing to do. Sadly, and unfortunately, many there are who choose to neglect and ignore such a priceless gift as salvation. (Heb 2:3).

Since tomorrow, and even the rest of today is not promised, if you have not claimed Jesus as your Savior, dare you not tarry to make that move in a one directional pursuit of the Lord. He is knocking! So answer the door. It's your move and yours alone.

> Jesus, God's only begotten Son,
> Redeemed us and paid the price,
> So make that move! Accept Him,
> And gain eternal life.

Jesus! His Name Says It All

For God so loved the world that He gave His only begotten Son, that whosoever believes in Him shall not perish but have everlasting life. (John 3:16).

Just because God loved us
Everlasting life is for all who receive God's Son.
Savior of the world, who to the
Utmost gave His life, a supreme sacrifice. Why? Because
Souls are worth saving.

As you can see, each first letter of the above poem spells out Jesus. Enough said.

Jesus Is Contagious

Among the God's there is none like unto thee. (Ps 86:8).

It is of no use whatsoever to make contact with Jesus if you do not allow yourself to be up close, and personal in your relationship with others because Jesus is contagious. All Believers know that it is far better to be 'Jesus stricken' than to be afflicted with 'Devil-itus' or 'Satani-tus.' Therefore, if you have contracted Jesus, be forewarned that He is highly contagious because His spirit infiltrates, and inundates every vein of your inner spirit to the utmost. Such being the case, do not quarantine your spiritual body from others, but dwell among them, and let them know that "nobody can do you like Jesus!"

> Sinfulness is a deadly disease.
> It will leave you ill at ease.
> And drinking the devil's toxic brew
> Will surely harm and poison you.

> Signed in blood, Jesus wrote,
> "I AM the only antidote."
> Sin sick souls have one prescription.
> The only cure all is redemption.

Jesus Personality

Be transformed by the renewing of the mind. (Rom 12:2).

As we know, it is true that everybody has an individual personality of their own. It not only labels us as who we really are, but it specifically identifies us as to whom we belong.

The world in which we live is a sin producing environment, and given our lifestyles, we are either saved, or unsaved, as revealed by our actions and the things we do, or choose not to do. As Children of the King, we undergo a new conversion, and when that happens, we are saved by His unsurpassable grace, and then a wonderful change comes over us, and we come forth as new creatures and assume the likeness of Jesus.

> That 'Jesus Personality'
> Will shine within your soul
> When you surrender unto Him
> And give Him full control.

Judges

Judge not, and you shall not be judged. (Matt 7:1).

The above scripture merely serves to remind us that none of us are in a position to judge one another. Absolutely none of us are fit to bang the gavel and pronounce judgment upon one another.

Remember the popular song, "Here Comes the Judge?" It is explained in (Matt 7:3), that we need to take a good look at ourselves before judging others. A classic example of such is revealed in (John 8:7). Jesus confronted the crowd that had gathered to stone an adulterous woman to death. The question He posed immediately dispersed her accusers one by one, until all were gone, save Jesus and the adulteress. Famous last words! "He who is without sin, let him cast the first stone!" As the saying goes, "who can afford to throw stones when we all reside in glass houses?"

> Be careful!
> Don't judge others of crime.
> You may be found guilty
> And have to serve time.

Killing Time

For when you die, you shall carry nothing away. Your glory shall not descend after you. (Ps 49:17).

Back in the day, famed singer, Otis Redding sang "Sitting on the dock of the bay, watching the tide roll away." It was a smash hit on the charts. But can we really afford to waste time like that? Often, the first impulse is to stall, put things on the back burner, and procrastinate. "Until I can set aside time to follow my dreams, I just don't have enough time right now to invest in fulfillment, but eventually, I will get around to it later on." You think?

Sooner than we can imagine, death will happen. So then, there comes a time when there is a dire need to take a step toward fulfilling your purpose and destiny along life's path, so quit horsing around and killing time. Time affords the opportunity to do your own thing and make your existence wholeheartedly worthwhile. Accept for yourself all that God has to offer, and then take advantage of the numerous possibilities He awakens within us as followers of Him, and then the Holy Spirit will teach you how to number your days and apply them to wisdom, as is so stated in the Holy Bible. What will you leave behind after your earthly departure? Not your glory! That's for sure!

> You don't have to kill time.
> Time will surely kill you.
> So live a life of purpose,
> And do all that you can do.

Known By Name

And the Lord said unto Moses, I will do this thing that you have spoken, for you have found grace in my sight, and I know you by name. (Ex 33:17).

On occasion, the thought may have crossed your mind about just how close you really are with Our Lord and Savior, Jesus Christ. Nothing seems to help us more than examining ourselves to ensure that all is "up tight" insofar as our personal interaction with God is concerned.

You may be sure that if you are blessed in the Lord and indeed highly favored, God knows your name.

> When grace and favor are given to you,
> Unthinkable things, God will do,
> For when Our Father, knows your name,
> Nothing in life is ever the same.

Launching Pad Power

Pray without ceasing. (1 Thess 5:17).

David affirmed in (Ps 55:17), that he would pray in the evening, in the morning, and at noon because he knew God would hear his prayers, and God did. One particular definition of the word, launch, means to plunge boldly or directly into action. Therefore, one should come boldly unto the throne of grace in order to obtain mercy and find grace to help in time of need. (Heb 4:16).

Since it is known that the prayers of the righteous avails much, we need to pray always with all prayer and supplication in the spirit as noted in (Eph 6:18).

Are you a prayer launcher? The more you pray, the more you create a solid platform and base upon which to release your prayers and propel them into action.

Day by day
And from minute to hour,
Launch your prayers with Holy Ghost Power.

Learned Behavior

Let this mind be in you which was also in Christ Jesus. (Phil 2:5).

When we look at the total picture in retrospect, a lot of time is invested in attempting to cue in on behavioral patterns of those with whom we are closely associated. As the saying goes, "I can read him like a book, or I know what makes her tick." Getting to know someone requires a whole lot of effort. Does it not?

So then, how does one get to know Jesus? And while it is true that no one can read the thoughts of God, we can still get to know Him better. How? An interesting thing happens when we faithfully invest and devote more time in studying the Word of God. He speaks to us through the Word, and the Word continues to increase our heavenly stock. We have a more hopeful outlook as we meditate upon and digest the Word of God. There is a trend employed throughout scripture that will teach us how to behave like Jesus. In that vein, it is possible to observe the behavior of Jesus, and learn how to be more like Him. It is wise to spend a sizeable part of life getting to know Jesus.

> All throughout the Bible,
> Jesus is a trendsetter,
> So daily study the Word of God,
> And you will get to know Him better.

Letting Go

Forget those things which are behind and reach for those things which are before. (Phil 3:13)

Wasn't it just yesterday when all heads used to turn my way?
I was so petite and small, and now, gained a few pounds is all.
Oh look! It's my favorite wrap around skirt. Fellows used to wink and flirt.
What happened to the good old days? Things have changed in many ways.

Oh my! Here's my old prom dress. All it needs is just a press.
For fun, let's see if it will fit. Nope! Looks like I was poured into it.
My fancy high steppers and mini skirt! Too short!! Too high! And my feet hurt!
I can't believe I wore those shoes. Everybody pays some dues.

Since nothing seems to fit anymore. It's time to shop from store to store.
No more tucking it in for a tight squeeze. I give up! Larger size! Please!
Free at last! I can give it away. Cause baby, it's a brand new day!
Gotta new wardrobe! Watch me style! I love who I am! Check out my smile!

I'm letting go! Don't think me strange! The time has come to make a change.
What does not matter, leave it behind, and do what does as time unwinds.
Hey! Silver fox! Looking real good! Just like a woman my age should.
'Sista girl' has got it together! A red hat, with a purple feather!

Lick the 'Flicts'!

A just man falls seven times and arises again. (Prov 24:16).

Whatever conflicts rise up to meet us, we can overcome them, for we are more than conquerors through Jesus Christ, our Lord and Savior. (Rom 8:37). So put on the whole armor of God, and courageously step out into the ring. (Eph 6:11).

Certainly, there are times when the challenger will appear to be extremely intimidating, gigantic, or seemingly undefeatable, but do not helplessly cling to the rope, or fearfully huddle up in a corner. Remember David slew Goliath, and that the Lord is on your side when foes rise up against you. (Ps 118:6).

> The adder may bite, and the bee may sting
> When you are challenged in life's ring,
> But when the enemy calls it a win,
> A fallen, just man, will rise up again.

Little Promise Keeper

Let us hold fast the profession of our faith without wavering, for he is faithful that promised. (Heb 10:23).

I was richly blessed after watching an inspiring episode from the classic Dragnet series, titled "The Christmas Story." Sergeant Friday, portrayed by actor, Jack Webb, always had a very uncanny way of speaking in riddles and driving the truth all the way home.

After futile attempts failed to locate and return a stolen, inexpensive, yet invaluable statue of Baby Jesus to the church, a very innocent culprit suddenly appeared and returned the missing statue of Baby Jesus back into the church in his little red wagon. When asked why he decided to take the statue of Baby Jesus from the nativity scene in the church, the little boy replied that he had promised Jesus that if he blessed him with a little red wagon, he would give Him the very first ride in it. The priest informed Sergeant Friday that the little boy was from a very poor family. Friday's comment was, "Is he Father?"

> When from up above he heard,
> A poor, little boy kept his word.
> He gave Baby Jesus, the very first ride.
> How rich a heart resided inside.

Lost Identity

Then shalt thou walk in thy way safely, and thy foot shall not stumble. (Prov 3:23).

How do we walk safely in the way and not stumble? First of all, walking in the way means to walk in the Light as a Child of the King. Stumble on the other hand, is choosing darkness rather than light. It is walking on the dark side that causes one to stumble and fall from a spiritual point of view.

The value of wisdom and what makes it priceless is that sound wisdom and discretion will allow us to walk safely and not stumble, for He is the Light ever illuminating the pathway ahead of us. Can we change our identity, and who we were born to be? Whatever your gender, God ordained it, and when we attempt to alter who we are, dark clouds surround us, and the way of life chosen is no longer safe as we continue to grope in darkness.

> A woman is born a woman, and a man is born a man.
> Male and female, created He them. It's all about God's plan.
> So be who you were born to be, much more and nothing less.
> Live within His Holy will, and He will surely bless.
>
> Do you struggle with lost identity?
> Ask the Lord to set you free.
> No one knows any better than you,
> Who you are, and what you must do.
>
> If the shoe doesn't fit, there is a reason,
> And life will bloom for only a season.
> So who are you, and what is your calling?
> Walk in the light! It prevents falling.

Lost Time

So teach us to number our days that we may apply our hearts unto wisdom. (Ps 90:12).

A DD214 is a military document that supports total time served during active service. Any period of inactive service, for whatever reason is recorded as time lost. It simply does not count at all.

Considering the fact that even the very hairs of your head are numbered according to (Matt 10:30), can you afford to waste time while engaged in inactive service for the Lord? I think not!

> Make each day count for the Lord.
> Who knows when death's bell will chime?
> You will not be rewarded
> For inactive service, or any lost time.

Lucky Hunches

Blessed and holy are they who have part in the first resurrection because the second death has no power over them at all. (Rev 20:6).

If you are one of those people who would rather count on lucky hunches instead of staking your claim on a sure thing, remember this! You will die, and that is a fact! So if you have been viewing winning the lottery as a foretaste of heaven, there is one catch. No place on earth is like heaven.

Some dream of winning combinations and play them in the lottery, while others solicit help from widely known psychics, hot tips, or other sources, and then follow their urges accordingly. But here is a sure winner every time. You have nothing to lose when you bank on God. Here's how! Take a chance with God! Get to know Jesus, and then receive salvation. After all, what better way could you spend eternity than escaping the second death which is hell, and receiving eternal life, which is heaven.

A lucky hunch will never win a ticket into heaven.
You must enter through the door. No seven come eleven.
It is all or nothing and the stakes are very high.
So have a hunch for Jesus, or prepare to die.

Lumpy Grits

Oh Lord, our Lord, how excellent is thy name in all the earth. (Ps 8:9).

There are some people who say and many more who believe that we call all the shots concerning how we choose to cope with life's highs and lows, and lumps in our grits. Someone once said, "Keep a spare tire, and you will never have a blowout!" While there is some truth in this belief given certain circumstances, even a spare tire will flatten when suddenly punctured by something unseen and totally unexpected.

We can do everything in our power to be the best that we are able, but when it boils down to it, we will more than likely run out of steam in attempting to press out all of those unsightly wrinkles all by ourselves. To place things in perspective, the bible reminds us to include God in every aspect of our lives because He indeed is as excellent as His name, and we are not.

If you need help,
And you are at your wit's end,
God can even out rough spots
And smooth them out again.

So don't throw in the towel,
Give up, or call it quits.
Just ask the Lord to help you
Stir those lumpy grits.

Majors and Minors

There is a time to weep and a time to laugh, a time to mourn, and a time to dance. (Eccl 3:4).

Life like music has its ups and downs, and highs and lows. A sudden sharp turn may render one surprisingly stunned and breathless, and an unexpected thorn may prick a high rising balloon causing the air to escape, and immediately everything in your world will suddenly go flat.

We might as well get right to the point of it all. Could it be that God gradually takes us slower, or moderately faster due to our (staccato) nature to so very easily become separated and detached? Without sharps and flats, music has no melody, and a life without God is certainly off-beat and ceases to flow rhythmically.

It's up to us to keep our eyes steadily fixed on God, the Conductor, and (legato), everything will be smoothly connected once again. After all, there are major and minor chords on every keyboard of life. So be patient! God will teach you how NOT to major, minor things.

> Whether deep down in the valley,
> Or way up high upon a hill,
> God controls highs and lows
> No matter how we feel.

May

I have fought a good fight! I have finished the course. (2 Tim 4:7-8).

More like Jesus, I want to be.
All of self, I surrender to thee.
Yonder kingdom beckons me.

Today is the day, I desire to become more and more like Jesus. Today is the day, I totally surrender unto Jesus. There is no other way. Self must die!

According to God's Holy Word, He has begun a good work in me, so I will labor while it is day, for surely the sun will set, and all labor must cease. When night comes, yonder kingdom will beckon me into a timeless place where those who are faithful unto death will obtain the prize having fought a good fight, and having stayed the course. With joyful anticipation, for all that is yet to come, thank you Lord Jesus! Find me, I pray, not slothful in business, but diligent in all labor, and so it is.

Man Overboard!

Lord! Save me! (Matt 14:30).

Peter courageously braved the danger of the perilous sea, and walked upon the water to meet Jesus. But there is another twist in this story. As long as Peter kept eye contact with Jesus, he walked upon the sea, but when he looked away, and saw the angry waves of the rolling sea surrounding him, faith failed, and he began to sink. Fearfully, he cried out! "Lord! Save me!"

When waves of affliction create havoc upon the sea of calm, God wants us to focus on Him and not the storm. Of course, it is easier said than done, but that is what true faith is all about. Isn't it?

When I must walk through the storm
Upon the troubled sea,
Will I have faith and believe
That God will rescue me?

Matter of Timing

Hope deferred makes the heart sick, but when the desire comes, it is a tree of life. (Prov 13:12).

God makes everything work out good and right in His own time.

Answer me, God,
You are taking too long.
"Settle down kid!
It takes time to grow strong."

But God, I'm impatient,
And I hate to wait.
"Trust Me!
My timing is never too late."

I need it right now!
Please! Do hurry!
"All cares are mine,
So why should you worry?"

Speed it up God!
Express it today.
"To rush is human.
Expect some delay!"

Step on it God!
A! S! A! P!
"Time is mine.
It belongs to Me!"

But God,
I'm used to having my way.
"Hang up kid!
Call it a day!"

Meant for Good

I am Joseph, your brother, whom you sold into Egypt. (Gen 45:4).

I share the following creation with you poetically. The following poetry highlights Joseph, and how God intervened for his good. Enjoy!

A young lad, known as Joseph, was only seventeen.
Yet he was wise beyond his years. He was a dreamer of dreams.
His older brothers envied him. Perhaps you wonder why?
He was conceived of Jacob's old age, and the apple of his father's eye.

There were many reasons why his own brothers were jealous of him.
Joseph proudly shared his dreams with the lot of them.
The more Joseph revealed his dreams, their hatred kindled all the more.
And their disdainfulness toward him was greater than before.

The strange interpretations of Joseph's vivid dreams
Meant he would someday reign above them all, as it would seem.
Joseph was young, gifted, and endowed with keen vision.
He loved his father, Jacob, who was also blessed with wisdom.

Now Jacob made for Joseph, a colorful, new coat.
How it irked his brothers to watch their father dote.
That huge, wide eyed, green monster was lurking angrily,
So they devised a wicked plan enraged by jealousy.

Destined to deceive and cause harm to another.
They plotted, and conspired against their own brother.
So they disrobed Joseph, and threw him down into a pit.
Then killed a goat, and dipped his coat into the blood of it.

When Jacob saw Joseph's coat drenched and soaked with blood,
Sorrow welled within his heart. His tears were like a flood.
For his dear son, Joseph, did Jacob mourn and weep.
Painful darts pierced his soul, and the wound was deep.

After many years had passed, a famine plagued Joseph's homeland.
So his brothers were in search of a helping hand.
They arrived in Egypt, where Joseph was in command,
Unaware their destiny was all in Joseph's hand.

He made it known unto them that he was Joseph, their brother.
Stunned, awed, and amazed, they fearfully gaped at one another.
"I am Joseph! The Ruler of Egypt! I am alive! God placed me here!"
Then he embraced them, and allayed their guilt and fear.

"I have suffered much, he said, so be it understood,
What was meant for evil, God meant it for my good."
His brothers bowed before him, unraveled at the seams.
Painfully, they faced the truth of their young brother's dreams.

Me? Let Go My Ego?

The Lord will resist the proud, but He will give grace unto the humble. (James 4:6).

Many of us there are who suffer from inflated egoism full blown out of proportion. Some have fallen prey, and addicted to the 'How Great I am, virus syndrome.' Satan targets victims who are egocentric and self centered because they are worshipers of vain glory. To self, Be the glory! Get the picture?

Should you discover that you are guilty of over indulging in too much self glorification, consider yourself an egoist who knows not whither he goes. Decide today, to put the glory where it truly, belongs. Back into the hands of God! If you choose not to give God the glory, the devil will surely steal all of your glory away from you, and claim it all for him.

Me? Let go my ego?
Oh! No! Not self centered me.
I'm just as proud and boastful
As I want to be.

I am totally conceited,
And strictly center ring.
I worship me, and all I am.
I glorify a self made king.

Midnight Special

And at midnight, Paul and Silas prayed and sang praises unto God, and the prisoners heard them. (Acts 16:25).

One of the greatest hindrances to overcoming difficulties is undoubtedly failing to praise the Lord in the midst of it all. I wish I could tell you that it is an easy thing to do, but it isn't. Still, when Paul and Silas were beaten and cast into prison, they refused to allow cruel indignities to lessen their faith in God to deliver them out of harm's way, and continued to praise Him through it all. What a classic example of how to hang on in there when all appears to be bleak and hopeless.

Because Paul and Silas were adaptable and unwavering as soldiers of the cross, not only were they miraculously released from prison, but the keeper of the jail and his entire household accepted the Lord, and all were baptized because of the unyielding faith, and unending trust of Paul and Silas in their Lord and Savior, Jesus Christ.

> Praise Him in the fire.
> Fail not to sing and pray.
> Trouble not your heart.
> God will surely make a way.

Mindful of Man

What is man that you are mindful of him, and the son of man that you visit him? (Ps 8:4).

In my lifetime, and likely in yours too, someone has planted a seed of wisdom to forever bloom in the garden of the mind; a thing remembered.

One of my most favorite grade school teachers, Juanita Rose, who taught at Dunbar Elementary School, posed a question which none of her students could answer at that time. What makes a man more valuable than an animal? As long as I live, I shall never forget the answer to that one particular unanswered question. Ms. Rose simply replied, "Man has a soul."

> What is man that he should boast?
> We should praise God the most.
> All flesh and blood will soon decay,
> But souls will never pass away.

More than One Way to be Rich

The Lord makes poor, and makes rich. He brings low and lifts up. (1 Sam 2:7).

There is much to be said about richness. Our Father is rich in houses and land, and interesting to note is the fact that His richness will never depreciate, or ever lose its value. You need never worry about a depression, regression, or inflation. There is no falling or sinking of God's currency, for His wealth is secure and will remain stationary forever.

There is no returning to the poorhouse once you have claimed prosperity in our Lord and Savior, Jesus Christ, for He will give you everything that even money cannot buy. Why remain poor when you can be richly blessed in the Lord? Claim your fortune and prosper forevermore.

> There are many things in life
> That money cannot buy.
> Rare and priceless treasures
> Await us, by and by.

Move on Over God

In all your ways acknowledge Him, and He shall direct your paths. (Prov 3:6).

Have you ever asked God to move over? When the Lord birthed this poem into my spirit; of course, I questioned Him about the title. "Are you sure this is the title you want me to use, I asked?" Each time; however, that I attempted to change the title, nothing seemed appropriate. As I suspected, many were offended, and whispers were heard when I announced the title of the poem. But after a visual presentation of "Move on Over God" all whispers were silenced, and the audience was richly blessed. Rosalyn Wheeler and Reva Robinson, two very young Saints of God so dear to my heart, have joined the angels, but "Move on Over God" blessed their spirits wholeheartedly, and to this day, the poem is a blessing to many. First of all, when we fail to acknowledge God, we invite Him to move on over, and instantly 'our seat belts' are no longer secure. Next, we tend to run stop signs, drive down one way streets, swerve around dangerous curves, and then due to careless driving, narrowly escape head on collisions unknowingly. Finally, last of all, we come to ourselves with too many near misses from fatal and otherwise unfavorable consequences, call on God, repent, and beg Him to resume driving because we had to learn the hard way why it is safer to drive under the influence of God. In the following poem, the impatient passenger invites God to move on over because He is driving way too slow, so God decides to take him up on the offer. Suddenly; however, the driver of his 'own soul' surprisingly discovers that he is in big trouble, and calls on God to bail him out. So he invites God back into the driver's seat and happily acknowledges God as His Chauffeur.

Food for thought: Have you ever asked God to move on over?

> Move on over God! You're driving way too slow.
> I have some miles to cover. So hurry up! Let's go!
> I have my driver's license, so let me have control.
> I'm an experienced driver, and I can steer my own soul.
>
> So move on over God! Let me in the driver's seat.
> Oh good! Now I can step on it and drive to my own beat.
> What? Pull over? Anything you say.
> Oh Lord! I've got a feeling, today is not my day.
>
> Driving license? Sure! Hold on just one minute.
> Let me find my wallet. I'm sure, I put it in it.
> Oh! No! Officer! I guess in all my haste
> Unbeknownst to me, it must have been misplaced.

Moving violation? What stop sign, and where?
Oh! The one that said CAUTION! SLOW DOWN! PROCEED WITH CARE!
Okay! So I was pushing it when I sped pass,
But ain't no way, I could have been that heavy on the gas!

Oh! Come on now, Officer! Don't issue a citation!
Dear God! Won't you, please, help me out this situation?
Please! Don't lock me up! I don't have a dime!
Oh! Dear God! Where are you? Please! Help me pay this fine!

God! You're back in charge! I'm giving up my seat.
Buckle me up for safety, and drive me down life's street.
You are my soul's best driver. Of this, I have no doubt.
I'm moving over God. Your passenger! Over and out!

Must Need Love Today

We love Him, because He first loved us. (1 John 4:19).

The world renowned actor and singer, Dean Martin always sang, "You're nobody, 'til' somebody Loves You." As we see, eye to eye, we can all identify with the greatest love of all. Jesus loved each and every one of us all the way to the cross, and there was no respect of persons. So when love seems far away, get up close and personal with Jesus. Go ahead! Let Him make your day.

I'm going around in circles,
It seems I'm getting nowhere.
My heart feels so heavy.
I'm weighted down with a load of care.

Why? Why do I feel this way? Where is love, love, today?

I'm standing at the crossroads,
Please! Help my uncertainty.
So many roads to choose,
But which is the one for me.

Why? Why do I feel this way? I gotta have love, love today.

I'm feeling so all alone.
But people are everywhere.
Lord! I need someone special
And some tender, loving care.

Tell me why? Why do I feel this way? I'm searching for love, love today.

I tried shaking away this feeling
That keeps on haunting me,
But shadows of my emotions
All seem to follow me.

Why? Why do I feel this way? I must need love, love, today.

Mustard Seed Faith

If you have faith as a grain of mustard seed, nothing shall be impossible unto you. (Matt: 17:20 & 21).

So often it is true that so many of us are needlessly living at a level of faith far beneath that which God wants for us. How many times we find that we are lacking when faith is warranted for whatever reason. Still, we have a humanly characteristic way of wanting to see a way instead of believing a way can or will be made, and that is not faith. Faith is complete and total trust in God, our Heavenly Father, to take charge of the situation, and work it out for our own good like no one else can.

Faith, when viewed individually, can work wonders, and according to our heightened level of faith, fasting and prayer life, so be it!

No matter who we are, or what our life circumstances may be, just a little bit of 'mustard seed faith' can, and will move mountains.

> Faith is not faith
> When you can see, and then believe it.
> Faith is when you cannot see.
> But still believe you will receive it.

My Favorite Valentine

There is a time to love, and a time to hate; a time of war, and a time of peace. (Eccles 3:8).

I always looked for ways to express my love to mama. It was Valentine's Day, February 14, 1992. After work, I paid mom a visit and presented her with a poem from yours truly, and that was not all. I treated her to a scrumptious 'take out' meal for two which we both enjoyed in the comfort of her home.

Now would be a good time to say that I spent years of quality time with mama not only on those special occasions, but we shared that 'special' mother and daughter connection down through the years. Seven years later, mom joined the angels, and I can truly say that I am grateful that God blessed me with many precious years of 'time to love' and enjoy such a lovable and unforgettable mom.

Mom, this is just a little note
Simply meant to say
That you are special to me
Not only just today.

You are the kind of mother
The world could use more of.
And I am so richly blessed
To feel a mother's love.

I count you as a blessing.
And when it's all said and done.
You will always win by vote.
You are number one!

Long ago, you taught me,
It was many a year.
"Always love, Jesus First,
And then, mother, dear."

Happy Valentine's Day! Mom, I love you!

Neat Freaks

Know you not that your body is the temple of God? (1 Cor 6:19-20).

"Cleanliness is next to Godliness" may be a somewhat trite and overused cliché, but frankly speaking, truer words have never been spoken. Any way you slice it, sin is dirty and unclean, and such will always separate us from God.

It stands to reason then that since most of us work at keeping our homes, and places of business tidy and neat, we as Fellow Believers, must strive, on a daily basis to keep our bodies clean as temples of God. After all, isn't that what matters the most?

How many times we find that it will soon be apparent to all that our housekeeping skills in keeping our temples clean as Children of God, will tell on us when the white glove method is applied and un-cleanliness is finally revealed. What am I saying here? What it will require each of us to do is nothing short of strict adherence to praying, reading, and doing whatever is required to keep our bodies clean as temples of God, and the most effective way to do this is to clean your temple every day through personal fellowship and daily worship with the Lord.

> Keep God's temple clean,
> And He will within abide,
> But if you fail to tidy up,
> He will remain outside.

Never Outnumbered

So he answered, Do not fear, for those who are with us are more than those who are with them. (2 Kings 6:16).

Hard as it is to let go and let God, Elisha remained undisturbed by the alarming report presented to him by his servant. A great host had come by night and compassed the city about with horses and chariots. It is of such importance that we rely on God no matter how insurmountable a situation may seem.

It is for this reason that Elisha reminded his servant that God is much bigger than any archenemy, or gigantic foe on the battlefield. God is far more interested in us believing what we are unable to see. That's faith! Still, Elisha prayed that God would open the eyes of his frightened servant, and so God answered his prayer, and the young man saw a mountain full of horses, and chariots of fire about Elisha.

> Perhaps the hardest thing to do
> When everything looks really bad
> Is to trust the Lord unwaveringly
> And stand assured, battle clad.

Never Trust a Snake

The serpent was more subtle than any beast of the field which the Lord God had made. (Gen 3:1).

As we know, Eve was beguiled and deceived by a deceptive snake in the Garden of Eden, and the fall of man was the end result.

I recall a story once told of a man who befriended a snake and brought him into his home to warm up. It was freezing outside, so he laid him in front of the fireplace. As soon as the snake warmed up, it raised up its head, and began to look at the man with a gleam in its eyes. Having noticed, the man said to the snake. "Remember now! "You promised not to harm me if I rescued you from the bitter cold." The snake slithered ever close and slyly replied. "I was talking then, but I'm acting now!" I shall never forget that story, and neither should you.

And while it is true that all snakes are not venomous, some will wrap around its prey, squeeze, and crush the living life out of its victim. By the way, there are people who similarly behave in like fashion. They tend to maneuver in a hidden, sneaky, and unusual, injurious way, and will recoil, and strike again without warning at any unexpected time, and their poison is deadlier than the bite.

> Take care! Beware of Snakes!
> Learn a lesson from Eve.
> A snake cannot be trusted.
> It is destined to deceive.

No Parole from the Hole

Depart from me, I know you not. (Matt 7:23).

God is the only one who can pronounce a death sentence. Let me make this a little easier to understand. Man can kill the body, but according to (Matt 10:28), God is able to destroy both soul and body in hell. Not only that, but think about this also. It is appointed unto man once to die, and then the judgment. (Heb 9:27). So make it your business to use time wisely. Number your days, and spend them suffering if you must, for all of the right reasons. (Ps 90:12).

And while it is better to suffer for Christ rather than as a thief, or murderer, the truth be told, each one of us are sitting on death row until we choose to accept our Lord and Savior, Jesus Christ, as the Redeemer of Salvation.

> There is no means of escape.
> It is from the grave, to the bottomless pit.
> All lost souls are hell bound,
> And that's the truth, so hear it.
>
> While time is on your side
> And death, still awaits,
> Oh! Sinner! Turn to Jesus,
> He is the Keeper of heaven's gates.
>
> There's a Warden with no pardon.
> He will grant no weekend pass.
> No parole, from the hole.
> Eternal damnation no one can outlast.

No Substitute for God

So the scribe said to him. Well said, Teacher, you have spoken the truth, for there is one God, and there is none other but He. (Mark 12:32).

Time and time again, many look for that Pot of Gold, "Somewhere over the rainbow." Over and over again, others search for a "Thrill on Blueberry Hill." And repeatedly, and superstitiously, people tend to "Knock! Knock! Knock on Wood" for good luck. Is it working?

If you are from the old school, surely you recall many of the oldies but goodies, and blasts from the past. Songs deliver messages. "Stop in the Name of Love!" God is love, so stop worshiping other Gods. There's only one, and it is Him. "What Becomes of the Brokenhearted?" God will heal and bless you coming and going if you obey and acknowledge Him. Let's face it! If the "Thrill is Gone Away," maybe you "Made Your Move Too Soon," away from the True God of Abraham, Isaac and Jacob. There is no substitute for God. "Whosoever is willing, let him come." That's the WORD. "Ain't No Way for God to Love You," if you don't Let Him.

> There is no substitute for God.
> He is the real thing,
> So climb the stairway up to Him,
> And kneel before the king.

Not Enough Time

Seek ye first the kingdom of heaven, and all other things will be added. (Matt 6:33).

Everyone knows that anything that is deemed worthwhile requires quality time for completion. Believers know that when planning their daily agendas, time must be set aside for Christian duties to promote the advancement of kingdom building here upon the earth.

God always has time for us, but we don't always have time for Him. Try as we may, it takes a made up mind to practice placing Jesus as top priority, above all else, at the very top of our 'things to do today list.' Not only is Satan good at making molehills into mountains, he specializes in management of 'Time Wasted Seminars.' He tells us we are too busy to be gainfully employed in being about our Father's business right now. That's procrastination! He promises us that there is always tomorrow, and that is a false promise which he cannot deliver, and then he dupes young people into believing that they have their whole lives ahead of them, but death is no respecter of age.

It's okay to set goals, make your dreams come true, reach for the stars, and all else that can be accomplished in one's lifetime, but know that when it is time to gather the harvest, there will be none if not enough time is spent laboring in the vineyard.

> Seek ye first the kingdom of God.
> Spend your time wisely, and be glad,
> For countless, manifold blessings,
> He will increasingly add.

Nothing but Noise

Take thou away from me the noise of thy songs, for I will not hear the melody of thy viols. (Amos 5:23).

As Christians, a daily desire to draw closer to God each day is certainly a natural inclination. As relationships deepen, praises increase, souls rejoice, and hearts overflow with thanksgiving, for it is a good thing to be joyful in the Lord.

The following scripture is one however, that cautions us to think sincerely about our praises unto God. "I know your manifold transgressions, and your mighty sins, so I don't want to hear your noise." (Amos 5:12).

With as much as lies possible within you, strike only the purest and sweetest notes in life's songbook and the music of your praise will not be noisy unto whom it is given.

> False and insincere praise
> Emits a shrill, discordant sound,
> But truthful, high praise service
> Will noiselessly, resound

One God Only

You shall have no other Gods before Me. (Ex 20:3).

Let's think for a moment about idols. Anything that we worship more than God is an idol. It's in our nature to desire pleasurable things, and we spend a sizeable portion of time invested in obtaining materialistic luxuries. No wonder we are told to seek first, the kingdom of heaven, and all other things shall be added. There are several questions to ask when it comes to honoring the one and only God. First of all, is God first above all else in honoring Him as the head of your life? The second question to ask is does your life reveal that you are doing what matters the most? Thirdly, is your commitment of the lasting kind?

If you have aligned your thinking with godly thoughts, the answer to the first question is yes. If you have sought deep spiritual insight into what is needed in order to please the Lord, then you have already decided whom you will serve. Then, you will do what matters the most, so the answer to the second question is yes. So then, if you have a God like mind, and desire to please the Lord by serving Him only, the answer to the third question must be yes, for only what we do for Christ will last when we are totally committed to the promotion of His Kingdom.

God said, "I am a jealous God!"
In case you haven't heard.
"I am the Lord, thy God!"
Read it in the Word.

One Pound Blessing, a Year Later

Wait on the Lord, be of good courage, and He shall strengthen your heart. Wait, I say, on the Lord. (Ps 27:14).

At its core, faith is hands off! God's got it! The news media announced in 2007, the birth of a tiny, precious baby girl. Weight, one pound!

There comes a time when courage is required to remain steadfast in meeting adversity, but if you learn how to wait on God, and trust Him to work things out, He will indeed strengthen your heart. The parents of the small infant continued to believe with stubborn faith that God would sustain their child's life even though the situation appeared somewhat hopeless as to a favorable outcome. But faith listens neither to doubt, nor to fear, not to disbelief, nor to uncertainty. Remember it is the very time to take a leap of faith when sight ceases. The baby's survival rate was more than likely beyond 'seeing' but not 'believing.'

In the greatness of their need, they amazingly discovered that God was greater than any fear that tested their trial of faith to see it through. And so, God stepped in at an unannounced time when there was the least appearance of a miracle. Surprisingly, a year later, the news media released the following update, Christmas day, 2008. The baby that weighed only one pound at birth, a year ago, was finally going home to be with her parents. Isn't that just like God to commonly appear in our greatest extremity to strengthen our hearts and to reward our having trusted Him to deliver according to His promises through the power of faith that works in all who believe and take Him at His Word.

> Just because her parents
> Remained persistent at God's throne,
> On Christmas day, their baby girl
> Was blessed, gift wrapped, and taken home.

Open Line

Cast all your care upon him, for he cares for you. (1 Pet 5:7).

Ever heard of the Open Line Telephone Company? Probably not, but I am sure services are provided for you by Southwestern Bell, or AT & T. The Open Line Telephone Company is unlisted, but it has always been, and still is, readily available for anyone who desires to use it at any time whatsoever, but so many fail to do so. Why? Beats me!

First of all, it's free. Secondly, the line is never busy, and thirdly, and most importantly, the person to whom the call is directed is always at home. No power failures! No interruptions! No malfunctions! The caller is guaranteed to reach the intended party without fail. How about dem apples?

Ever attempted to reach a friend while burdened with a load of care,
But the phone just rang and rang. No one at all was there.
So then, you called another friend hoping someone would be home.
"Please record your message. Listen for the tone."

Finally! Someone answered. "Hello! Please! Hold on!
I will be right with you. Don't hang up the phone."
A 'call you back tomorrow' will not bail you out today.
Especially, when you want help, and need it right away.

Wake up! It's time to face the facts, for often you will find
That most friends are much too busy to share what's on your mind.
Get your act together! There is an Open Line.
It's free of charge, available, and you can use it anytime.

A T & T has special rates. Southwestern has them too.
Yet there is one phone service, for which bills are never due.
So next time you need someone to chat with for a while,
Why not call up Jesus? Will He not hear His child?

There are no busy signals. You will always find Him home,
And ready to receive your call, so why not try this phone?
Too bad the service that is free is seldom selected, preferred, or chosen.
The Open Line is Heaven's phone on which few words are spoken.

There will never be a problem to get a call through.
The Open Line will always be available for you.
All you really need to do is just pick up the phone,
And dial J-E-S-U-S! **HELLO! YOU'VE REACHED HEAVEN'S THRONE!**

Parachute Prayers

Pray without ceasing! (1Thess 5:17).

Many choose not to pray, and if you are one of those people, beware! Failure to pray is like telling God to roll over, and play dead. The less we pray, the more we become the devil's prey. Some people only pray when things happen, while there are others who pray in order to make things happen.

An interesting thing happens when we invest time in prayer. It pays off! When the enemy comes in like a flood, and things come to an alarming pitch, and there is turbulence on board, and everything seems to be spinning out of control, and you feel as though you are headed for a nosedive, or a crash landing, there is a means of escape. Bail out! Prayer is the only parachute that guarantees a safe landing in the midst of it all.

> A very active prayer life
> Will ensure beyond a doubt,
> That your parachute will open,
> And God will bail you out.

Play Me Back!

Search me! Oh! God, and know my heart. Try me, and know my thoughts. (Ps 139:23-24).

As a Christian, the desire to draw closer to God should be incorporated into our daily rounds. One of the ways that we can begin to draw closer to Him each day is to improve the quality of our everyday living. And while it is true that none are without fault, living as holy as possible will make us more like Him each day.

The reason we are so often spiritually blind sighted is that we become self absorbed instead of spiritually centered. What is needful then, is for God to shine the light of heaven on our souls that we may better know, for our own sakes, our major shortcomings, and indwelling secret sins. All you need do is say, "Lord! Play me back! He will! And many will discover that we have denied Him like Peter, or betrayed Him as did Judas. But the grace of God is fully demonstrated when we kneel before Him with a contrite heart, and confess our faults whether ankle deep, knee deep, or above our heads, so to speak. When we see ourselves as we really are, our Lord and Savior, Jesus Christ will in spirit taught ways prepare us for the highest, and holiest of service through righteous living here on earth.

> Play me back! Lord Jesus! Tell me all I said
> That uplifted someone's spirit, or lowered someone's head?
> Play me back! Lord Jesus, until I see in me,
> A reflection of your likeness, as you would have me be.

Plug Up the Leaks!

Let this mind be in you which was also in Christ Jesus. (Phil 2:5).

No one knows the mind of God, but the Holy Ghost will help you to think with a God like mind. You shall grow spiritually stronger the longer you strive to live holy.

How do we live holy? When we try to live holy, and fail in our trying, what next? God has commanded us to sanctify ourselves therefore and be holy. (Lev 20:7). It is not a suggestion but a requirement that is expected of all who are called by His name. There comes a time when there is a need to re-consecrate and rededicate our sainthood to sacred use. Unholy things tend to distract us and poke holes in our Christian attire, and there begins a slow leakage process until the seepage becomes noticeable to those around us. Then what? Simply ask God to plug up the leaks! It's a God mind thing. Practice keeping your mind stayed on God, and when that happens, peaceful holiness is the end result. (Is 26:3). God empowers us to do those things which we set our minds and hearts to do when we give our minds and hearts to Him. (Phil 4:7), and that is the only way to live holy.

> Want to live holy?
> Ask God to plug up all those leaks.
> It is not what we say as Christians
> But what we do that boldly speaks.

Policy Holders

Remember how short my time is; for what futility have you created all the children of men? (Ps 89:47).

It was David who said remember how short my time is. According to the Word of God, the brevity of life, and passage of time is likened unto a vapor and a weaver's shuttle, and that is why staying in touch with God on an intimate level should be an everyday thing. So on your daily to do list don't fail to include spending quality time with God.

Born again Christians are Policy Holders. A policy, that is, a Certificate of Insurance, is immediately issued to you upon your date of conversion and profession of your faith. Let's discuss premium. A premium is defined as a prize awarded for a particular act or something that is offered free or at a reduced price as an inducement to buy or purchase something. Now read John 3:16. It should be clearly understood that the prize awarded to us through the death of Jesus is salvation. Jesus had to die because there was absolutely and positively no way that we could, even with a reduced rate of which there was none, become a Policy Holder. No not one! No one but Jesus could purchase salvation for us, and so He did.

Salvation is offered free of charge. Are you a Policy Holder? Are you covered under God's Redemption Plan? If not, you need to make that move. Invest in the Salvation Insurance Plan that will take you out of this world, and into the next with a lifetime guarantee of eternal life forever throughout eternity.

> The same as a Life Insurance Plan
> On earth must stay paid up,
> As Policy Holders of Salvation,
> We too, must stay, 'prayed up.'

> To all Non Policy Holders,
> Sign up today! Don't wait!
> Lay hold unto salvation.
> Tomorrow may be too late.

Pop Hopper

I can do all things through Christ which strengthens me. (Phil 4:13).

Saddle up! Hang on! You are in for the ride of a lifetime when you hop on Pop.

Who or what is a Pop? So real to me is my Heavenly Father, that I fondly adopted the phrase, "Hop on Pop!" as an affirmation. Why? God can take us to heavenly places we have never been before right down here on earth, and allow us to do things we never imagined possible within our realm of capabilities. When there is a challenging job to be done, a 'right now' goal to be reached, or an urgent demand that is heavily imposed, and strictly enforced, I always tell my kids, if you want to gain momentum and yardage to cross the finish line, saddle up and Hop on Pop!

> When you tend to veer off track,
> God can always bring you back.
> Hop on Pop! Hop on Pop!
>
> When everything is in a tizzy,
> And your flat soda needs some fizzy.
> Hop on Pop! Hop on Pop!
>
> Awake from your sullen stupor
> And become a Super Duper.
> Hop on Pop! Hop on Pop!
>
> Drowning cares in a bottle
> Won't help you function at full throttle.
> Hop on Pop! Hop on Pop!
>
> Whenever God is included in it,
> Ride on! Ride on! The sky is the limit.
> So Hop on Pop! Hop on Pop!

Power of the Cross

And Jesus came and spoke unto them saying, all power is given unto me in heaven and in earth. (Matt 28:18).

The following poem was written to uplift those who are confined, and are serving out their sentences as mandated by law. As an active member of the Prison Ministry, I witnessed the outreaching and touching of the lives of numerous inmates through the power of the cross.

No longer in confinement,
Your soul has been set free.
Through the power of the cross
There is no captivity.

No matter where you are,
Confess your faults sorrowfully.
Give your heart to Jesus.
Grace will grant you liberty.

Incarcerated? Serving time?
Don't count it as an unfound loss.
Jesus died to set us free.
Claim the power of the cross.

Prairie Fire Lies

The lip of truth shall be established forever, but a lying tongue is but for a moment. (Prov 12:19).

It is impossible for God to lie, but not us. Some attempt to sugar coat untruth by calling it a little white lie. But a lie is a lie, and lying is one of the seven things God hates.

A prairie fire spreads very quickly, and can very easily become an uncontrollable, raging inferno. The swifter and wider it spreads, the greater its destruction, and lies can be likened unto the same. (Prov 12:22), so reads as follows: Lying lips are an abomination to the Lord, but they that deal truly are His delight. So tell the truth, and put out the fire!

One lie calls for another,
And when finally through,
All of those twisted versions
Don't even make sense to you.

The truth can be repeated,
But never will a lie,
For lies cannot be told the same
No matter how you try.

Praise Reports

Then sang Moses and the children of Israel this song unto the Lord, and spoke saying, I will sing unto the Lord, for He hath triumphed gloriously; the horse and his rider has He thrown into the sea. (Ex 15:1).

Praise report! Pharaoh's chariots, his host, and even his chosen captains were drowned in the Red Sea, for the Lord is a man of war, and the Lord is His name. (Ex 15:3-4).

Often my children call me with a Praise Report. In eager anticipation, I always await the good news. "Hurry I say. Tell me! What has God done now?" And while it is true that God does phenomenal things for us too numerous to mention, yet there are times when He moves in such a way that we can't help but give Him the glory and shout it from the rooftop. The truth be told, God is good all the time! He is not a split second, haphazard God, but an on time, sure shot God, and the exciting things about His grab bag full of surprises, and unexpected blessings, is that it is all far deeper than we can begin to imagine. So begin the process of recording and sharing your expressions of praise with those around you. After all, this is what God wants.

> More than we can phantom,
> God has it all in store.
> So share all your praise reports
> And He will bless you even more.

Pray Unto Deliverance

Pray without ceasing. (1 Thess 5:17).

Prayers of deliverance often fall into the category of "this too shall pass" situations which require long overdue waiting periods of undeniable trust and rest assured patience. What happens when God chooses not to hurry with quick responses to which we have all grown accustomed in this rapid pace, jet set, 'right now' world of today? We become so easily discouraged, and prayers begin to decrease in number, and faith begins to dwindle down because earthly patience is of such a short term nature. (Eph 6:18).

> There are no unanswered prayers.
> God consumes all of our cares,
> But when He chooses not to hurry,
> Don't despair, fret, or worry.
>
> When a prayer is placed on hold
> Don't throw in the cards and fold.
> Don't give in, give up, or give out,
> Or pray less, and begin to doubt.
>
> God says, "I'm not finished! Wait!
> Don't mark me by a calendar date.
> I answer by my own timetable.
> "Pray on, dear child, for I AM able!"

June

Surely goodness and mercy will follow me, and I will dwell in the house of the Lord forever. (Ps 23.6).

Joyfully view heaven's glory.
Untold is the silent story.
Never ending ecstasy!
Everlasting eternity!

Being in companionship with Jesus, in this life, is but a glimpse of heaven's radiant glory. Paul mentioned that eyes have not seen, nor have ears heard, the silent, untold story of the glory at last to be revealed when Jesus comes again, and claims His own into everlasting eternity. We will be clothed with immortality, and never ending ecstasy will happen in glorious heaven where will be worn the incorruptible crowns of life. When time for us will be no more, what a blessing to know that we shall be able to stand upon life's mountaintop, and view the Promised Land, enter in, and so dwell in the House of the Lord forever.

Prayer Way is a Stairway

Evening and morning and at noon will I pray, and cry aloud, and He shall hear my voice. (Ps 55:17).

The best way that anyone can begin the day
Is to take a little time to kneel down and pray.
It only takes a moment to pray and tarry there.
Your whole day will be nestled in the cradle of your prayer.

But if you fail to call on Him and everything goes wrong.
Prepare to be defeated, for you cannot stand alone.
Often weighted crosses are extremely hard to bear
But nothing is too heavy to lift to God in prayer.

So take a little time to pray, no matter what the reason.
Prayer does not go out of style, nor does it end by season.
Bend your knees! Bow your head and meditate in prayer.
Then rest assured undoubtedly that God will meet you there.

Let the name of Jesus resound throughout the air.
What the world needs today is power driven prayer.
You can make the enemy retreat and steal away,
And even Satan weakens the more we kneel and pray.

So meet God in the morning, and greet Him every day.
Wonders will never cease when you fail not to pray.
Miracles will happen! Prayer will unlock doors!
Prayer will give you strength to do unfinished chores.

Prayer way is the stairway that leads to up above.
Prayer is a special gift given with true love.
Prayer is a weapon, so wield it every day.
Amazing things will happen when we kneel and pray.

Prodigal Tendencies

I will arise and go to my father, and will say to him," Father, I have sinned against heaven and before thee." (Luke 15:18).

The prodigal son demanded of his Father that he be given all due him and then he departed with his portion of wealth out into the world and engaged in riotous living. If ever there was anyone who was green and trusting, it was the wayward son. He wined and dined with all his newfound friends until all his fortune was completely wiped out. How few indeed realize that when all the money is gone, so are the ones who enjoyed partying with you.

The end result of a fast paced life lost its beat much too soon, and all he heard were the echoes of his own footsteps walking down a lonely and deserted road that led him nowhere at all. At the end of his rope, busted, disgusted, tired, lonely and hungry, the prodigal son wallowed in the hog pen of the school of hard knocks. Finally though, he came to the realization that his Father could rescue him from skid row if only he would, with a contrite heart, repent and beg forgiveness for all the sins he had so willfully committed. To make a long story short, his Father recognized him from a long distance away, and eagerly extended open arms of forgiveness to his long lost son who found his way back home.

How often do we as Children of the King experience an urge to walk on the wild side, party down, and let it all hang out, merely to enjoy a taste of worldliness. Much like the prodigal son, most of us will wallow in the hog pen until rudely awakened to the fact that our Father can alter any circumstances in our lives if we are willing to confess our faults, repent, and honor Him as Lord of all, and then of course, He will lovingly embrace His lost sheep, and welcome them back into the fold.

> Father, I have sinned,
> But I want to come back home.
> Forgive me my transgressions,
> I will no longer roam.

Pulling the Plug

Yea though I walk through the valley of the shadow of death, I will fear no evil, for thou art with me, thy rod and thy staff, they comfort me. (Ps 23:4).

There are differing opinions when it comes to DNR. (Do Not Resuscitate), and there are so many 'what ifs' when a decision must be made to pull the plug, and let our loved ones slip away when death appears imminent due to a hopeless, irreversible condition, or uncontrollable circumstances. Yet there are times, however, when loved ones themselves release us from having to make that kind of crucial decision. But even when such is the case, still, it leaves the family members completely devastated whenever the plug is pulled, no matter whoever chose the option to do so.

When the unavoidable, unexpected happens, and someone you love has slipped into a permanent vegetative state, and seemingly there is no hope of regaining any operative functions, and there is no advanced directive regarding such a move; suddenly, you are faced with a brain dead, 'Dear God, what shall I do?' type of situation, and then the decision is yours alone to make.

Once the decision has been made, and the plug is pulled, it is human to feel guilt ridden, and second guess yourself into wondering if you made the right move, or if you closed a door that should have remained open.

There is comfort in the Word! So let not your heart Be troubled. Read (John 14:1-3), and dry your tears.

> No matter how sick loved ones are,
> We want to hold them close and cling,
> But when we finally let them go,
> They rejoice to meet the King.

Put Your Shoes on Baby!
You Got Big Feet Now!

For everyone that uses milk is unskillful in the Word of righteousness, for he is a babe. But strong meat belongs to them that are of full age, even those who by reason of use have their senses exercised to discern both good and evil. (Heb. 5:13& 14).

Back in the day there was a song that went "Put your shoes on Lucy! You're a big girl now!" What am I saying here? It is important that we do not stunt Christian growth by failure to move on up a little higher and take it to the next level. Can you imagine a baby Saint flopping around in great big shoes that are way too big to stay on his feet? One must grow in order to boldly parade around in high stepping shoes to tread upon scorpions and squash the enemy. So grow into your Gospel shoes! Too many are still milking around with the Word when they should be eating the meat of His Word which is a continual feast.

> The time has come to eat the meat,
> And let go of the cow.
> So put your shoes on baby,
> Cause you got Big Feet now!

Quiet Words Speak Loudly

Words of the wise quietly spoken should be heard rather than the shout of a ruler of fools. (Eccles 9:17).

A word to the wise is sufficient. How often have we heard this said? Yet, it is anything but trite, overused, or commonplace. The wise will hear and receive instruction, but a fool will not do so.

A comparison is made in (Eccles 10:2-3), of a wise and foolish man. A wise man's heart is at his right hand, but a fool's heart is at his left. A plumb fool is devoid of wisdom, and sooner or later, everyone will know that he, or she, is a fool.

>Speak words of wisdom quietly.
>There is no need to shout.
>It only takes a whisper.
>The truth will come out.

Rain in the Forecast

And Joshua said unto the people, you cannot serve the Lord, for He is a holy God, He is a jealous God; He will not forgive your transgressions, nor your sins. If you forsake the Lord and serve strange gods, then He will turn and do you hurt, and consume you, after that He had done you good. (Joshua 24: 19 & 20).

How do we prepare for the onslaught of rain? We listen to the weather channel, and if rain is in the forecast, we grab our rain gear and umbrellas in preparation for the expectancy of downpours of heavy showers of predicted rain. Additionally, we check the windshield wipers to ensure keen visibility throughout rainy seasons.

Rain from a spiritual point of view, is defined as a heavy and continuous descent of anything. Joshua explained to the Israelites that as long as they obediently adhered to the Covenant, God would continue to bless them. Also he made it crystal clear that if they ignored the Covenant, they could expect rain in the forecast; that is, a down-pouring of God's wrath upon Israel.

We too, must faithfully remain committed and true unto God as His Followers, and all that He represents in our holy walk as those who are called by His name. If not, get ready! It's gonna rain!

> There is rain in the forecast
> When we fail to follow through,
> So faithfully keep God's Covenant
> As He would have us do.

Read the Small Print

You must study to show yourself approved, unto God. (2 Tim 2:15).

Have you ever wondered why so many who sign contracts are often overwhelmed by the element of surprise relating to their contractual agreements? Of course, the answer to this question is failure to read the small print.

It is especially true now that in a world of unfair tactics, numerous shenanigans and underhanded deals, the time has come to pay close attention to the handwriting on the wall. Read the small print! Even the devil knows that it is what you do not read that will entrap you, and hold you captive by your own written consent. Think about it! Read your bible, and don't fall prey to Satan's devices, for they are many. Do not sign anything at all before you take the time to read all of the small print in its entirety. It could be a matter of life, or death.

> Needless pain and anguish
> Alertness can prevent
> If only we will take the time
> And read the 'small print.'
>
> It is what we fail to read
> In living day, to day,
> That cleverly may conceal
> Signing lives away.

Rendered and Hindered Prayers

And whenever you stand praying, if you have anything against anyone, forgive him, so that your Father in heaven may forgive you your trespasses. But if you do not forgive, neither will your Father in heaven forgive your sins. (Mark.11:25 & 26).

Any old day will do to make amends before submitting your personal prayer requests unto the Lord. So do so, and He will wipe the slate clean. Examine your life, and if you are out of fellowship with a loved one, friend, co-worker, or whomever, your rendered prayers will be hindered. Many areas in our Christian way of life require constant maintenance. We all want a meaningful fellowship with God. We can have this kind of relationship by praying without ceasing. But in doing so, we must not become hollow and hypocritical when we kneel down, or fold our hands in prayer before God. (Matt 5:23 & 24) illustrates aptly how and why we can prevent our own blessings from coming forth. And while some are admittedly difficult to contend with, do not lay your gift upon the altar until you have made peace with that person. Then return, and offer your gift unto God. When we forgive, God will do likewise. (Matt 6:14-15).

> Some gifts are unacceptable.
> Have you sown discord?
> Do not hold a grudge
> And then appear before the Lord.

Reason It Out

Come now, and let us reason together, says the Lord, though your sins are like scarlet, they shall be as white as snow. Though they are red like crimson, they shall be as wool. (Is 1:18).

Life will not feel as fragile or fragmented when you talk it out, and share what's on your mind. The more you hold things in and attempt to cover it all up, the less likely you will rise above whatever is swiftly dragging you down deeper and deeper into the dark dungeon of despair. Of course, you can always seek out professional help, but the greatest win to be gained is running to Jesus, and reasoning things out with Him. While others are desperately attempting to figure you out, and to understand what makes you tick, Jesus already has your number and He knows not only every suck hole that is pulling you under, but He also knows how to keep your boat afloat. So get to know Him better. After all, He created you in His own image, and surely, He is the sound voice of wisdom and reason. Candidly speaking, it takes every ounce of strength we have to wage the battle of mind games. Remember, Satan has declared war! So strive to overcome his tactics. When God is on your side, you are unbeatable.

God has known all along
The kind of person you can be.
"Come let us reason together, He said.
Talk it over with ME."

Remember God Perfects

But may the God of all grace, who called us to his eternal glory by Christ Jesus, after you have suffered a while, make you perfect, establish, strengthen, and settle you. (1 Pet 5:10).

What is Peter saying here? How are we made firm and secure? Suffering pounds us into a stable condition, so that we can stand. Suffering strengthens our saintly muscles so that we can withstand pressure and not give way during trials and afflictions. God establishes strength through suffering and then He restores calmness and settles us down, again, and again, and again.

> God will shake us up
> With many whirlwind situations
> To establish strengthen and settle us.
> He builds strong and firm foundations.

Rerunning the Reruns

So teach us to number our days that we may apply our hearts unto wisdom. (Ps 90:12).

How many times will you watch those same old movies over, and over, again and again? How many countless times have you already seen those reruns? How many times will you "Play it again Sam?" Come on now! You already know every punch line, and the outcome is certainly no surprise to you at all. So what is up with that? Why so much attention and time given spent watching reruns? It was ingrained in my brain to faithfully watch every rerun episode of the very popular Matlock Series. Not to mention repeat Life Time Thrillers. Consequently, one day it occurred to me; however, that long ago since, I could have devoted all that rerun watching time to bringing closure to all those unfinished and incomplete projects on my 'things to do list' whenever I decided there was time to get around to it. So I opted to turn off the set and got down to real business.

Time spent unwisely is wasted doing unproductive things instead of doing what matters the most. Sooner or later, one should realize the precious gift of time, and at some point, begin to value time as an invaluable, precious commodity.

> Too soon, before you know it,
> Death's bell will surely chime.
> So think about what matters most.
> Then do it with your time.

Right Angle! Wrong Approach!

And I, if I be lifted up from the earth will draw all men unto me. (John 12:32).

What could possibly be more rewarding than "Bringing in the Sheaves" and saving souls? As Believers, we are mandated to do so, and above all else, it is our greatest mission here on planet earth. Many well meaning Saints; however, have the right angle, but the wrong approach. An angle is defined as an attempt to get something by artful means, but when it comes to saving souls, we need God's help to perfect the art from the right angle of spiritual preparation and proper training. Approach, on the other hand, means to come nearer or to solicit the interest or favor of. The wrong approach is the finger pointing, holier than thou method. Do not scold them, or ask them why they do not attend church. Tell them none is perfect save the Father, and then tell them why you attend church and enjoy worshiping in and out of the Lord's House. Now that is impressive, and much more humbly received. What am I saying here? When recruiting for Jesus, simply lift Him up, and let His Word do all the talking. Forget about the angle. It is all in the approach. Happy Soul Hunting!

> There's a right way, and a wrong way.
> Simplicity will teach the lost.
> When none of us could pay the Ransom,
> Jesus died, and paid the cost.

Root Bound

And in the morning, as they passed by, they saw the fig tree dried up from the roots. (Mark 11:20).

When once healthy and thriving, green leaves suddenly turn brown, and begin to fall away one by one, there is indeed a big problem somewhere. So then, it becomes necessary to check out the root of the problem, or is the root itself the cause of the problem?

As we know, a root is defined as the "usually underground portion of a plant that serves as support, and draws food and water from the surrounding soil, and then stores food for proper growth." What good is a tree; however, if it does not bear forth fruit? Unless we remain deep-rooted in enriched soil constantly cultivated by the Holy Spirit, unhealthy symptoms will appear and begin to stagnate and stunt proper Christian growth in the spiritual garden of life.

Consequently, when a plant begins to droop, sag, and show signs of rapid deterioration, it is safe to assume that one should get right down to the root of the problem. Are you maintaining a healthy, eat right diet of the Bread of Life for proper nutrition? Are there too many roots in the pot? Has the fountain of Living Water ceased to flow resulting in dry rot roots?

There is only one true support system, and that is Christ Jesus. To remain spiritually healthy, you must eat the Bread of Life which is the Word of God, and you will have a continual feast, but when there are too many roots in the pot there is inadequate space to expand, and those invading and unwelcome roots must be uprooted so there will be enough room for spiritual growth to continue to thrive and survive. Is your soul root bound? Are you suffering from root rot? Eat the Bread of Life and stay healthy! Drink the Living Water, and thirst no more!

> We are the branches.
> He is the Vine. So let your soul take root.
> Unless we abide in Him,
> We can bear no fruit.

Run and Tell That!

We are Ambassadors for Christ. (2 Cor 5:20)

There lies before us a challenge to accept the Great Commission. "Go and teach all nations, baptizing them in the name of the Father, Son and the Holy Ghost, and teach them to observe all things commanded by our Lord and Savior, Jesus Christ, and to remember the promise, Lo! I am with you always even unto the end of the world." (Matt 28:19-20).

Many there are who enjoy being the bearer of bad tidings. Honey! Guess what? Another fallen celebrity! Yes! There are talebearers who faithfully love to reveal deep, dark indiscretions of 'would you believe' mouthwatering, juicy, bring um down gossip, before a stunned audience of listeners in the public arena of life. What a shocking element of surprise to be the first one to deliver a powerful 'T.K.O' about you know who.

Hold up! Why not consider delivering the only good news that really matters, and that is, Jesus saves! So run and tell that! The name 'Jesus' means that He will save us from our sins. He did! (John3:16)! Now run and tell that! We were bought with a price; therefore, glorify God in body and spirit. (1 Cor. 6:19-20). Run and tell that!

> God don't need gossip birds
> To repeat all they heard.
> He wants carrier pigeons to spread the news
> That Jesus is the one to choose.
>
> No one else could pay the fee,
> So Jesus died to set us free.
> The 'Chosen One' stepped up to bat.
> Salvation! Redemption! Run and tell that!

Saints of Assembly

Do not forsake the assembly. (Heb 10:25).

No matter what one endeavors to do, strives to become, or struggles to maintain, support is always needed in order to see us through to the end of it all. From a 'pat on the back' to 'hang on in there kid,' or even just a simple, 'don't give up!' goes a very long way. Support is extremely vital and absolutely necessary even for the survival of the fittest Christian Believers, and Warriors of the Saints of God.

The new kid on the block, or new recruits of the kingdom, rely upon well-seasoned soldiers of the cross to encourage and help them to remain within the constant flow of faithfully adhering to their newly committed way of life when surrounded by the assembly of a God fearing congregation. Strength is derived from unity. No wonder it is required that we should assemble ourselves together as often as we can.

> We must support each other.
> Do not walk alone!
> In unity there is strength.
> Don't try to make it on your own.

Satan is a Fisherman

Let no man say when he is tempted, I am tempted of God, for God cannot be tempted with evil, neither does he tempt any man. But every man is tempted when he is drawn away of his own lust, and enticed. (James 1: 13-14).

Without fail, Satan faithfully baits his hook, and throws his line into the river of life. We do not know what he will use as bait, but one thing is certain and that is, whatever the bait, it will appear to be deceivingly delicious, irresistibly juicy, and bewitchingly enticing enough to allure us to grab hold, and immediately sink our teeth into it. Beware! The Bible warns us not to be ignorant of Satan's devices, for there are many. He desires to reel you in like a helpless fish, and then toss you into his pail with all the other 'catch of the day' felled prey. Never underestimate the Tempter! He is clever, but the Christ in you can resist him.

Refer to (James 1:15). "Then when lust has conceived, it brings forth sin, and sin, when it is finished, brings forth death." Not many of us are living at our best, but needless to say, Satan loves to go fishing, and we all know what happens to caught fish. Don't we?

> Whenever you are tempted
> To nibble at a baited hook,
> Pause for just a moment,
> Then take a closer look.
>
> Perhaps you will discover
> That you should back away.
> All that looks good isn't!
> Don't become the devil's prey.

Saul's Séance

And when Saul saw the host of the Philistines, he was afraid, and his heart greatly trembled. And when Saul inquired of the Lord, the Lord answered him not; neither by dreams, nor by urim, nor by prophets. (1 Sam 28:5-6).

When Saul discovered that God had departed from him because of disobedience, he disguised himself and consulted a Medium, or one who has power to summon the dead. The woman inquired of Saul whom she should bring up, and Saul requested Samuel. Saul expressed his concerns about the Philistines to Samuel, and told him that God had departed from him, and then asked what he should do since God no longer answered him. Samuel informed Saul that since he had distanced himself from God, his kingdom had been given to David because of his disobedience relating to Amalek, and that Israel would be delivered into the hands of the Philistines. He further informed Saul that tomorrow (the next day), both he and his sons would be with him. (Surely die). Reference (1 Sam 28:7-20). There are times when we also tend to walk away from God, but remember should that happen, there is always a price to pay at some point in time on down the line.

> Saul was God's anointed,
> But he strayed away.
> Of course, God will forgive,
> But there's still a price to pay.

Seeing Clearly

For God has not given us the spirit of fear, but of power, and of love, and of a sound mind. (2 Tim 1:7).

We are generated by His power. We are showered with His love. We are endowed with a sound mind. What occasion is there then for fearfulness? Learn to meet God on a more intimate level and share your innermost thoughts and feelings, and through these experiences, you will become closer to God. Let your whole being receive, and accept for yourself all that God has to offer.

A remarkable thing happens when Jesus happens to us. As the song goes, "On a clear day, you can see forever and ever-more." Also popular recording artist, Johnny Nash soulfully sang, "I can see clearly now the rain is gone." So when we choose to believe God for the best when things are hanging in the balance, He will either remove the obstacles, or lead us safely around them. And have we not seen this in many lives of those who dare to trust God and take Him at His Word. We see things more clearly when we begin to see through the eyes of God.

> Even when there are stormy skies,
> We can see clearly through God's eyes,
> And after the downpour of rain is gone,
> Sunshiny skies reveal heaven's throne.

Seeker Rewards

But without faith it is impossible to please Him, for he who comes to God must believe that He is a rewarder of those who diligently seek him. (Heb 11:6).

For a lot of us, the thought of seeking may seem to be a long drawn out process, but seeking after God cannot be over emphasized.

Even if you have not yet found the time to seek after personal longings, know that time invested in a diligent search for Jesus is of the highest priority. God's concern is with our willingness to seek after Him first so that all other things may be added. (Matt 6:33). When we are able to do this, and to approach the day as if only God matters, He will respond and reward us in ways unimagined.

Seek Him now!

> It pays to be diligent.
> Search high and low for the Lord.
> Surely you will find Him
> And claim your reward.

Send me!

Also I heard the voice of the Lord saying, whom shall I send, and who will go for us? Then said I, here am I; send me. (Is 6:8).

There's a soldier in God's Army. Her name is Cloteal.
She is destined and determined to do the Savior's will.
It is far from easy to stand up, pray and fight,
But Cloteal is a Warrior, empowered with strength and might.

No demonic forces can block or hold her back.
She's fully clothed in God's armor, and ready for any attack.
The old flesh was crucified. She answered to God's call.
She's anointed and appointed. God is her all and all.

Whether she is in the air, on land, or out to sea,
Her steps are ordered by the Lord to march on victoriously.
Even the devil knows her name, and when he sees her coming,
The Spirit of God within her backs him up, and sends him running.

Honoring Apostle, Cloteal Morgan, Redemption Ministries

Serial Sinners

Help Lord; for the godly man ceases and the faithful fall from among the children of men. (Ps 12:1).

The awful truth is that sin is like a rampant disease out of control, and the world we live in is, of course, a sin producing environment. Serial sinners are those who repeatedly veer off track, are spiritually weak, prone to immoral behavior, and overcome by carnal actions.

Let us view from a spiritual perspective that in order to advance God's purpose in a sinful world, the quality of a Believer's lifestyle must be holy. It is an effrontery to holiness, to fall prey to sinful charades once God's divine powers have given us all things that pertain unto godliness, having called us to glory and virtue. (2 Pet 1:3-4). Satan's charms are irresistibly magnetic, but resist we must if we are to uproot satanic harvest as Soldiers of the Cross.

> Sin is addictive.
> It can destroy the soul.
> Do not go back into the night.
> God has made you whole.

Seven by Seven

It is not in me. God shall give Pharaoh an answer of peace. (Gen 41:16).

Joseph was indeed an interpreter of dreams, and when he was summoned to appear before Pharaoh, he interpreted his dream and stated that God was the one who revealed it unto him. Then Pharaoh said to his servants, can we find such a one as this is, a man in whom the Spirit of God is? (Gen 41:38).

Pharaoh dreamt a strange dream. It caused his heart to quiver.
He dreamed that he stood by the Nile River.
There came up from the river seven fat fleshed kine.
They were very healthy, and all were good and fine.

Suddenly! Seven more appeared, but they were very poor and lean.
Such in the land of Egypt as Pharaoh had never seen.
The unhealthy animals devoured the healthy kine.
The dream sent creepy shivers up and down Pharaoh's spine.

Again he dreamed of seven ears of corn in one stalk, full and good
That appeared before him where he watched and stood.
Then, seven ears of withered corn, blighted by the East wind,
Destroyed the healthy grains of corn, and left it poor and thin.

Many were summoned to appear on the troubled scene,
But Joseph was the only one who could interpret Pharaoh's dream.
"There will be seven years of plenty, he said, and seven more years of having not.
In those seven plenteous years, you must store up and save a lot."

King Pharaoh was satisfied, and so God moved His hand.
Joseph was appointed by the king to rule over Egypt's land.
God knew that there would be a famine in the land,
And all of Joseph's loved ones, would need a helping hand.

Seven Shameful Days

And Moses cried unto the Lord saying, "Heal her now! Oh God, I beseech thee!" (Num 12:13).

Miriam was the sister of Aaron and Moses. Even as a girl, she was very wise, and persuaded the Egyptian Princess who discovered her hidden Hebrew, baby brother, Moses, to seek out a Hebrew woman to nurse him. Approval granted, she returned with her mother, the mother of Moses. Miriam was also known as a Prophetess, and was appointed as a leader in the nation.

Although Miriam was a woman of accomplishment, there came a time when divine intercession was extremely warranted on her behalf. Unwisely, she rebelled against Moses because she was jealous of his influential leadership style, and she, along with Aaron, conspired to undermine Moses because of his marriage to a foreign woman. But when Miriam attacked God's chosen one, the outcome was anything but ideal. She was stricken with leprosy, so Aaron pleaded with Moses who in turn became Miriam's intercessor, and after seven days as a leper outside of the camp, Miriam was restored and healed of her leprosy. Can anything be nobler than having a powerful intercessor in your corner?

> Sometimes it may seem
> That there is nothing we can do.
> Thank God for intercessors,
> They can send a prayer on through.

Shine!

No man, when he has lit a candle, covers it with a vessel, or puts it under a bed, but places it where others may see the light. (Luke 8:16).

The following poem was written for the United States Postal Service, Gateway District, (Adopt a Child Campaign) in the year 2000.

In a grim corner of the world,
Huddled in a dreary place,
A child is in need of love,
So please, light up a happy face.

Shine!

Have you a heart made of gold?
Outshine darkness today.
Come hearthside! Warm up a child!
Chase gloomy shadows away!

Shine!

Light up the world! Let there be light,
For somewhere, way out there,
Are rare and priceless, hidden gems
Of treasure unearthed through foster care.

Shine!

Now blow out the candles,
And make one wish come true worthwhile.
Turn a flicker into a flame.
Share the light! Adopt a child!

Shine!

Shortcutting Prohibited!

Know this; the trying of your faith works patience. (James 1:3).

Now that we think about it, there does come a time when impatiently, some may attempt to find shortcuts when it comes to Christian duty. But we know only too well, that we cannot get to heaven 'back stepping' once we are called and committed to moving forward in His name. Giant quantum leaps are totally out of the picture, for we must patiently persevere and continue to walk in alignment with God's holy will, moment by moment, step by step.

With stronger faith, deeper love, and highest and holiest service, we must take the long way around, and travel the full distance of the upper road on the narrow way that leads us through the straight gate unto heaven's door.

> There are no known shortcuts
> As we make our journey home.
> We must travel the full distance
> To reach heaven's throne.

Show and Tell

And the gospel of the kingdom shall be preached all over the world, for a witness unto all nations and then shall the end come. (Matt 24:14).

Not long ago when my two children were of school age, they were required to bring an item or toy to class on Show & Tell day. They would show and tell their teachers, and classmates all about the object, toy, game, or whatever they had selected to share with them on Show & Tell day.

How many of us today as followers of the Master, show and tell others about the Good News Gospel? Some of us, more often than not, are guilty of placing our personal experiences of holiness on the shelf only to gather dust. If such is the case, you need to regroup and rethink things through. We should be ready to show others Christ on parade! How so? By witnessing and compelling non-believers to accept Jesus as their personal Savior, we are showing and telling the world that we are grateful to be among the chosen as citizens of His kingdom. How many ways He loves us! Fellow Believers! We may not all be ordained to preach the gospel, but we can all show, and tell. Hallelujah! Amen!

> If God is Lord over your life,
> Then surely all is well.
> Stand up! Be a witness!
> Speak up! Show and tell!

Shut Yo Mouth, or Change the Subject

Keep your tongue from evil and the lips from speaking guile. (Ps 34:13).

Interestingly, some people who simply talk too much have a tendency to repeat the same things, over and over, and over again. Boring! When that happens, eventually they come to the end of the truth, and begin to lie and gossip in order to retain the attention of the listeners. If such is the case, it is advisable to practice the art of golden silence, and simply brainstorm for a moment, or two. What subject could you talk about and always end up telling the truth, "the whole truth, and nothing but the truth, so help you God?" God is the only one who can not lie, so why not talk about Him. It is guaranteed that you will never run out of truthful things to say. He is absolutely honest and breathtakingly amazing. The proof is in the pudding. So eat it, and talk about Jesus. Talking about a Superman; Jesus walked upon the water! He commanded the wind to obey Him, and it was so! He even raised the dead, and most importantly, Jesus died to save us all, and yet He is still the same as yesterday, today, and forevermore. Top that!

> A tongue that wags like a dog's tail
> Might not escape the flames of hell.
> So shut yo mouth! Honey Chile,
> Or change the subject for a while.

Siege Mound

Therefore thus says the Lord God, Behold I am against you Tyrus, and will cause many nations to come up against you, as the sea causes its waves to come up. (Ezek 26:3).

God is much too powerful for any kind of resistance, or any force of defensiveness where we are concerned when He is calling the shots. Tyrus rebelled against Jerusalem, and so God allowed an enemy, Nebuchadnezzar, King of Babylon, to heap up a siege mound (mighty fort) and reign victoriously over Tyrus. (Ezek 26:8). There was no turning loose. There was no breaking free, and there was no escaping from God's wrath. It was not an unexpected disaster for Tyrus; however, because a message from God's Prophet, Ezekiel, to Tyrus in person, warned him that it was gonna rain! And when God allows the enemy to reign, it is lights out! Party over! So don't shoot the messenger! Simply obey God.

    The enemy successfully
    Built up a siege mound,
    And Tyrus was defeated.
    There was no shelter around.

Silence the Rocks

Rocks will cry out! (Luke 19:40).

Can rocks cry out and praise the Lord? You Betcha! Do not allow inanimate, lifeless objects to glorify God because you have failed to do so. Let everything that has breath praise the Lord. (Ps 150:6).

With a welcome sigh of relief, many thank the doctor for a favorable report concerning their health situation, but God is the one who heals all of our diseases. (Ps 103:3). With a round of applause, we gratefully commend the banker for that much needed, approved financial assistance, but God is the one who provides. (Jehovah Jireh), Gen 22:8 &14). So often, we are prone to lose sight of the fact that God merits and wants us to continually praise Him from whom all blessings flow. Read (John 3:16). This, to me, is all the reason we need to praise the Lord without ceasing.

> When we fail to praise the Lord,
> Surely the rocks will cry out.
> So let us lift up holy hands,
> And praise God with a mighty shout.

July

For I am the Lord, I change not. (Mal 3:6).

Joy can be yours today.
Unclaimed love will waste away.
Love the Lord with all your heart.
You will never grow apart.

If you are up close, and very personal with God, you can say, joy is mine! If you have accepted Jesus into your heart as your personal Savior, you have claimed His love, and you can say that, love is mine! As you continue to honor and cherish a life-long fellowship with Jesus Christ, you can say that, I will never walk alone, for an unchangeable God has promised never to leave you alone even unto the end of the world. Remain fully persuaded that nothing can separate you from the love of God.

Skinny or not, here I come!

I can do all things through Christ who strengthens me. (Phil 4:13).

If you are completely dissatisfied with the size and shape of your body, change it! But by no means should you allow Satan to kill your body softly by duping you into resorting to advertised quick fixes for guaranteed instantaneous results. It's okay to have a body to die for, but is your life worth the price of anorexia or bulimia?

If you want to have the bodily shape you have always desired, go to God for it, but remember, He works inside out. Once your spiritual body shapes up, your mindset of how you view your physical body will eventually change as you will begin to focus more on what is inside of you than out. God will grant you the discipline to eat well balanced meals, diet sensibly, and melt away fat, a pound at a time.

> Ask God to shape your body, and very soon before you know it,
> All eyes will follow you when your body starts to show it.
> Don't bargain with the devil to promenade on scene.
> Ask the Lord to help you strut, a healthy, lean cuisine.

Simpler Times

Be content with such things as you have. (Heb 13:5).

One need only look back to see how far we have come. There was a time when simplicity was golden. But nowadays, admittedly, even the best life has to offer is never satisfying enough for most of us today.

It was rub-a-dub, dub
In a big tin tub, and I was squeaky clean.
There were no bathtubs, so I played in the suds.
Life's purse was thin and lean.

I ate fatback and greens, and ham hocks and beans.
There was cornbread and buttermilk too.
But when times were hard, we thanked the Lord!
And God always pulled us through.

There were home grown tomatoes, and fresh picked potatoes,
And doctor visits were few.
Clothes hung on a line, and for only one dime,
We bought a whole lot of candy too.

Now I bathe and scrub in a luxury tub.
The bathroom is spacious, and wide.
We have come a long way. It's a brand new day.
The 'out house' is now inside.

I eat taters and steaks, and thank goodness sakes,
I can choose what I want to eat.
My reward, is knowing the Lord
Still provides daily bread and meat.

We skimp and scurry, grow food in a hurry,
And feast on a microwave meal.
We may be more wealthy, but far less healthy,
For simpler times cured many an ill.

Sit This One Out!

Trust in the Lord with all your heart, and lean not unto your own understanding. (Prov 3:5).

There will be times when you will stand at the crossroads of life, and not have the foggiest notion in which direction to head out. What next? What should you do? The hardest thing ever, nothing! Stand still! Wait! And know that He is God. (Ps 46:10). True enough, doing nothing is difficult. But to trust your own instincts without a vision in sight will only lead you down the wrong path, and farther away from the direction in which you should go.

Such crucial decision making choices should not be a flip of the coin, or heads or tails type of thing. Do not give in to your impulses, rash conclusions, or otherwise ill advised, solicited advice. When in doubt, wait it out!

> Confused, indecisive?
> Step back from the plate.
> God says, "Trust me! I got this!
> Sit this one out! Wait!"

Sleepless Nights

It is vain for you to rise up early, to sit up late; to eat the bread of sorrow, for so he gives his beloved sleep. (Ps 127:2).

Why lay a tossing, and turning in your bed
While whirling, twirling thoughts, go spinning through your head?
Curl up with Jesus, and drift right off to sleep.
He is more than able, a weary soul to keep.

Nighty night!

Sleepwalking Saints

And that knowing the time, that now it is high time to awake out of sleep; for now is our salvation nearer than when we believed. (Rom 13:11).

Some Saints are wide awake and definitely on fire for the Lord. But in contrast, many have fallen asleep on the job, and the fire has gone out. So stir up the cinders and keep the fire burning.

> We must remain awake.
> Do not fall asleep.
> Be about God's business,
> For we have a charge to keep.
>
> Keep working in the vineyard.
> Lip service is merely talking.
> Do not be found guilty of
> Slacking, and sleepwalking.
>
> Wake up! "Smell the coffee!"
> There is no time for slumber.
> Oh! Sleepyhead! Remain alert!
> And you'll be counted in heaven's number.

Soap Opera Affair

We spend our years as a tale that is told. (Ps 90:9-10).

There are those who wander blindly clinging on to **The Edge of Night**,
But only Jesus is the way. He is **The Guiding Light**!
Some people live in a fantasy world built upon **Ryan's Hope**,
But in their **Search for Tomorrow**, find they cannot cope.
Many seek a **Dallas** lifestyle, or head out to **Falcon Crest**,
But Jesus is the only one in whom we may have rest.
The WORD is**, All My Children** who are washed in the blood of the Lamb
Are truly **The Bold and The Beautiful**, and belong to the great I AM.
The Young and The Restless, and the old and foolish too,
Live their lives aimlessly. They don't know what to do.
We have but **One Life to Live**, but **Another World** is sure to come.
So be about God's business. Don't leave your work undone.
Who needs **General Hospital**? No emergencies up there!
All of God's Children will rejoice without a care.
So if you want to be an heir of the Royal **Dynasty**,
God says, "Here am I! Come on! Follow me!"
And so are **The Days of Our Lives** that we live like a tale that is told.
The Recording Angel sees and writes all we do on heaven's scroll.
You must be born again, or look forward to disaster.
If you don't accept HIM, HE is not your MASTER.

Solo Conversationalist

The grace of the Lord Jesus Christ, and the love of God, and the communion of the Holy Spirit be with you all. Amen (2 Cor 13:14).

We should ever be mindful of what qualifies us as Christians. How we behave outside of the church during the weekdays can seriously handicap our communion with God if we are inconsistent in how we come across with maintaining daily communion with God through fervent prayer and meditation.

If you talk to God each day, then this message is not for you, but if you don't listen up. Been talking to yourself lately? Each time you fail to talk to God, you begin to start talking to yourself, and when you commence to talk to yourself, you become the only voice of reason, and when that happens, nothing seems to make sense anymore because you don't have all the answers, and God does.

The Word of God voices the felt need to talk to God. Pray without ceasing. (1 Thess 5:17). When all attempts to figure things out seem hampered, hindered, and crippled, perhaps you are a solo conversationalist who talks to yourself, and no one answers, but you.

No one knows the mind of God, but when you open up and talk to Him, He is not an unresponsive God. He will answer you. He will talk back to you, so don't hold back. God wants to hear from you, but most importantly, listen to what He has to say, for He will reveal the deepest, and darkest, untold mysteries of all that you could ever begin to comprehend, or phantom, without Him. So stop talking to yourself! Commune with God, and the grace, and love of God, and the gift of the Holy Ghost will indeed be with you always.

> A Solo conversationalist?
> Why not kneel and pray?
> God is more than interested
> In all you have to say.
>
> Go ahead! Talk to God
> And when you don't know what to say,
> Let your heart speak for you.
> It's more sincere that way.

Somewhere to Lay My Head

And Jesus said unto him, foxes have holes, and birds of the air have nests, but the Son of Man has nowhere to lay His head. (Luke 9:58).

When a certain man said unto the Lord, "I will follow you wherever you go," Jesus replied unto him that the Son of Man had nowhere to lay His head. If ever there was anyone who had nowhere to lay His head, it was Jesus. As such things go, He was despised, rejected, denied, and betrayed. Still, he remained dutifully committed and free of unproductive thoughts. In single-minded determination, He remained spiritually centered and focused on the cause for which He came into the world, to seek and save the lost. (Luke 19:10).

Give me a quiet place, somewhere to slip away.
It's a noisy, twirling world. Let there be peace today.
I need somewhere to lay my head.

How heavenly to know, a place where we can go
To ease a troubled mind, and let it all unwind.
I need somewhere to lay my head.

There's a hidden, sacred space, where to behold his face,
And feel deep peace within, over, and over again.
I need somewhere to lay my head.

On gentle wings of a dove, He'll lift you high above.
All worries will come to cease in the stillness of His peace.
I need somewhere to lay my head.

"Foxes have holes, and birds have their nests."
And there is a secret dwelling of rest.
I need somewhere to lay my head.

Songs and Praises of Deliverance

Now when they began to sing and to praise, the Lord set ambushes against the people of Ammon, Moab and Mount Seir, who had come against Judah; and they were defeated. (2 Chron 20:22).

Jehoshaphat the King of Judah became fearful after hearing the news that a great multitude was headed his way, so he sought the Lord and proclaimed a fast throughout all Judah, and prayed unto the Lord, and the Lord responded with a message of deliverance. "Fear not! Face your enemies. There is no need to fight, for the battle is not yours! It's mine!" So all they needed to do was to stand still and watch God work it out.

And so King Jehoshaphat appointed singers as they went out before the army to praise the Lord, and when they began to sing and praise, the Lord fought Judah's enemies, and they were defeated. (2 Chron 20:24-25).

> God will fight your battles,
> For Him, nothing is too hard.
> He will bring deliverance,
> So sing on, and praise the Lord.

Stay in walkie-talkie Range

The Lord will hear thee in the day of trouble. (Ps 20:1).

One consequence of getting too far out of range is that you stand the risk of not being warned of pursuant danger lurking just ahead of you. It is of no use whatsoever to rely on faulty equipment when you have distanced yourself from God. You must stay in close touch with Him to receive warning signals in order to avoid pitfalls, snares and traps that unexpectedly lie in wait just around the very next bend, or fork in the roadway of life.

Great emphasis should be placed on the fact that Satan will create static and interference on the line, for he is the Prince of the air. But be encouraged, for God's ears will always hear the cries of the righteous; therefore, stay in close proximity, and the airwaves from the upper flow currency will successfully be transmitted to you in the day of trouble.

> Stay in walkie-talkie range.
> Do not venture too far out,
> So that when God warns you,
> Satan cannot tune you out.

Stick a Fork in me! 'I'm Done Already!

And not only so, but we glory in tribulations also knowing that tribulation works patience. (Rom 5:3).

As you know, we live in a jet set, turbo charged, fast paced world; therefore, we expect most things to be completed within a given time frame, but guess what? God never hurries, yet "He's an on time God! Yes! He is." However, when the enemy comes in like a flood, being still in the presence of the Lord, and waiting patiently for Him to act is extremely challenging when we have grown accustomed to microwave, push button and instantaneous results, but God is a slow motion God. More than often, He will take us into the dark room where we must wait until the picture is fully developed, but in our haste and eagerness to grab the picture and walk away, we end up with a premature image in our mindset. The 'stick a fork in me, I'm done already, I hate to wait syndrome,' is a catchall for many begun and unfinished, back burner, bottom of the pile, get around to it dreams, that never become realities.

When we learn how to wait on God; however, and avoid self activated actions, we find that we will emerge with a sharp, clear, and completed image to focus upon.

> Stick a fork in me! I'm done already!
> Hurry up for goodness sakes!
> God tested me, found me undone,
> And put me back in the oven to bake.

Stop Downsizing God!

Is anything too hard for the Lord? (Gen 18:14).

We may view a situation as hopeless, but there is no failure in God! With that in mind, doubting that He can produce extraordinary results is like whittling God down to our size. Actually, our Heavenly Father will wrought phenomenal blessings if only we can believe them into existence beyond the shadow of doubt.

Let us remember whom we are communing with. Lack of trust in God is attributable to receiving a flat soda without the fizz. We receive only what we believe according to the power that works in us. (Eph 3:20). We have been trained not to pursue what seems illogically outside of the realm of our capability to accomplish, but realistic goal setting pales in comparison to (Phil 4:13). I can do all things through Christ which strengthens me!

We may ask above and beyond meager expectations, and rest assured that there is no such thing as unattainable goals to discourage, or frustrate us when we stand upon the promises of God.

> Stop cutting God down to your size.
> Have greater faith, and claim the prize.
> There is nothing too hard for Him to do,
> But trust and faith is up to you.

Sunny Side Up

My brethren, count it all joy when you fall into divers temptations. (James 1:2).

Most of us have had the experience of dealing with the aftermath of unforeseen occasions, uneventful situations, and fiery trials that knock us to our knees so unexpectedly. Surprisingly, we are left breathless, bedazzled, and bewildered.

You may have very cheerfully anticipated a sunny side day, bright and speckled with promise, but suddenly, without warning, your private world spins out of control. Everything is topsy-turvy, and once again, golden dreams and unfulfilled desires are placed on the back burner once again, and temporarily abandoned in the midst of it all.

Far beyond what is expected, when the yoke of life becomes hard boiled instead of soft and easy over, just remember that too many sunny side up orders, and soft boiled experiences, will undoubtedly render you much too fragile to graduate from the School of Hard Knocks.

> Don't let the cloudy days of life
> Rain on your sunny disposition.
> God wants you to toughen up.
> That is His intention.

Tangible Untouchables

Shun the appearance of evil. (1 Thess 5:22).

It is a good thing to remember that as Children of the Light, the only way we can win others to Christ is to stay out of the darkness ourselves. Do you ever experience the call of the wild? Certainly! But when tempted, there is always a way out if we remain spiritually centered in God, for He will not allow Satan to sift us as wheat because Christ prayed for us that our faith would not fail us when the walls appear to be closing in on all sides, and seemingly, there is no way out.

As Christians, we are still able to hear the haunting melody and sensuous music of Satan's fife playing to enchantingly seduce us into unrighteousness, but all such 'tangible untouchables' are off limits to us, and we must fight to shun the appearance of evil as best we can. Resist the devil, and he will flee from you.

> Don't heap up unrighteousness.
> Sin is way too heavy to handle.
> Think about it long and hard.
> Your soul is much too precious to gamble.

Tax Free Salvation

I will greatly rejoice in the Lord. My soul shall be joyful in my God, for he has clothed me with the garments of salvation. (Is 61:10).

Somewhat amazingly, how long the Lord waits upon those who do not believe to consider salvation. A great deal is said about salvation all throughout the Holy Bible. The following scripture is one that really drives it home. Neither is there salvation in any other, for there is none other name under heaven given among men, whereby we must be saved. (Acts 4:12). That is, no other name than Jesus. So how then can anyone neglect the gift of salvation? (Heb 2:3).

A new revelation dawned upon me while enjoying the luxury of an over sea's Ocean Cruise. I went shopping, and immediately noticed that no taxes were included on my bill for any of the items I had selected for purchase. No taxes! Hold that thought! The greatest gift ever given is salvation, for we were purchased with a price by our Lord and Savior, Jesus Christ, who paid the debt 'in full' upon the cross of Calvary, and He has loved from the cross even until now, but in the same breath; however, he cares for only one thing, and that is, that we will believe in Him and accept His gift of salvation, gift wrapped in blood, and tax free.

> Tax free salvation!
> The greatest gift one can receive.
> Accept Christ as your Savior.
> All you need do is just believe.

That Kind of Love

What greater love than that a man should lay his life down for a friend. (John 15:13).

Dying for a friend! As we know, there is no love commensurate with the love of God. His love is unequalled, unmatched and unsurpassed, for when we were yet consumed of sin, He gave His only begotten son to save us from eternal damnation.

Exhibiting a loving spirit means that we have come to know Jesus, for God is love. When love reaches out to encompass others, we are then known as His disciples. (John 13:35).

They nailed Him to the rugged tree,
Scoffed and scorned, and bruised for me,
So that I might endlessly
Lay hold to eternity.

A crown of thorns adorned His head.
Oh! Slaughtered Lamb! My Savior bled.
He purified my sinful soul.
He washed me clean, and made me whole.

Upon the cross of Calvary,
He bore the weight of enmity.
Jesus Christ was crucified.
Love held Him there until He died.

Love is shown in many ways,
But I will praise Him all my days
For giving me that kind of love,
I was so unworthy of.

All the way to the cross
He died for me just because
No one else, but He above
Freely gives, 'that kind of love.'

That's mine!

God so loved the world that he gave his only begotten son, that whosoever believes in him will not perish, but shall have everlasting life. (John 3:16).

In this day and age, one of the greatest pleasures in life is claiming salvation. It gives us a long lasting peace of mind in knowing that eternal life is a promised and guaranteed gift from the Lord.

In school, as students in the classroom, we were always instructed to write our names on all of our personal belongings in order to avoid confusion, and claim proper ownership. As you know, all school crayon boxes were identical, and even popular lunch boxes were tagged due to similarities of design, and as a matter of fact; without a doubt, a classmate or two were sure to wear a look alike coat same as yours. But just one quick look inside, and it was claimed with a "That's mine!" Why? Everything was personalized.

No one is excluded from the gift of salvation; however, many there are who will not receive it because they are unwilling to accept it. Salvation is the same gift presented time, and time again, to any willing recipient, and it is not offered to one this way, or to another that way, but it is offered to everyone in the same like manner. No matter who steps forward to receive it, it will always add up to one thing, and that is eternal life. It is one personalized gift presented unto all, and you know that it is yours because He has written your name upon it, and it is so recorded in the Book of Life.

> Have you claimed salvation?
> Do not run out of time!
> Receive the Lord, Jesus Christ,
> And say, salvation is mine!

Temporal and Eternal

For our light affliction which is but for a moment, works for us a far more exceeding and eternal weight of glory. (2 Cor 4:17).

As I watched the very popular Young & the Restless Soap, a comment was made by one of the leading stars that immediately captured my attention. "Short term pain is long term gain." I couldn't help but think about Paul when he was bombarded by trials on every hand.

In the above mentioned scripture, Paul stated that light afflictions are only temporal, and will pale in comparison to the long term gains to be inherited eternally in the heavenly kingdom above us.

Be not dismayed when trials beset.
Remain patient and never forget
That nothing temporal will ever compare with the glory to be revealed over there.

The ABC Sermon

Preach the word! Be instant in season, and out of season. (2 Tim 4:2).

Always remember, you are the apple of God's eye.
Be bold for Jesus, and lift His name up high.
Christ is the one who has everything you need.
Don't expect a harvest if you do not plant a seed.
Every good teacher must have a lesson plan.
Fail not to be a friend as often as you can.
Go where God so leads to get the message through.
Help comes from the Lord. He will deliver you.
I is a 'me' word, but unity means one and all.
Just remain faithful, and answer to His call.
Kingdom building is what we ought to do.
Love your neighbor, the same as God loves you.
Motivate all students to do their very best.
Never be satisfied until all have passed the test.
Open doors of wisdom! Read and feed the mind.
Procrastination will keep you far behind.
Question not the Lord, but obey all His commands.
Realize the whole world is still in His hands.
Sow good seeds of kindness every single day.
Trust the Lord with all your heart when you kneel to pray.
Understand that Jesus moves in His own way.
Victory is yours and mine. Time to shout! Hey! Hey!
Wisdom means to ask when you do not understand.
X out doubt and worry, and put it all in His hands.
"You will fall for anything, if you choose not to stand."
Zap out the enemy! Preach all over this land.

The Devil in Me

But God is faithful, who will not suffer you to be tempted above that ye are able, but will with the temptation also make a way to escape. (1 Cor 10:13).

Some time ago, comedian, Flip Wilson, made popular the saying, "The Devil Made Me Do It!" Of course, we laughed, but the truth be told, the devil spends a lot of quality time making spectacles out of us, and then, of course, he has the last laugh. The devil has a dire need of willing vessels to use in order to create havoc, react foolishly, and remain unwise. Many there are who do not disappoint him, and that is not a laughing matter.

If you think you can out maneuver the devil without Christ, think again! When you are bold enough to say, Satan! Get thee behind me! Be sure that Christ the Lord is backing you up.

> When Satan offers you a deal,
> Please! Don't shop around, or buy it.
> Your soul will end up in a pan
> And then, he will cook and fry it.
>
> When you appear before the Lord,
> The devil knows full well
> That you may blame him for your faults,
> But it won't keep you out of hell.

The Empty Seat

Set your affection on things above, not on things on the earth. (Col 3:2).

God can very easily and effectively communicate with us in inexpressible and phenomenal ways. Let me explain. Mama was a well seasoned Veteran in the Army of the Lord. Although she wore many hats, she was always ready and willing to surrender to God's agenda. Her mind remained focused and set on things above and beyond this world.

Of the many dreams mama shared with me, one in particular, I desire to share with you now. She told me that she dreamt of an empty seat, and oddly enough, somehow mama knew that the vacant seat was meant for her, but for some unknown reason, the seat was unoccupied. The seat was nameless, but it was numbered, and mama wondered why she wasn't in her seat. Needless to say, mama prayed, and she prayed and she prayed. Finally, she dreamed the very same dream all over again with one exception; however, this time the seat was no longer empty, but mama was in her seat. God gave mama the peace that passes all understanding. Perhaps the dream was only a test, but as can be seen, mama passed it with flying colors.

> None of us are good enough
> Even at our best,
> But when we are determined,
> We will surely pass each test.

The Faithful Fruitful

But the fruit of the spirit is love, joy, peace, longsuffering, kindness, goodness, faithfulness, gentleness and self-control. Against such there is no law. (Gal 5:22-23).

Faith, or faithfulness, is the seventh Fruit of the Spirit mentioned in the book of Galatians, and as we already know, without faith it is impossible to please God.

There is a growing need
To cultivate and plant a seed
That it may spring up from the root.
Faith is among the Spirit's fruit.

Fresh picked faith every day
Will multiply when you pray,
So dutifully stay on the job,
And faithfully labor for God.

Believe in what you cannot see.
Then keep the faith that it will be.
God in turn, will surely reward,
So just stay faithful in the Lord.

Be fruitful in your faithfulness,
And the Husbandman will surely bless
The fruit of His Spirit to ripen in you,
Fully developed, mature, and true.

The Hem of His Garment

And when the men of that place had knowledge of Him, they sent out into all that country round about, and brought unto Him all that were diseased. And besought Him that they might only touch the hem of His garment; and as many as touched were made perfectly whole. (Matt 14:35-36).

Wherever Jesus went, the word got out and in ways few people ever experience, many came to Jesus, and were immediately made whole. A woman with an issue of blood, (Luke 8:43-48), Blind Bartimaeus, (Mark 10:46-52), and the faith of friends who lowered a man stricken with palsy down through the rooftop so that he could be healed, (Mark 2:1-12), all had one thing in common, they were all stubbornly persistent, and had the faith to believe that healing would happen upon contact with Jesus and it was so.

When physical contact with Jesus is not possible, such as it is today, how do we still manage to reach out and touch the hem of His garment? Let me refer you to (Luke 7:2-9). The Centurion believed that it was totally unnecessary for Jesus to come to his servant in order to heal him, but only speak the word, and it would happen. No wonder Jesus marveled at him and said, "I have not found so great faith, no not in Israel." And so his servant was miraculously healed because of the Centurion's unwavering faith in Jesus.

> Jesus is still healing today
> All manner of sickness and disease,
> So reach out and touch the hem of His garment,
> And put your mind at ease.

The Heart of a Harlot

Now Joshua the son of Nun sent out two from Acacia Grove to spy secretly saying, Go view the land, especially Jericho. So they went, and came to the house of a harlot named Rahab, and lodged there. (Joshua 2:1).

Listen to understand that God considers every single detail of our lives, and far deeper than we can imagine, no matter who we are, or what we have done, He never fails to seize the opportunity to intervene on our behalf. It was no accident that the spies happened to lodge in the house of a prostitute, for God knew her heart. To illustrate my point, Rahab hid the spies from the King of Jericho, and then she shared her feelings about the God of Israel with them. "Your God, she said, is God in heaven above and in earth beneath." And then she asked, that her kindness toward them be rewarded, by sparing her, and also her family from death. Her request was honored, and the same scarlet chord used to lower the spies down through the window, was the same scarlet line used as a sign that God would spare not only her, but her father and mother, and all of her brothers and sisters from harm's way. Yes! God knew the heart of a harlot, and when He knocked upon the door of her heart, Rahab answered Him.

> Rahab hid the spies
> From the King of Jericho,
> And asked to be rewarded
> For the kindness she did show.
>
> She did not ask for riches,
> Expensive oil, or spice,
> But only that God would spare her
> And each loved one's life.

The Mask

Then God said, Let me make man in our image. (Gen 1:26-27).

Don't hide your greatness! You are incredible!

Faces mirror the soul's reflection.
Masks are worn to hide imperfection.
We do not want others to see
The real you, or true me.

Masquerade never goes out of season.
A mask is worn for most any reason.
Behind a false smile lurks evil and danger.
We laugh it off to cover up anger.

The artificial mask is unreal.
We hide behind it to conceal.
So deeply hurt, but no one knows.
Masks are worn like every day clothes.

No matter how we try to disguise,
God sees through each mask with soul-searching eyes.
We are naked and exposed to His view.
You can't hide! He sees the real you.

He nurses our wounds, and feels our pain.
He eases our sorrows when tears flow like rain,
And when everything seems out of place
He even invades our personal space.

Wearing a mask? There is nothing to fear.
Take it off now! Jesus is here!
Remove the false face. Let God's glory shine through.
You were made in His image, so why not be you?

The Same Pay

So when evening came, the Lord of the vineyard said to his steward, call the Laborers and give them their hire, beginning from the last unto the first. (Matt 20:8).

Some people believe that they should receive a greater reward than others, and that is largely because they have faithfully worked as Christian Laborers in God's vineyard all along. But in reading the parable found in (Matt 20:1-16), we find that the system of merit God used to determine how each Laborer was paid, surely supports the fact that He does not always reward us according to our expectations.

Some came early, some came late,
And others at the close of day,
But the owner of the vineyard,
He turned not one away.

Truly it's a blessing to be employed by God,
And serve Him very faithfully while working on the job,
But He is more concerned about those who have not come,
And seeks to have them harvesting before the day is done.

The Talking Ass

And the Lord opened the mouth of the ass, and she said unto Balaam, what have I done unto thee, that thou hast smitten me these three times? (Num 22:28-30).

Some time ago there was a popular movie titled, "Francis, The Talking Mule." There was also a T.V. show about a talking horse called "Mr. Ed." Long ago; however, God actually opened the mouth of an ass, and that folks, was neither non fictional, nor animated. God's anger was kindled against Balaam because he was disobedient and failed to follow through as God had commanded him to do so. Let's focus on the ass and why Balaam struck his beloved animal three times. First of all, unknown to Balaam, the ass saw an angel of the Lord standing in the way with a drawn sword in his hand, and so the ass turned aside out of the way into a field. Strike one! Next, the angel stood in a path of the vineyard with a wall on this side, and a wall on that side, so the ass thrust herself unto the wall, and crushed Balaam's foot against the wall. Strike two! Finally, the angel took it a step further and stood in a narrow place which made it impossible to turn either to the right hand or to the left, so Balaam hit the ass with his staff a third time. Strike three! Consequently, the ass spoke. "What have I done for you to hit me three times?" Balaam replied to the ass that "she had mocked him to the point that had he a sword in his hand, he would have killed her." The ass in turn spoke yet again. "Haven't I been faithful thus far, and have I ever caused you any harm?" Balaam's only answer was no! Suddenly the Lord opened Balaam's eyes, and finally, he saw the angel of the Lord standing in the way with a drawn sword in his hand, so he bowed his head and fell on his face. Then the angel asked him the very same question as the ass had posed unto him. "Why did you strike your ass three times? Your ass saw me and then turned from me three times, and had she turned not, I would surely have slain you, and spared the ass."

God deals with disobedient folk.
He opened the mouth of an ass, and she spoke.
God used an ass to deliver His word,
And you can believe, it was finally heard.

The Tongue Tamer

But the tongue can no man tame, it is an unruly evil, full of deadly poison. (James 3:8).

It is of no use whatsoever to foolishly believe or to think that mankind is able to control such a little member like the tongue. I don't think so! Let's face it!

An unbridled tongue is not of God. (James 1:26). Now what does that mean? It means that death and life are in the power of the tongue, and they that love it shall eat the fruit thereof. (Prov. 18:21). It means that unless we ask God to let the words of our mouths and the meditations of our hearts be acceptable in His sight, (Ps 19:14), we will set things ablaze, for the tongue is like a fire that will defile the whole body and set on fire the very course of nature ignited by sin. It means that there is a bridle for the horse, a muzzle for the ox, and a tongue tamer for man. So pray without ceasing that God will keep the door of your lips, and you will then possess a wholesome tongue which is indeed a healthy tree of life. (Prov 15:4).

> Put the tongue out of business!
> Close up the gossip shop,
> Or God will do it for you.
> The evil tongue must stop!

The Wisdom of Babes

And Jesus said to them. "Yes. Have you never read, out of the mouth of babes and nursing infants you have perfected praise?" (Matt 21:16).

During my early childhood years, I recall mama sharing a story she once heard about a little girl who was scolded by a parent for ironing on the Sabbath day. Looking confused and somewhat perplexed, replied the little tot. "Now don't you suppose the good Lord knows that this little iron ain't hot?"

The reason we are so often knocked off our feet by little babes is that wisdom spoken by small children humbles us to the point of melt down. Even children know that God knows the difference between play acting and the real thing. Now handle that.

> Out of the mouth of babes
> Come praise, wisdom, and sound truth,
> So take the time to listen up.
> God speaks through youth.

There it is!

But as it is written, eye have not seen, nor ear heard, nor have entered into the heart of man the things which God has prepared for those who love Him. (1 Cor 2:9).

It has been stated that "we are heavenly beings having an earthly experience." Whoever penned those words is more than a gifted genius. There was a saying taken from a very popular song back in the days of the nineteen nineties. "Oops! There it is!" In other words, the undisputed truth is indeed undeniable. There is absolutely nothing earthly that can in any way experience anything heavenly until a transformation has taken place. No wonder then, we moan and groan to shed mortality in exchange for a glorified, immortal heavenly body. (2 Cor 5:1-2).

> Earth has nothing priceless
> That it can give, or offer me,
> But heaven is a gift from God
> That can be shared eternally.

August

He that keeps you will not slumber. (Ps 121:3).

> **A**ll things work out for those who love the Lord.
> **U**nthinkable things, He is able to do. Nothing is too hard!
> **G**ood Shepherd is His name. He will never fall asleep.
> **U**nder His protection there is refuge for all sheep.
> **S**cores of human eyelids will close at the end of day.
> **T**rust God! He won't fall asleep, or snooze along the way.

In this day and age, God's promises are just as true as ever. He keeps right on blessing and working things out for the good of all His children. According to the power of faith and belief, we have to trust God unquestioningly above all that we can think or even begin to imagine. Absolutely nothing is too difficult for God. As His children, we may rest assured that He is the 'Good Shepherd' who will always safeguard the Sheep of His pasture. Human eyelids will eventually close, but the eyes of God are everywhere beholding the bad and the good. He is a Keeper who never sleeps, nor slumbers.

Thoughts of a Roman Soldier

Then said Jesus, Father, forgive them, for they know not what they do. (Luke 23:34).

Alas! How very strange indeed that now at the sixth hour,
Such darkness I have never seen causes me to cower.
Could this be an omen of what is yet to be?
And what is this dreadful feeling taking hold of me?

It is now the eighth hour! Oh! I can hardly see.
I sense a wrongful foreboding rapidly engulfing me.
Oh! No! He gave up the ghost! He hung His head and died!
Surely! It's the Son of God whom we have crucified.

The veil of the temple has been rent in twain.
We have crucified the King. Oh! Blessed be His holy name.
Hark! The earth beneath my feet moans, and shakes, and quakes.
He is the Savior of the world who died for all our sakes.

I heard Him tell the thief just before He died,
That he would in Paradise join Him at His side.
Did I not hear them mock Him as he bowed his thorn pricked head?
Then they pierced Him in His side, and He profusely bled.

Did I not hear Him whisper a plea for me, and you?
"Father, Please forgive them, for they know not what they do!"
Did I not see God's glory illuminate my Savior's face?
I witnessed through my guiltiness, His unfailing grace.

Oh! Dear God! Woe is me!
Yet I am grateful just because
Jesus also died for me.
His blood redeemed me at the cross.

Threefold Cord

For in him dwells all the fullness of the Godhead bodily, and you are complete in Him who is the head of all principality and power. (Col 2:9-10).

While in today's world there are differing opinions about the Trinity, do not allow the "I beg to differ syndrome' to toy with your mind. Again and again, the truth is, the Father, the Son and the Holy Spirit, are three individual personalities, yet they are unified as one in God. This is known as the Trinity, and that is that. First and foremost is the primary person. God stands first and His function is one of complete control over the universe. He has the authority to execute judgment. Because of his great, undying love for us, the second person of the Trinity has the role of the Savior. Jesus Christ died for our sinfulness that we might receive salvation through redemption of His blood. The third person of the (3 in 1) God head connection, is the Holy Spirit. The third person descended only when Jesus ascended upward to the throne of God. Such being the case, we are highly privileged to commune with an easy to reach, and not a distant or detached God. So be joyful!

As mentioned in the Word, a threefold cord is not easily broken. It stands to reason that all three persons of the Godhead work together harmoniously and effectively to bring about desired and miraculous results.

> The Godhead is three in one.
> Oh! Blessed Trinity!
> What an awesome threefold blessing
> That amazes you and me.

Time Out for Play

When I was a child, I spoke as a child, understood as a child, and thought as a child, but when I grew up, I put away childish things. (1 Cor 13:11).

It should come as no surprise that many have never outgrown their childhood days. In much the same fashion as children, many of us are afraid to step forward and do the things we know we should without a reassuring thrust, or nod of approval from others. Then too, having been forewarned repeatedly, some insist on touching a hot stove that continues to burn them upon contact. Listen to understand, we can be physically mature adults with the mind of a child, and we can also be spiritually immature, and remain baby Saints. When God commands you to move forward, it begins with the first step on your own. Don't worry! He's watching you! And whenever He warns you to shun the appearance of evil, or suffer the consequences, grow up, and do as you are told. All Believers begin as baby Saints. Those who put away the toys; however, understand that time is out for play, and no longer drink milk any more, but change into adult Saints who feast upon the meat of His Word, and emerge as mature Saints of God.

When I was a child, I spoke like a child,
And often when playmates passed by,
Like a bee stings, I said hurtful things,
Poked fun, and made some cry.

I was only teasing though
But in a very childish way,
I was snubbed, made up and hugged,
And then, I proceeded to play.

With a child's heart, I was innocent,
My thoughts were without understanding.
I was guiltless and free, and life then for me,
It was carefree, and so undemanding.

Those gone by days no longer exist.
A child, I never again will be.
I am now fully grown, with a mind of my own,
And I face accountability.

Now who will tell me what to do?
Who dare will direct my way?
God will skin my hide, to help me decide
That time is out for play.

Tribute to America

Who Himself bore our sins in His own body on the tree, that we, having died to sins, might live for righteousness, by whose stripes you were healed. (1 Pet 2:24).

September the eleventh!
A day we shall never forget!
American lives were taken away.
They paid the ultimate, unjust debt.

America watched in terror.
We were taken by surprise.
Airplanes fell, smoke arose,
And darkened, glowing skies.

Buildings crumbled! Cries rang out,
And the earth stood still.
The terrorists had their way
But it was not God's will.

No longer will the enemy
Triumph on American sod.
We will stand as one nation;
We pray, under God.

We circulate "in God we trust!"
So then it must be true,
That we have faith in God alone,
And He will pull us through.

Red is for the precious blood
The Lamb of God so freely shed.
Blue is for His stripes and wounds,
Nail prints, and thorn pricked head.

White stands for purity.
All sin is washed away.
Hey Red! Hey White! Hey Blue!
America! Let's pray!

Trust Drive It

This thing is from me. (1 Kings 12:24)

Many of us have grown accustomed to comfort riding our way through life. Such being the case, there is a desire and tendency to attempt to test drive everything that comes our way even when God Himself is the Sender.

Admittedly, we want to check things out and know the full extent of what to expect, so that we can determine if we are well wadded and cushiony enough to absorb shocks in order to ensure comfort riding along life's thoroughfare. And then, there are those of us who want a storm proof system in place because few of us if any, enjoy riding out the storms of life in discomfort. Not so. Self effort always hinders. Each day God gives us something to look forward to and whether it brings abundant joy, or extraordinary difficulties, we cannot override the strong currents of adversity that shake us from daydreaming into reality, or avoid the thundering rent of a storm, but must ride on through it anyhow. God does not provide storm proof covering!

Keep in mind that through it all, God commonly appears in greatest extremities; therefore, you must look to Him alone and 'trust drive' whatever He sends your way. No matter how rough the ride may be, one thing is certainly true and that is, none of us will ever joy ride our way into heaven.

> You cannot ride to heaven
> In a First Class, comfort seat.
> But you'll be glad you trusted Him when your journey is complete.

Trust in Jesus

Trust in the Lord with all thine heart, and lean not unto thine own understanding. (Prov 3:5).

Trusting Jesus means to be absolutely sure that He will deliver all that He has promised He would. Decide today, to trust Him all the way, for He will reward all who place their trust in Him.

Oh! What blessings to receive
When we trust Him and believe.
Come what may within your life
Almighty God will suffice.

Unrestrained winds may blow,
Tossing cares to and fro,
But He commands the storm at will,
And it obeys. "Peace! Be still!"

Stand firm! Hold fast to your belief.
Surely! Jesus is relief.
Rely on Him, whatever the plight.
Lean on Him with all your might.

Teach your heart to depend
On Jesus, a forever friend,
And all concerns will come to cease.
Be still! Trust Him! He gives peace.

Trust Your Nose

Eat thou not the bread of him that hath an evil eye, neither desire thou his dainty meats. (Prov 23:6).

Ever heard the expression, something just doesn't smell right? Instinct is defined as a powerful motivation or impulse, so if something looks inviting, but doesn't smell right to you, trust your nose! Walk away! When the sensor beeps, respond to its signal. The reward comes to us when we realize that with each victory over a temptation, it becomes all the easier to resist next time it happens again.

Keep in mind that there are only two kinds of trouble. Good and bad. Often, God will send trouble and allow it to break us down in order to build us up. Consider that as good trouble. Bad trouble; on the other hand, is the trouble we ourselves call up and then later on down the line, we wish we could hang up on it. One thing about the Devil is that once you dial him up, he has your number and next time, he will call you. Now that's the kind of trouble you can smell.

Think about it! Tell me now,
How do you suppose
A dog evades an enemy?
He learns to trust his nose.

Turn the Bed Loose

A little sleep, a little slumber, a little folding of the hands to sleep, so shall thy poverty come on you like a prowler and your need like an armed man. (Prov 6:10-11).

If you want to experience prosperity first hand, get out of bed! Become an early riser! "Arise and shine!" Yes! An early bird will indeed eat the worm, but a late bird will only nibble at the core of a left over apple. So when opportunity knocks, answer the door. God will bless you, and prosperity will be yours.

> There are those who love to lie dormant in bed
> Whose bellies will hunger and not be fed.
> When you rise up late, and dibble and dabble,
> Someone else will eat your apple.

Turning Dimes

We know not what shall happen tomorrow. What is life? It is like a vapor that appears for a little time, and then vanishes away. (James 4:14).

Many believe that life turns on a dime. Actually, the truth is, life turns on Jesus. Candidly speaking, taking chances each day without Jesus, is like flipping a coin in order to determine your destiny; heads, or tails? The stark reality is that death, an unseen, constant companion, is closer than close but the good news is; however, that Jesus claimed victory over death on Calvary. So then, the big question so often asked is, "GOT JESUS?"

> Is living risky business?
> Well! It all depends.
> If you belong to Jesus,
> Eternal life never ends.
>
> Life here may not continue to turn.
> Why trust your fate on a dime?
> Get to know Jesus!
> Don't run out of time!

Twelve Stones

And those twelve stones which they took out of the Jordan, Joshua set up in Gilgal. (Joshua 4:20).

Joshua commanded twelve men from every tribe of Israel to carry a stone with them to the lodging place where they spent the night. These were not only memorial stones unto the children of Israel, but they were also 'forget not to remember stones' to remind them to tell future generations that God allowed Israel to cross over Jordan on dry land. Never forget to remember the God of Israel.

In our life experiences of today, what stones have we laid to remind our children and grandchildren of God's unfailing goodness to us. There should always be something left behind to remind others of how God worked wonders during our lifetime here on planet earth.

What better gift to leave behind
Than a personal testimonial stone,
So loved ones will rely on God
Long after we are gone?

Twice Blessed

Let them praise His name with the dance; Let them sing praises to him with the timbrel and harp. (Ps 149:3).

I can truly say that I have been twice blessed in knowing that praying for our children is the best gift they will ever receive from parents. Eva Marie Tabb, the second of my two children, heralded her entrance into this world on July 30, 1973. And, of course, I prayed for my precious, little baby girl, as I had prayed for her big brother.

> Dads just love those baby girls
> With dimpled cheeks, bows, and curls.
> On July 30, nineteen, seventy three,
> Along came, Eva Marie.
>
> Another soul for God to keep,
> Another babe to rock to sleep,
> And a beautiful woman to behold
> When she grows up and leaves the fold.
>
> Once again, I prayed a prayer
> And twice again, God met me there.
> "Bless my daughter, dear Lord, I pray.
> Order her steps from day to day."

Yes! I am twice blessed to say that Eva Marie is the world's best daughter, cherished sister, loving wife, super mom, hardworking, creative, and gifted in the artistry of dance. But most importantly, she is a Child of the King.

Beautiful feet are anointed to praise the Lord in the dance.

I love you, my daughter. MOM

Unblessed Food

Give us this day our daily bread. (Matt 6:11).

Some people think that skipping grace is irrelevant and unimportant. Not so. Let me show you why this is true. Often bargain merchandise is labeled "As Is." So then, in some way, one realizes that an imperfection does indeed somehow exist. In other words, buy at your own risk. In the same vein; however, unblessed food is also eaten as is, at your own risk. Unblessed!

Some may think it no big deal
To consume an unblessed meal,
But when all is set in place,
Please! Take time to say the grace.

Even when dining out,
One should always think about
The food you are about to eat.
Bless it all, including the treat.

Most meals are prepared by a loving hand,
But still, you need to understand
That some may tamper, or deal in pranks.
So eat! Drink up! But first, give thanks.

There is food contamination
And any unhealthy situation
Can spoil fruit, veggies, or meat,
So bless your food before you eat.

Fold your hands! Bow your head!
Thank God for your daily bread.
Make it a part of your everyday living.
Always bless your meal with thanksgiving.

Undo

Create in me a clean heart, oh God; and renew a right spirit within me. (Ps 51:10).

The computer has an 'undo' icon, and whenever it becomes necessary to restore a document back to its original state, all you need do is hit the icon button, and it works like magic! How much easier our lives would be if we could backtrack and undo some of our hasty, spur of the moment actions during our daily rounds and encounters with others along the way. But there is a way to reprogram those split second decisions. Instead of wasting time continuing to stew over those less than stellar moments, and regrets, try Jesus! David was a man after God's own heart, yet he always repented, and he continuously begged the Lord to undo him and spiritually renew him every time he fell from grace, and displeased his Heavenly Father.

> We are not empowered
> To transform or renew,
> But God can change anyone.
> He is more than able to undo.

Unction at the Junction

But you have an anointing from the Holy One, and you know all things. (1 John 2:20).

In the second chapter of the First Epistle of John, verse 19, John penned these words: They went out from us, but they were not of us; for if they had been of us, they would no doubt have continued with us, but they went out, that they might be made manifest that they were not all of us.

There is much to be said here. Let me explain. First of all, they were all at the holy junction, seemingly joined together, but all were not gathered together in His name. So what I am trying to get you to see is that there were (tares), or unsaved non-believers, among the (wheat), or those who were saved, and who also believed. Secondly, since they were unequally yoked, they could not identify with the true believers of Jesus Christ, and so the Anti-Christ, veered off course and departed from the junction. Thirdly, the reason is more than obvious why the unsaved could not measure up, or see eye to eye, the ultimate purpose of godly togetherness because they were ungodly, so they were exposed, and rightly so, but those who are appointed, anointed, and have that unction for the Holy One, will stay the course and finish the race.

> The soldiers in God's Army
> Don't surrender, or retreat.
> Meet Him at the junction.
> It is where true Believers meet.

Undressed

Put on the whole armor of God, so that you may be able to stand against the wiles of the devil. (Eph 6:11).

Do not miss your morning glory, or things are bound to get real gory. Upon rising early in the morning, do you begin your day with coffee? Why not sip Jesus first? Like C & H sugar, He is pure cane sweet to your taste buds. Artificial sweeteners won't keep your voice 'Sweet N Low' and nothing can 'Equal' the real thing! You need Jesus to prepare you to meet the world each day, and there are no substitutes for God. Your faith, like 'Folgers' should be mountain grown, and if you acknowledge Him early on, you will find that just like 'Maxwell House Coffee,' He is good to the very last drop! So don't depend on coffee to pick you up because Satan will knock you down! Gusty winds of opposition will chill you to the bone, and when things get too hot to handle, the devil will melt you down when you are unprotected out on the battlefield. So whatever you may do each morning, make it a habit to put on the whole armor of God, and you shall victoriously overcome.

I hurriedly rushed into a new day.
I didn't take time to kneel and pray.
In all of my haste, I failed to dress,
So who did I think, I would impress?

I sipped some coffee, then rushed through the door
Not knowing what was lying in store.
I did not meet God at His throne;
Therefore, I was on my own.

The cold world made me shiver, and shake
As I drifted along like a snowflake,
And the torrid flame of adversity
Was so piping hot, it melted me.

I fought in the battle,
But I was undressed.
I was naked, unclothed,
Stripped bare, and stressed.

Because I failed to dress today,
`Sin took over, and had its way.
Satan laughed! He knew me not,
So he aimed his bow, and took his best shot.

Smack dab in the middle of Satan's mess,
The harder I fought, the more he did press.
I was wounded in battle, weak, weary, and slain.
The whole day was all in vain.

What is the moral of this story?
Things don't have to be grim, or gory.
Just be sure that when you rise up,
You salute the Lord with your very first cup.

Don't wait until the end of day
To take a little time to pray,
For Satan will, without a warning,
Catch you undressed come any morning.

Unforgivable

Peter asked the Lord how often should one sin against him and be forgiven by him. Instead of seven times as quoted by Peter, the Lord replied, "Seventy times seven!" (Matt 18:21-22).

Many there are, who allow those who have offended us to continuously ignite flames of Satan's timber to burn within our unforgiving hearts by refueling the fire until at long last, it consumes us as the end result. We should not over indulge in holding grudges, getting even, or to an even greater extent, ignore the "seventy times seven" reply of our Lord and Savior, Jesus Christ, for to do so will compel our Heavenly Father to withhold our forgiveness as well. (Matt 6:14-15).

It would be so horrible
If God would hold a grudge;
Just stand, and shrug His shoulders,
And then refuse to budge.

How terrible a circumstance
If God would cut no slack,
And while asking for forgiveness,
He would simply turn His back.

We have grace and mercy
Because the Savior lives,
And Thank God for Jesus.
Through Him, God forgives.

Unknown

Whither shall I go from thy spirit? Or whither shall I flee from thy presence? (Ps 139:7).

I have often thought of fallen heroes of war. Probably, the most significant single thing that stands out in my mind is the unknown. Countless slain soldiers of war are honored and remembered simply as the unknown soldiers. Some who enlisted to aid their country by serving in the armed forces are now missing in action and others perhaps, are laid to rest in unmarked graves as unknown soldiers.

Annual services are held to commemorate those who gave their lives during warfare for the good of their country. On Memorial Day, and Veteran's Day, flags are flown at half staff, and traditional, honorary gun salutes fill the air, and colorful wreaths of fresh scented flowers, adorn the resting places of the known, and unknown soldiers, all of whom were so dearly loved by someone. No one; however, is unknown to God. Whether living or deceased, we will always remain identifiable to our Creator.

> The grave is where my body sleeps.
> My soul is with the one who keeps.
> Oh! Wounded Spirit! Free from pain.
> No one here knows my name.
>
> "The good die young," so I am told.
> The Reaper claims both young and old.
> Here am I, a hero unsung,
> Yet no one knows my bell has rung.
>
> This is my country; "land of the free."
> Fail not to remember me.
> I fought to save sweet liberty.
> Oh! Where is my identity?
>
> Long may the banner wave!
> Honor the unknown in the grave.
> Here I lie, so honorably,
> And only God knows it's me.

Untouchable Souls

Have you considered my servant, Job? (Job 1:8).

The cold hard fact of the matter is there comes a time when faithfulness to God will be tested in the severest way. When commitment to God will challenge us through long corridors of adversity, and lead us way down into deep and dark dungeons, and gloomy chambers of satanic activity.

Recall if you will, Job's bout with the Devil. With God's spoken permission, Satan robbed Job of his wealth; grieved him of his loved ones, disrobed him of royalty, and humiliated him before his wife and friends. But through it all, God's servant, Job, remained unrelentingly faithful to God. So then Satan recoiled and approached the Lord, yet again. "Now do one more thing! Allow me to trouble his flesh!" And God concurred with one exception. "Do not touch his soul!"

The reason we are so often bulked by difficulties is that for our own sakes, God will permit troubles, and trials to happen to us, so that He in turn may be glorified if like Job, we are able to patiently trust God and wait it out until our change comes.

> Satan wields his power
> Full force to gain control,
> But God is still in charge.
> Satan cannot touch your soul.

Upward and Onward

But Jesus said, suffer little children, and forbid them not, to come unto me, for such is the kingdom of heaven. (Matt 19:14).

Promises are easily made, and just as easily broken, but the promises of God are everlasting even throughout eternity. One of the most memorable experiences of Church School is memorizing, and studying God's Word as youngsters, and reciting all His written promises. From the Beginners Class into adulthood, we are assured that God cannot lie, and He will never ever fall short of His Word. He will not break a promise, and so it is.

> We were promoted in Sunday School Class.
> Upward and onward, how the years pass.
> Remember all that has been spoken.
> God's promises are never broken.

Veteran's Preference

I have fought a good fight! (2 Tim 4:7).

Have you considered that all soldiers enlisted in Christian combat will be entitled to Veteran's Preference after spiritual warfare has ended?

When the smoke clears and the battle is finally won, those who have exercised courage and braved danger through an unexpected turn of events, performed feats of bravery and sustained injuries from opposition of the enemy while in the heat of fighting for the promotion of the Kingdom of God, will be justly rewarded for having endured hard times as Veterans of the Cross.

God has His set times, so begin to visualize a victorious celebration to honor those Veterans who have faithfully served even unto death in the Christian Army. The Commanding Chief Officer will adorn His Heavenly Brigade with honors due, and will single-handedly applaud each one for their voluntary enlistment and personal effort as a committed soldier in the Army of the Lord. So become a retired Christian Veteran. It pays off eternally.

> When the battle is over,
> And the war is won,
> God will reward all Veterans
> And say, "Job well done!"

Waxed Cold

And because iniquity shall abound, the love of many shall wax cold. (Matt 24:12).

It is of no use whatsoever to bury your head in the sand, or roll over and play dead, and pretend that all around you is well, for it is not. There are wars and rumors of war, and love is waxing colder from day to day. At an ever accelerating pace, crime is on the rampage. Immoral behavior lifestyles are at an all time high. There are too many missing children. Gun happy snipers have invaded the malls, and too many college students are walking on eggshells, fearing for their lives, on once safe college campuses. When will a fellow student decide to go on another shooting spree? And teachers in classrooms are also sitting targets.

Where is natural affection? Many love pleasure more than God. (2 Tim 3:1-5). The handwriting is on the wall, and the worst is yet to come. Perilous times have arrived, and we are living in the last days. So how then, do we arrive at a breakthrough solution? Feeling threatened and hemmed in on all sides will not uproot satanic harvest, but prayer changes things. We shall grow stronger the longer we pray. Kneeling down to pray over matters will always make a significant difference in the world of today, and prayer will also empower Believers to humble themselves, and continue to 'walk in the way' so that God will hear our prayers as we turn from our wicked ways, and heal the land.

> Be not dismayed or troubled,
> Nor allow your hope to dim.
> Jesus is coming back again,
> So rest assured in Him.

Way Back Then

Remove not the ancient landmark which thy fathers have set. (Prov 22:28).

The church of way back then is still a landmark for the church of here and now!

No one else could praise the Lord,
The way they did. No! Not like them,
And how it blessed our souls to hear
A good, old fashioned, country hymn.

Give me a down home country church.
Everything was simple and plain.
Nope! Folk didn't have a lot,
But they chose not to complain.

They were not concerned about
Glamorous types of stylish hair.
They just made it their business
To always show up there.

God is not a wardrobe God.
So there was no one to impress.
There was a time, most only had
One 'Sunday-go-meeting' dress.

There was no flair for fashion.
No decked out, designer suit.
All God's folk wanted to know
Was if your soul had root?

It took much more than dressing up
In stunning fads and looking cute
To shake that old devil off,
And give sly Satan, the boot.

Some Pioneer Christians walked to church,
And then they dusted off their shoes.
They were grateful to arrive on time
And hear the Gospel of good news.

The Ushers were in place
And positioned at the door
To welcome Saints and Sinners in,
And then, they praised God all the more.

Some families rode in wagons,
And could hear old Reverend Ike,
Miles before they got to church,
And way back then, there was no mike.

The quartets and the choirs
Never sang off-beat.
No organ! No piano!
They clapped their hands, and stomped their feet.

There were no fancy accolades.
No prolonged service to honor the dead.
The Saints preached their own eulogies
By the kind of lives they led.

Saints of God were laid to rest
And they were buried in the churchyard.
All tombstones simply read;
"I am now with the Lord!"

Those who did not know the Lord,
The Saints would give their arms a pinch,
And soon they would be taken up
To tarry on the Mourner's Bench.

Way back then, Saints never played church!
Serving God was a full time position,
And if we want to make it to heaven,
We too, must have that old time religion.

What Do You Do?

Now unto him that is able to do exceeding abundantly above all that we ask or think according to the power that works in us. (Eph 3:20).

What do you do when you completely run out of rope to cling to? Seek out God, and then ask Jesus to give you some more rope. God is more than able to solve your problems which seemingly appear to be hopelessly unsolvable. In Jesus, you can cope, for He is hope. "So be the next one in line for your any day now miracle." Let's face it! Challenges will come, and you will be compelled to go a mile with your adversary. Yep! Someone is going to yank your chain, but do not allow them to pull it out of the socket. Accept the challenge and walk two miles with your enemy. It is important to note; however, that one can not react that way unless the same spirit is in you, that is in Jesus Christ, our Lord and Savior. According to (1 Peter 3:4), the ornament of a meek and quiet spirit in the sight of God is of great price.

What do you do when the road runs out and you're at the end of the rope?
Who do you turn to for help, and how will you manage to cope?

Who will perform the miracle and turn the water into wine?
Who will save the royal feast so that all may drink and dine?

What do you do when someone offends? Do you turn the other cheek?
When you are judged and wrongly accused, what words are you given to speak?

When out of rope, clutch the True Vine. Jesus is a safety net.
Are you troubled? God is a present help, so why haven't you trusted Him yet?

Jesus turned water into wine, so come and feast at the banquet table.
Miracles will never cease! Wine and dine, for He is able.

Not the weak, but the mighty in Spirit is able to turn the other cheek.
Walk away a conqueror! The world belongs to the mild and meek.

Ways to Praise

Because thy loving kindness is better than life, my lips shall praise thee. Lord, I will bless you while I live. I will lift up my hands in thy name. (Ps 63:3-4).

There are countless ways,
We can praise the Lord.
We can worship Him all alone,
Or worship together, on one accord.

We can praise God at anytime,
Any place, or anywhere.
No scheduled appointments!
Just meet the Lord in prayer.

We may praise God silently,
Or honor Him through dance.
But by all means, praise Him!
Glorify Him given each chance.

Praise Him on the job.
Praise Him as you move along
Praise Him with the cymbal,
Or salute Him with a song.

Praise God in the morning.
Be it noonday, or at night.
Every time you honor Him,
Things will work out right.

God is worthy of all praise.
Let everything praise the Lord!
Magnify His holy name.
High praise, He will reward.

When it Tickles, Laugh

And as the ark of the Lord came into the city of David, Michal, Saul's daughter, looked through a window and saw King David leaping and dancing before the Lord, and she despised him in her heart. (2 Sam 6:16).

There's no question that David knew the significance of the Ark of the Lord, and so he could not help but dance with all his might and leap for joy, for there was every reason to rejoice over such a tremendous blessing. So how then could Michal remain untouched by the blessing of the Ark in the city of David? A mighty foothold to the devil is undoubtedly failure to focus on God. Michal was so fixated on what she saw as a blatant display of King David shamelessly leaping around uncovered, and getting his dance on, that she dismissed the fact that he was giving God the glory and praising Him for returning the Ark of God to the city of Jerusalem. You will surely find the same is true today. Many will react indifferently to high praise worship, but the Word tells us to quench not the Spirit. Shout on!

> When it tickles, laugh!
> God's blessed people should have no shame.
> So get your praise on,
> And glorify His holy name.

What's Eating You?

Cast your burden upon the Lord, and He shall sustain thee. (Ps 55:22).

Many have an unending desire to lose weight by controlling their appetites and watching what they eat. But what about what's eating you?

It is important that we do not allow back-to-back bouts of depression, stress, or anxiety to unknowingly eat away at us like imperceptible, tiny tape worms, until we are completely overwhelmed and totally despondent.

Which is of greater importance, to watch what you are eating, or to watch out for what is eating you?

> Greedy overeating will result in gaining weight.
> One must be determined to push away the plate.
> But heaviness of Spirit is much too heavy to bear.
> What's eating you will weigh you down, so go to God in prayer.

Whoever Heard of a Peaceful Enemy?

By this I know that God favors me, because my enemy does not triumph over me. (Ps 41:11).

Ever hear the saying, "Hold your friends close, and your enemies even closer?" How true it is. Who indeed ever heard of a peaceful enemy, and how in the world is that possible? When a man's ways please the Lord, He makes even his enemies to be at peace with him. (Prov 16:7).

Why enemies? Let's answer this question with a question. Why not? If you are not a friend of the world, Satan is already your enemy, but the good news is that God is your friend. Which way would you rather have it be? If it had not been for the Lord on your side, the enemy would prevail over you. But when we obey God's word, we will have power over our adversaries, and heap coals of fire upon their heads. (Prov 25:21-22).

> Only God can make peace
> And tame your enemy.
> He makes all enemies peaceful.
> So claim each victory.

Who is who in God's World?

A good name is rather to be chosen than great riches and loving favor rather than silver, or gold. (Prov 22:1).

Now that we think about it, everybody wants their name to count for something good in this world. There is nothing of any lasting good to be gained from riches, but a good name seen in a somewhat different light will last forever and always, for whatever we do for Christ will last.

In a very real sense, who would not love to be featured in 'Who's Who?' Accolades and personal recognition are extremely important to us. We are destined to eternity in one way or another, and what is significant is that our good works will follow us into the kingdom of heaven. How many ways God loves us!

Want a good name? Live for Jesus and your name will be listed on the honorary roll of Who's who in heaven up above. Now that is indeed an honor bestowed.

> Many seek after riches
> And value silver and gold,
> But a good name is priceless,
> So let the truth be told.

Wilderness Voices

And John said, I am the voice of one crying in the wilderness, make straight the way of the Lord. (John 1:23).

After a span of four hundred years of silence, came a voice crying in the wilderness. It was John the Baptist.

Even in today's society, there are still voices crying in the wilderness, and boldly proclaiming the Good News Gospel to all who will hear the Word, and obey the voice of God. There are preachers, and teachers, evangelists, and missionaries, and ambassadors for Christ. Yes! He is on His way back! So keep you house in order!

God's grace and mercy is so great that the world will not know its end until the Gospel has been delivered unto all.

Are you a voice crying in the wilderness?

> I groped in darkness along the way.
> My soul was lost in hopelessness,
> But then I heard the voice of God.
> He called me through the wilderness.

Wipe My Tears

And God shall wipe away all tears from their eyes, and there shall be no more death, neither sorrow, nor crying, neither shall there be any more pain, for the former things are passed away. (Rev 21:4).

My precious granddaughter, Danielle, who was only age three at the time, suddenly appeared before me with tears streaming down her small, angelic face. She said to me, "Beba! Wipe tears! I just fell down!" With arms outstretched, I embraced her with a comforting, granny hug, and then with a gentle touch of soft tissue, once again, all was well.

What a blessing it is to know that we have a loving Heavenly Father who will also in due time, wipe all tears away.

What a joy it is to know
That when we kneel to pray,
There are no tears of sorrow
That Heaven cannot wipe away.

September

Arise! Shine! For thy light has come. (Is 60:1).

Shine! Others will see the Light.
Enemies lurk throughout the night.
Place your lamp in view so that all might see
The true light of Jesus
Everywhere you tend to be.
Make sure the outreach lighthouse is on and beaming bright.
Be on the lookout for someone lost and searching for the light.
Every child of God, so let your Light shine.
Real love is saving souls. Souls like yours and mine.

Why should we remember all of this? (In Matt 5:14), Jesus refers to a city on a hill that cannot be hidden because of its Light. How can we hold up the Light? We can best do this by striving each day to let the glory of the Lord shine through His Believers as witnesses in a very dark world. And if this hits home, check out (Matt 5:15). A candle should be placed on a candlestick and not under a bushel. So please, don't make light of the Light. Shine on and glorify the Father, Son, and Holy Spirit.

Wise as an Owl

If any of you lack wisdom, go to God for it. (James 1:5).

Some may think that the saying, "wise as an owl," is a trite expression that is somewhat stereotyped and overused, but failing to obtain wisdom may omit to be disastrous. If you, of your own accord never wise up and seek after wisdom, your reasoning will, of course, be void of understanding, for only the Lord, is the Giver of wisdom, and out of Him comes knowledge, and understanding.

Nicodemus, a ruler of the Jews, lacked understanding until Jesus explained to him the following revelation. "Except a man be born again, he cannot enter the kingdom of heaven, for that which is born of the flesh is flesh, and that which is born of the spirit is spirit." (John 3:1-6)

No matter how educated one may be, or how scholarly our achievements, there is no knowledge in the grave to which we are headed. While many are worldly wise, still they see through closed eyes! What is needed then is seeing eyes, and hearing ears for the Word of God. Wisdom is the principal thing; therefore, get wisdom, and with all of your getting, get understanding. (Prov 4:7).

> If we search for wisdom
> Like prospectors sought after gold.
> We will acquire knowledge of God.
> He teaches both the young and old.

Workers for Hire

Abound in the Lord's work, and your labor will not be in vain. (1 Cor 15:58).

Most of us are working! But there is a big question to be asked. Who are you working for? Listen to this! The cold hard fact of the matter is that too many are laboring in vain, so be sure that you are not counted in that number. Obviously, if you are not working for God, then you are on the devil's payroll, and all your work is fruitless, unproductive, and of course, in vain and will amount to nothing when Harvest time finally rolls around.

In a nutshell, to be gainfully employed in the Lord's vineyard will reap unmatched, eternal value because serving the Lord will definitely pay off eternally. The benefits of laboring for the Master is only fully demonstrated when the season of the Harvest comes, and we shall reap of the fruits of our labor. Work for God! You'll be glad you did!

> What a shame to labor
> From sunup to sundown,
> Only to discover
> Vain labor earns no crown.

Worthy of Reward

Well done thy good and faithful servant. (Matt 25:21).

There are no crowns without crosses, and there are no gains without losses. Living for a better day? Keep walking the narrow un-crowded way.

> There are heavy crosses
> To bend and weight us down,
> But without some suffering
> There will be no crown.
>
> One should not anticipate
> That heaven is easy gain.
> You will be persecuted
> And endure hardship and pain.
>
> Live to do God's will,
> And stand upon His Word.
> Spread the Good News Gospel.
> Don't stop until all have heard.

Pass Him On!

And this gospel of the kingdom will be preached in all the world as a witness to all the nations, and then the end will come. (Matt 24:14).

A very simple act of kindness was extended to me from a customer at Aldi's grocery store. As I was about to deposit a quarter into the slot in order to retrieve a shopping cart, someone approached me and handed me a cart. When I attempted to give him my quarter in exchange for the cart he said, "Someone blessed me with this free cart, so now I'm doing likewise."

A remarkable thing happens when we establish a relationship with our Lord and Savior, Jesus Christ. A glorious transformation develops into a characteristic way of reflecting Jesus in all that we do and say, as we become new creatures in Christ Jesus. Since Jesus makes all the difference in the world to us, and through us, we should feel honored to pass Him on to others.

> If to Jesus you belong,
> Witness as you move along.
> Tell someone along the way
> How Jesus brightens up your day.
>
> Spread God's love all around.
> Let glad tidings happily resound.
> Why not let the whole world know
> How you came to love Him so.
>
> Fail not to do your part.
> Don't lock the joy within your heart.
> Tell the message! Share the news!
> When God is for you, you can't lose.
>
> Do not place God on a shelf
> And keep Him all unto yourself.
> Let others know how blessed you feel.
> Serve the Lord! Keep it real!

Wrong Way! Do not Re-enter!

But ye are a chosen generation, a royal priesthood, a holy nation, His own special people, that you may proclaim the praises of Him who called you out of darkness into His marvelous light. (1 Pet 2:9).

Once we have stepped out of darkness into the marvelous light, we must continue and strive to remain spiritually focused through daily interaction with our Lord and Savior, Jesus Christ. Remain constant in prayer and by all means, shun the appearance of evil.

Be not unequally yoked together with unbelievers, for what fellowship has righteousness with unrighteousness? And what communion has light with darkness? (2 Cor 6:14). Satan is diabolically clever in seemingly hopeless situations. He will offer quick fix solutions for our trials in order to con, deceive, and take us right back to where we started from. Just remember that as Believers, we are Children of the Light, and commit to the point of no return! No turning back! No turning back!

> When we remain committed
> With a Christ like, made up mind,
> We can tell the devil,
> In Jesus' name, to get behind!

You Have Come a Long Way!

I have been young, and now am old, yet have I not seen the righteous forsaken, nor his seed begging bread. (Ps 37:25).

The baby boomers have come a long way. Even when it seemed we had less, God always blessed us with more. Amazingly, there was always more than enough! Back then, and up until now, God always makes a way somehow. Those from the 'Old School' can identify with the following poem.

We wore penny strollers and bobby socks. Lou Father Times and Dave Dixon were jocks.
When parents and teachers spanked your caboose, there was no such thing as child abuse.
The next door neighbor disciplined you. Then mom and dad followed on through.
Although teeth may have gritted, talking back was not permitted.

The girls jumped double Dutch rope, and Baby Boomers knew nothing of dope.
Boys shot marbles across the cement. We didn't have much but we were content.
Prime time fighters were punching blows. We tuned in to "The Shadow Knows."
The radio blasted "The Squeaking Doors" as we huddled close on hardwood floors.

Yes! It was the best of times! There was lots of candy for only a dime.
Even if you had only one nickel, you could buy a large dill pickle.
At long last, we watched TV. "Me Tarzan, You Jane" was great to see.
We watched "Howdy Doody" and "Clarabelle" and "Hop-along Cassidy" blazed down the trail.

Dick Clark's American Bandstand was a favorite in TV Land.
Chubby Checker did the twist, and Panthers raised a Black Power Fist.
Poodle clad skirts and sloppy shirt tails swayed to the music of the Shirelles.
Baby Boomers shifted into high gear when soulful Aretha sang in their ear.

The great Impressions and mighty Temptations rocked the world across the nation.
Dining out was no big deal. White Castle! The affordable meal!
Delores Williams! What can I say! Honey Child! You have come a long way!
Fifty years! Healthy and strong! Happy Birthday! Keep moving along!

(In loving memory of my dear friend, Katherine Holmes, who requested this poem be composed to celebrate her daughter's special birthday, some time ago.)

Hindsight

Forget those things which are behind and look forward to the present. (Phil 3:13).

There is absolutely nothing at all that we can do about experiences we have already encountered other than to learn from past mistakes how to prevent them from re-hatching as recurring errors.

How is your spiritual eyesight? If you tend to view the crystal ball of the past pondering and reliving yesterdays over and over again, you are suffering from what is known as hindsight. Regretting and fretting over what should have happened and did not, or wishing you could change what did, is time invested unwisely. As you walk along your life-path, continuously looking back into the far distant past will adversely affect every aspect of visible blessings to look forward to. Hindsight will rob you of your vision and lead you blindly groping into the future. A sure cure for elimination of such a disease is to become nearsighted and focus on what is smack dab ahead of you. The rest of your life!

> Change the lens of your camera.
> Focus in on all that is new.
> Each day affords another chance.
> Become a better you.

How Long Will You Sleep?

As a thief in the night, so is the coming of the Lord. (1 Thess 5:2).

It is time to wake up and stop dreaming your life away. Be forewarned that day dreaming and sleepwalking can actually consume an entire lifetime. Oh! Sleepyhead! Awaken from your lazy stupor and get up and be about something. Sadly, you are addicted to the sleeping sickness of lackadaisicalness, and the whole world is continuously passing by as you are prone to drift aimlessly through the slumber land of nothingness.

Time is running out, and what is needed is a life changing transformation wake up call. No longer should you waste such an invaluable resource at your disposal, and such a priceless gift as time. The nightmare of all nightmares will be to awaken and discover that you are no longer asleep, but dead, and to come to the realization that you accomplished absolutely nothing with the time God gave you while on earth.

> Some need a rude awakening.
> How do you spend your time?
> Who knows when life's 'ticking clock',
> Will sound its final chime?

Kick in a Heavenly Direction

I have fought a good fight. (2 Tim 4:7-8).

It is all in the game! This time the ball is not in your court. It is out in that long 100 yard rectangular field of opposition. Yes! Be prepared to be tackled by the enemy whose job it is to prevent you from gaining yardage for the Kingdom of God, and scoring points unto the final victory. The offense will assail you in order to gain possession of the ball, but the defense will help to withstand any physical or spiritual challenges there are to be met as you, with a spirit of boldness, continue to lunge forward.

> If you are aiming for a field goal,
> Kick in a heavenly direction.
> Defensive angels are all around,
> And they will safeguard your protection.
>
> Only God can block the devil's pass,
> So allow Him to touch down.
> Hold on to that ball!
> Your prize will be a golden crown.

Do You Believe in Magic?

Blessed are they who have not seen and yet believe. (John 20:29), and who realize that all things are possible because of their faith. (Luke 1:37).

It has been stated that the hand is quicker than the eye. So watch out! The devil is a crafty and extremely clever magician. He can wave his magical wand of deception and trick you with beautiful, optical illusions to invade your mind and entertain your thoughts. In him lies the power to mesmerize your soul with mystical fantasies that will have a spell binding effect upon your imagination. Don't buy it! Pray instead to have Godly vision and spiritual insight to see things as they really are.

Allow the God Spirit to magically enrapture you. No! Not Black Magic, sorcery, voodoo, or witchcraft. Not that kind of magic at all. But magic like the parting of the Red Sea that led the Israelites to safety, and then surprisingly closed, and drowned all of their enemies in close pursuit behind them. God can do marvelous, spectacular, and unbelievable things without the use or practice of charms, spells, or rituals. He is supernaturally God all by Himself. Be therefore enthralled by the mystical magic of His authentic, all powerful, awesomeness.

> The devil's game is camouflage.
> His web is woven to deceive.
> God, like magic, can perform
> What eyes can't see, yet hearts believe.

Have You Tried God on for Size?

I know that my redeemer lives! (Job 19:25).

No alterations are necessary insofar as God is concerned. Our Lord and Savior, Jesus Christ, is evenly proportioned to outfit any soul. Try Him on for size, and you will see. Amazingly, you will find that He is a perfect fit because truthfully speaking, one size fits all!

Long ago, when the fabric of our souls had become far beyond 'slightly imperfect' and were fit only to be discarded, God selected His Tailor, our Lord and Savior, Jesus Christ, to mend the broken seams and torn remnants of our sinful souls by stretching wide upon the Cross of Calvary in order to restore our materialistic souls, (those who are markedly more concerned with material things than with spiritual values) brand new. We all were stitched back into shape by the sharp, penetrating needle of salvation. Admittedly, it is far easier to confess wrongdoing than to experience the consequences of it eternally. Salvation! It's yours for the asking.

> Try Jesus on for size.
> He is proportioned to fit all.
> When we were yet imperfect,
> His love repaired us all.

Staying Fit

Bodily exercise is to no avail. (1 Tim 4:8).

The best way to burn energy is to exercise 'God—fully.' Faithfully, we strenuously exert our physical bodies in order to maintain a highly achieved level of physical fitness. Although such a vigorous program is extremely advantageous from a healthy point of view, such energy is only useless if the promotion of spiritual fitness is not exercised as well.

From the earliest of our existence, the outward man is destined to perish, and no exercise ritual, no matter how powerful, can alter the inevitable. Therefore, it is wise to incorporate spiritual exercise into your daily workout routine schedule.

> The best way to stay fit
> Is to develop a workout plan
> And exercise religiously as often as you can.

Overweight?

Cast all your cares upon God and lose weight. (1 Pet 5:7).

How is your spiritual figure shaping up? If you are weighted down by numerous cares and cumbersome burdens, you are definitely overweight, and will continuously experience uncontrollable weight gain at an alarming rate.

Bulky fat tissue of worry weight
Will increasingly add pound after pound,
So let God flatter your figure,
And slim you all around.

Lube Job

He anoints my head with oil. (Ps 23:5).

There are many things that can slow us down and cause us as Christian travelers to lose ground on the Highway to Heaven. Actually, unanticipated factors can hinder us on our journey upward. Numerous problems clamor for our attention while we are heaven bound. All problems will not resolve themselves though some will. But one thing is certain, spiritual vehicles are in dire need of constant lubrication, or dryness will set in and engines will begin to stall and run sluggishly. To ensure that such is not the case, proper care of all transportation needs is required. When was your last lube job?

> Stop at the service station.
> Get inspected by God,
> And while you are there
> He will give you a lube job.

Fresh

Oh! Spirit of the living God, fall fresh upon me. (Titus 3:5).

Only the empowering presence of God is able to preserve the Saints by constantly retaining renewed freshness on a daily basis. So do not allow the devil to contaminate, or spoil your soul. Begin each day with a fresh outlook and brand new start. Commune with the Holy Spirit upon rising and it is absolutely guaranteed that your spirit filled contents will not wither, grow stale, or lose its portion of fresh anointing as the day wears on.

> Commune with God every day,
> It only takes a wisp.
> God's fresh anointing Spirit will fall fresh,
> And keep you cool and crisp.

Contentment

Learn in whatsoever state to be content. (Phil 4:11).

If often you're given to complain,'Grumplestiltskin' is your name.

Great is God's faithfulness, for His compassions are daily renewed, and His mercy is long lasting unto us. (Lam 3:22 & 23).

When sudden downpours of raining adversities blot out the sunlight from view, it is so easy to complain, to murmur and to mumble, but choose to begin each day with joyful expectation, and remember that God gives unsurpassed attention to every detail of your life's journey. How many times have we heard the chant, "Rain, rain, go away! Please come back another day?" It is our Lord and Savior, Jesus Christ who orchestrates the events of life. Of course, life seems at its best on sunniest days when all is warm and fuzzy, and bright with promise, but when the skies are overcast, and the sun plays peek-a-boo, and hides its face behind dismal and dark clouds, everything seems to fade to black. Is not this the time to praise and rejoice and look for visible glints of light to come shining through the darkness?

> Here comes another dreary day.
> The sun is gone. The skies are gray.
> When nothing seems to go your way,
> God can light the night like day.

Saving Our Roots

Chasten thy son while there is hope, and let not thy soul spare for his crying. (Prov 19:18).

Do not label the Word of God as antiquated, or outdated. Heaven and earth will pass away but the Word of God is forever. (Matt 24:35). So dust off those Bibles and go back to the basics. Train up a child in the way he should go and when he is old, he will not depart from it. (Prov 22:6).

Modern methods have proved to be extremely unsuccessful in altering disobedient behavior among children, but the chastening rod of correction will save a disobedient child's life from destruction. Even God Himself corrects out of love when it is deemed warranted. Let it also be said that we as parents, or overseers, must strive to walk upright before our offspring, for they are clones of our mirrored reflections and will surely mimic our every action in a 'monkey see, monkey do' fashion. Remember, the home is the classroom! Train up your child! You'll be glad you did.

> Fail not to train your children.
> Spare not the rod across the back.
> Live upright before them
> And their lives will stay on track.

Making Music for the Lord

Sing unto Him a new song; play skillfully with a loud noise. (Ps 33:3).

Were we harmonious as chirping birds, our life songs would become living symphonies. Voices singing praises unto the King of Kings will always rise above all others. So allow the melody of your heart to play sweet refrains throughout your entire lifetime, and the echo of the music of your soul will continue to resound long after your voice is silent in the quiet hush.

Shun the keys of disharmony! Such music is composed and directed by Lucifer, and will only serve to sow discord among brethren. Go with the flow of heavenly music, for it is soothing to each heart, and pleasant to all ears.

> Satan's music is way off-beat.
> It is served on a platter of deceit,
> But making music for the Lord
> Is the best song you will ever record.

Calling All Runners

Commit thy way unto the Lord. (Ps 37:5).

Many of us today are moving so fast, we fail to see what we should see, and miss hearing what is most important to be heard as we journey through life.

Scripture is certainly consistent about reminding us that the Lord Himself, made the 'seeing' eye, and also the 'hearing' ear. But the fact of the matter is over the course of your lifetime and mine, more often than not, there are eyes that do not see, and ears that do not hear. Be still! Do you see and feel the glorious presence of the Lord all around you? Hush! Can you hear a still, small voice crying out in the wilderness of this world?

Look! Listen! Jesus is tenderly calling for all interested parties to voluntarily enlist into the Running for Jesus Marathon. Commit to accept the challenge!

> First of all, be fully convinced,
> Then sign on the dotted line.
> Stay in the race with a made up mind.
> Make your commitment for a lifetime.

Be Strong

Quit you like men be strong. (1 Cor 16:13).

After commitment comes preparation. Do not believe that you have begun to realize or understand the role of a Christian Athlete. From the moment you decided to enlist, God began to prepare you for the tedious journey stretching out miles ahead of you. How so? He subjects your spiritual body to intense and strenuous workouts beyond what is imaginable. Make no mistake about it, one must exercise, practice, condition and flex those saintly muscles through constant God body building techniques and vigorous activity in order to compete as a Christian athlete. The spirit is willing, but the flesh is so weak, and subject to fall short of crossing the finish line at the end of the race.

But there is joy in running for Jesus, for He alone is the joy and the strength of life. Once He has called you, let Him prepare you. Expect victory, for He will always cause you to triumph.

> Let there be able-bodied runners
> Who will not lag, or slack.
> With recoiled resiliency,
> They always bounce right back.

Jet Lag

Will not thou deliver my feet from falling that I may walk before God in the light of the living? (Ps 56:13).

And now the race is on! Many Believers start out early on running for Jesus with the youthfulness of vim, vigor and vitality pulsating beneath super charged, flapping wings. Eagerly, energetic legs race swiftly forward to face the challenge of daily endurance with enthusiasm.

As time passes by; however, once 'pep in the step' feet will tend to have a much slower 'glide in the stride' but there is no room for jet lag runners in God's program. Therefore, in order to avoid stiffness, flabbiness, and maintain rock solid, one must continue to maintain a healthy spiritual diet by eating the Word of God, drinking plenty of Living Water, and avoiding occasional lapses of inactivity. With a determined attitude, holy composure will remain intact. As we know, it is a long distance race, and we must run it for the long haul. Failure to do so will result in weaving and bobbing in a zigzag motion which is guaranteed to render you unsteady and throw you completely off balance. Enemies are waiting for you to stumble along the way, but should you falter in your trying, don't stop! Keep on running! God will keep your feet from falling.

> Continue to press forward.
> Aim for the mark of His high calling.
> You may stagger along the way,
> But God will keep your feet from falling.

Stumbling Blocks

Now thanks to God who causes us to triumph in Christ. (2 Cor 2:14).

Not surprisingly, obstacles will be thrown into your pathway as you continue to race forward as a member of the Running for Jesus Track Team. According to scripture, the enemy will always meet you at the threshold of any great work, but God always interposes most effectually when that happens. How so? God's blessings are far larger than you may know, but it may become necessary to leap over towering hurdles placed by the enemy to arrive at that point and claim your blessing. Unlike Superman, you might not successfully leap over stumbling blocks with a single bound, but not to worry! The Lord will give you hind feet to help you over each hump, one day at a time. (Ps 18:33).

Victory today is yours! "Ready! Get set! Go!"

> The devil's unfair tactics are
> Everywhere you will compete.
> When stumbling blocks are in the way,
> Jump over them! Land on your feet!

Stay United

And if a house is divided against itself, that house cannot stand. (Mark 3:25).

While uniqueness of individuality is highly commendable, a divided house will surely fall, and a divided team will never win. Christian athletes must remain united, or a no win situation will be the end result. A stronger spirit of united teamwork will be fostered by running together with one sole, highest purpose in mind, and that is to stay in the race with the end in sight. Under no circumstances whatsoever should you ever attempt to run the race as a solo contestant. You cannot, and will not win the race alone all by yourself.

Satan seeks to divide, and then conquer. He is more than aware of the stamina of a 'united in God' force. Not sole focus! Team focus! There is strength in numbers! Should you fall behind, your teammates will assist you, so please, do not forsake the assembly with a solo flight. You will crash and burn. Remain united!

> Don't let the devil divide the team.
> Stay together and round the bend.
> A team divided cannot stand.
> It will fall apart at the end.

The Real Thirst Quencher

But whosoever drinks of the water that Jesus gives shall never thirst again. (John 4:14).

It is important that we do not allow unpleasant circumstances to deter us from completion of our daily rounds as Christian Marathon Runners for Jesus.

One must continue to be sustained by a refreshing Spirit in order to maintain endurance; for sooner or later, constant racing through the terrain in the scorching heat of the glaring noonday sun, and passing through the barren, dry, and dusty desert, will require that restoration of the soul is deemed necessary. But continue to hold on, keep on running, and stay in the race, for out of your belly shall flow rivers of living water if you persist to run on, and faint not.

> That old Devil will attempt
> To parch your tongue bone dry.
> He aims to dehydrate your soul
> And drain you, by and by.
>
> When you are tired and thirsty,
> Jesus is a steadfast Clincher.
> Not only will He give you rest,
> But He's the real Thirst Quencher.

Holy Boldness

And if I be lifted up, I'll draw all men unto me. (John 12:32).

Have you holy boldness? It takes a bold athlete to go for the gold. It takes a daring soul to champion a cause. It takes determination to make it unto the finish line. Going for the gold as a Christian athlete, means to run for Jesus all the way. To champion a cause for the promotion of God's kingdom here on earth, means to lay it all on the line for that reason, and to remain committed to the purpose for which you are running, means to give it all you've got until the battle is won.

Sometimes failure may appear to be imminent when the enemy begins to close in at an alarming heel's length pace, but do not despair. And while discouragement will be encountered to a considerable degree while engaged in running the marathon, hold your head up high, and keep on running. Holy boldness is required to display the blood stained banner, so lift the banner high, and run on. God is on your side, and He will not allow Satan to overtake you, nor defeat you.

Reach out and entice others to run.
Put God on proud display.
Many will see Him magnified,
And join the team along the way.

The Middle Man

Lord, you have been our track meet dwelling place in all generations. (Ps 90:1).

Once again, combined teamwork cannot be over-emphasized. There are times when only two, or three will be gathered together to run on in the name of the Lord. But have heart! According to God's Holy Word, still there are more than enough to comprise a winning team, for where two or three are joined together in His name, Jesus will always be the man in the middle.

Behold how good and how pleasant it is for Christians to run together united in the Lord, and to set the pace for future champions in the making.

> From hand to hand, throughout the land,
> Pass on the ancient landmark baton.
> It will indeed, so serve the need, and compel new comers to run.

No Cheering Squad

Jesus healed ten lepers, but only one returned with thankfulness to glorify Him for His goodness. (Luke 17:17-18).

Few there are who are willing to give God the glory He truly deserves. Not surprisingly, seldom if ever, will you be applauded, or honored with a standing ovation, or numerous medals for winning souls for Christ. I say to you, stay in the race! Run on with the torch! Continue to light up the world! Finish strong! Your reward is not here on earth below, but in heaven above. Your good works will follow you into the Kingdom of Heaven when your earthly journey is complete.

Those who run for Jesus
Will have no earthly Cheering Squad,
But angels up in heaven are shouting,
"Go for God!"

I Run for Jesus

But he who sins against me wrongs his own soul; all who hate me love death. (Prov 8:36).

You cannot out race the stop watch of death, but you can outrun hell if determined to run for Jesus and cross the finish line. If you are not a member of the Running for Jesus Marathon, Satan showed up and convinced you to run his way. So if you are continuously running in the race and getting nowhere at all, the time has come to ask yourself; "Why am I not moving forward?" It is impossible to move forward when you are a member of a backward team that is steadily running away from God. In order to run for Jesus, you must press forward toward Him, and never look back again.

Whether you have decided to run for Jesus or not, you are still in the race, but on the wrong team. Sad but true, there is a race that many will run unto death, so if you must run on anyhow, why not run for Jesus and inherit eternal life.

If you constantly lag behind
As time continues to unwind
Perhaps the race you are striving to win
Is a race, you should not have entered in.

Lend you ears! The truth be told,
So totally in depth,
If you're not running for Jesus,
You have chosen to love death.

Giants & It is finished!

Where offense might abound, grace did much more abound. (Rom 5:20).

Needless to say, always size up the competition. David did, but the size of His God in Him was greater than that of his oversized, gigantic enemy. Never underestimate one's opponent. Goliath did. A somewhat trite and overused expression is "The bigger they are, the harder they fall," and in Goliath's case, David's God made a believer out of them all.

Daniel survived the lion's den! Joshua won the battle of Jericho, and the walls went tumbling down! The Hebrew Children were thrown into the fiery furnace, but God made it fireproof. What more need be said. When God is on your side, don't worry about your enemies in hot pursuit and gaining yardage. Surely Satan and his followers are chasing after you, but don't let fear hold you back. Remain focused! Keep your eyes on the prize and keep on running. Stay in the race! Trust me! God is the only Giant you need to fear if you fail to cross the finish line at the end of the race.

> Gusty winds of opposition
> And threatening storms will surround you.
> Stand, and face it all head on,
> And God's grace will abound you.

It is finished!

Well done thy good and faithful servant! (Matt 25:21).

More than anything else, you need to run on and live in God's Will, until the Head Coach cries out it is finished! In every day are found distractions to blindside your finest intentions, but the biggest mistake any one can make is to withdraw from the higher power.

All too often, we begin to feel threatened and hemmed in on all sides as the miles continue to stretch out ahead of us. Actually, the closer we get to the sought after prize, the more the tempter attempts to bind us, and try to hold us back. It would be an unspeakably sad outcome to fall short of the goal when the finish line is closer than close, and still not claim the victory. Don't give place to impatience. It takes every ounce of strength one has to stay in the race. Don't quit! Cross over the finish line and shout, it is finished! Hallelujah! Amen!

Eternal joy awaits thee,
So run with the winning team.
Keep your eyes on the prize.
Let nothing come between.

The race will not be over
Until the angel sings,
"Enter into the joy of the Lord,
And receive the King of Kings."

October

The Lord is my rock and fortress. (Ps 18.2).

Only God can make a difference in one's life.
Christ made the ultimate sacrifice.
Trust Him. Give Him your every care.
Omnipresent God is everywhere.
Blood of Jesus sanctify!
Empower Lord! Hear my cry.
Rock of refuge, please stand by!

Heavenly Father, we are conscious of your being, and only when we choose to partake of your Spirit will we become new creatures in Christ. All the way to the cross, the sacrificial Lamb of God was slain, and whoever is willing to come and accept Your Son Jesus, will have everlasting life through salvation. The name Jesus means that He will save us from our sins, and so it is! Right now! We trustingly cast all our cares upon You, Lord Jesus, and we stand undoubtedly reassured that You Lord, are an omnipresent, inescapable and all powerful Overseer of all humankind. Sanctify us, dear Lord we pray, and set us aside from worldly temptations. Empower and strengthen us from on high. Oh! Rock of refuge, strong tower and mighty fortress! Amen

Basic Training

He prepares a table before me in the presence of my enemies. (Ps 23:5).

Do you have what it takes to be a soldier in the Army of the Lord?

There will come a time when Christian Soldiers will be in the presence of their enemies, and that is why there is a dire need for basic training. There will always be spiritual wickedness in high places, so one must be spiritually fit to endure the severe hardship of Christian Combat against the enemy. In the pathway of duty, one must successfully complete Basic Training. No weak kneed recruit will ever march in God's Army.

> Life is not always a breeze.
> We lie not on feathery beds of ease.
> God prepares a table purposely in the presence of the enemy.

Enduring Hardness

After various stages of suffering, only then will God perfect that which concerns you, and establish, strengthen, and settle you. (1 Pet 5:10).

Enduring hardness is not at all an easy undertaking, and that is why tolerance is born in God's Boot Camp. Now is a good time to mention that you will ford streams, run miles, climb mountains, swim rivers and be subjected to extremely harsh weathering of every kind in order to condition your spiritual body and prepare you for what is yet to come. It is not effortless ease, but spiritual fortitude, that endures hardness. From that point on, God will perfect your imperfections, establish your goings, strengthen your stamina, and peacefully, settle you down.

> Therefore endure hardness.
> Be a good soldier of the King.
> Set aside affairs of life.
> Give Him your all and everything.

Study

Study to show thyself approved unto God! (2 Tim 2:15).

God can impact your world. Let Him!

If you fail to study the strategy outlined by the Commanding Officer in Charge, how will you ever meet His approval? How will you know what to do, or what not to do, when face to face with the enemy? God will show you the next move, and the one after that, but here's how it works. You must read and study His Word, and follow the instructions to the letter. His Word is the bridge that will carry you over safely, and His Word, is the map to follow once you have entered into war zone territory. Shameful to say, one cannot rightly divide the Word of Truth if it is to you unknown; therefore, study, and there will be no shame in your game.

> You must study to show yourself approved,
> Good Workman and Soldier of the Cross.
> Rightly divide the truth of His Word.
> All worldly gain count as loss.

Hold Fast

For if we sin willfully after having received the knowledge of truth, there remains no sacrifice for sins. (Heb 10:26).

Yes! God will thrust you into a situation you never imagined possible, but still will allow you to remain steadfast and immovable. Sometimes it is all you can do to hang on. Oh! Soldier of the Cross! Do not desert your post. Though it can be a challenge, strife carries with it a special joy. You will become a Victor in the strife when you gallantly fight on in the name of our Lord and Savior, Jesus Christ. According to scripture, be not weary of well doing, for you will reap in due season if you faint not. Time is running out, so run that you may obtain the prize. (1Cor.9:24).

> The devil wants traitors
> Who will surrender, and bow unto defeat;
> Who will steal away, walk backwards, and are prone to cowardly retreat.

God's K.P.

No chastening for the present seems joyous, nevertheless, after it yields peaceable fruit. (Heb 12:11).

We need to take seriously the consequences of following orders and obeying them as we should. There lies before us, a spiritual war to be won. The big question to be asked is how do we view God as a disciplinarian figure from a Christian Soldier's point of view? Without chastisement, we would not remain partakers of holiness, whereby Satan and his battalion would render us completely helpless, as he comes to steal, kill and destroy all who serve and worship the one and only true and risen Savior; therefore, we should never despise God's wielding rod of correction where we are concerned. At those times, we should be all the more thankful to receive punishment when it is indeed warranted.

> Go ahead! Peel those potatoes.
> Do your time! Pull K.P.
> Better than fall in deceitful hands
> And die with the enemy.

Battle Clad

And the evil spirit answered and said, Jesus I know, and Paul I know, but who are you? And the man in whom the evil spirit was leaped on them, and overcame them and prevailed against them, so that they fled out of that house naked and wounded. (Acts 19:15-16).

Look at the total picture in retrospect. We can easily identify the fact that God's sovereign power was absent to those who claimed such power, but had none. Understandably, even the ungodly know God's armored, battle clad, Soldiers of the Cross. So unless you are fully clothed with the whole armor of our Lord and Savior, Jesus Christ, don't challenge the devil. He knows a fake soldier when he sees one.

> When you make the devil mad,
> Be sure that you are battle clad.
> Put on the whole armor of God,
> Lest you be smitten by Satan's rod.

Is the Lord on your Side?

If it had not been for the Lord who was on my side when men rose up against us, we would not be victorious. (Ps 124:2).

The more closely you walk with God, the more fully He will bless your life. One of the advantages of soldiering in God's Army is to know that you can attempt what seems unattainable to you, and stand assured that it will come to pass. So when things come to an alarming pitch on the battlefield, it is good to know that the Lord is on your side. Through fiercest challenges and through the greatest of difficulties, God is more than the entire world against you, and He will always cause you to triumph. Forward march!

> Satan would sift your soul as wheat.
> But God, he cannot defeat.
> If it had not been for God on your side,
> The devil would surely skin your hide.

Are You Tough Enough?

Though He slay me! Yet will I trust Him. (Job 13:15).

When multiple trials are buffeting the soul, somewhere in the inner recesses of your being, trust what your heart, and not what your head tells you to do. It was Job's wife who suggested that he curse God and die when the going got rough. Job; however, had trusting confidence in God, and so he decided against all odds to wait until his change had come.

God wants to fill us with his fullness and this can be best done by boldly refusing to renounce Him when sustained injuries cause us to bleed and suffer, and hardships weigh heavily upon us. Remember that the enemy can do no more than God allows him too. There is a limit where God's approved consent is concerned. The devil could not touch Job's soul. Nor can he touch yours. Are you tough enough? Run on in His name.

> Though He slay me!
> Yet will I trust Him.
> When my change comes,
> I will wear a royal diadem.

Rest for the Weary

Come ye, yourselves apart into a desert place and rest a while. (Mark 6:31).

No challenges are greater than constantly pressing through pain and feeling the impact of fighting against Satan's Warriors. The flesh is weak! Combat is far from easy, and hanging on rarely is. But even when circumstances indicate otherwise, God will not allow his troops to sink to a point beyond recovery, but He will call all soldiers away into a desert place when it is absolutely deemed necessary to do so, for he is a peace giving, all sufficient God. He will allow us to steal away on wings of tranquility from the midst of heated warfare, for He gives His beloved rest. "Come apart, My Child, and rest!"

God endowed with wisdom
Surely always knows
When bone weary soldiers
Are in need of sweet repose.

Unity

Do all things without murmurings and disputing. (Phil 2:14).

Few take time to think things through, but for those who do, guiding principles include dwelling together in unity. Do not remain ignorant of Satan's devices for they are many, and he will aim at our most vulnerable points. It is wise to concede the fact that you cannot handle satanic forces all alone. Being of one accord, and uniting for the same purpose will eliminate bickering and confusion, bring about cohesiveness, and greatly minimize the power of the enemy.

> Wherever there is division,
> The devil wins the game.
> So stand together united.
> And fight on in Jesus' name.

Wilderness Temptations &
Wise Time Management

He will deliver the godly out of temptations. (2 Pet 2:9).

On the battlefield for the Lord, prepare to be tempted by the devil as was Jesus in the wilderness.

Resolving to live by values based on the principles of God, and attempting to be in total alignment with the vision and mission for what purpose we are called is far from easy. There are innumerable hungry and enticing wilderness temptations floating all around us, but the bible says, essentially this; "Man does not live by bread alone, but every word that proceeds out of the mouth of God." (Matt 4:4).

> When wilderness temptations
> Are floating all around,
> Have heart and keep on standing.
> You're on solid, Holy Ground.

Wise Time Management

Dear Lord! Teach us to number our days, that we may apply our hearts unto wisdom. (Ps 90:12).

Time management is vitally essential to every soldier of the King. We stand reminded that we are dust, and flowers of an earthly field. (Ps 103:15). For what is life? It is even a vapor that appears for a little time, and then vanishes away. (James 4:14). Therefore, it is wise to value precious time spent in the promotion of God's kingdom.

There is every reason to run on in His name. We, who are Children of the Light, are destined to fight on, for we are encouraged that though the passage of time will eventually dissolve our earthly tabernacles, we have a home eternal in the heavens. (2 Cor 5:1).

Knowing that time is running out, we awake out of sleep for salvation is near, the night is far spent, and the day is at hand; therefore, let us put on the armor of light. (Rom 13:11-12).

> Time is winding up!
> Passing moments, we cannot save,
> So invest your time wisely
> From life's cradle to earth's grave.

Day Breaking Experience

Therefore, if any be in Christ, he is a new creature. Old things are passed away. Behold! All things are become new. (2 Cor 5:17).

All Believers undoubtedly undergo day breaking experiences as we dawn into new creatures of Christ. No longer willing to be conformed to the norms of this world, we are miraculously changed and are spiritually transformed by the renewal of our minds as we aspire to walk in the newness of the light striving to prove all that's good and acceptable, and the perfect will of God. (Rom 12:2). Thereby renewed in the spirit of the mind, we emerge as recreated, brand new creatures in righteousness and true holiness. (Eph 4:22-24).

> Loosed from the power of Satan
> And rescued from the night,
> How sweet it is to be transformed.
> So amazing is the Light.

Point Me to the Light

The night is far spent and the day is at hand. Let us therefore cast off the works of darkness and let us put on the armor of light. (Rom 13:12).

There comes a time when we must choose between light and darkness. There are numerous choice points in life, but none so awakening, as stepping out of darkness into the marvelous light. There you have it. The Light has no fellowship with darkness.

At this point, it is adequate to note, that all who willingly choose to receive the gift of salvation are no longer children of the night, but children of the day, and are walking in the pathway of the Light.

Are you living in a sinful world of darkness? If so, Jesus can point you to the Light.

> Dearest Lord and Savior,
> Please! Point me to the Light.
> I have drifted aimlessly.
> I'm lost in the dead of night.
>
> Time is so far spent,
> And the end is close at hand.
> Lead me into the Light.
> Let me hold your hand.

No More Darkness

But you are a chosen generation, a royal priesthood, a holy nation, a peculiar people that you should show forth the praises of him who has called you out of darkness into his marvelous light. (1 Pet 2:9).

There should be no more room for darkness to invade the Light. As a chosen generation, we must persist to shun the appearance of evil at all times. Few of us, if any, fall into the category of total abstinence, save Jesus alone, but as peculiar people, we must continuously fall out of love with the world, and all that is of the world, and constantly fall in love with things that are not of the world, and remain in love with our 'First Love.' (1 John 2:15 & Rev 2:4).

> There is spiritual wickedness in high places.
> The devil wears many faces.
> But once you have stepped into the Light.
> Do not go back into the night.

Morning Joy

Weeping may endure for a night, but joy comes in the morning. (Ps 30:5).

The onset of an early morning sunrise is an indescribable beauty to behold in its glorious splendor. Such is the illustrious, brilliant, illuminant presence of our Lord and Savior, Jesus Christ, who after having guided us through the desolate, unwelcome, pale and overcast shadows of the night time season, lovingly heralds the advent of the long awaited morning light. The storm has subsided. The night has passed away. And now, the welcome Spirit of God's Son rising and shining above us all, through us all, and in us all, is warmly received, for the overwhelmingly radiant change, is beyond compare.

> Weep not! Oh! Weary one.
> Endure the darkness throughout the night.
> Joy will greet you in the morning.
> Hold on! Here comes the Light!

Can You Make It Through the Night?

The Lord is my light and my salvation. Whom shall I fear? (Ps 27:1).

It is most definitely the sole purpose of the Ruler and Prince of Darkness to keep you confined in the dungeon of darkness forevermore. Actually, the Tempter desires that no one ever be rescued from captivity and drawn into the Light of day. The more the Light comes shining through, the less Satan has a hold on you.

Let it be known; however, that it is not always Satan who permits darkness to envelop you. More than occasionally, it is God! When diver temptations foresail and troubles reign, count it all joy. (James 1:2). When a sudden illness invades your life, or someone you love, and causes deep anxiety or great concern, is not His grace sufficient? (2 Cor. 12:9). When the untimely, unexpected death of a precious loved one lowers your spirit down into the gloomy chamber of mourning and bereavement, just remember that the Lord gives, and the Lord takes away. Blessed be the name of the Lord. (Job 1:21). Truthfully speaking, dark trials illustrate aptly how darkness serves to draw us even closer to the Light.

> Sore pressed by heavy burdens.
> Blinded by a starless night?
> Have heart! Hold on until morning.
> Everything will be alright.

Let Your Light Shine

Let your light so shine before men, that they may see your good works, and glorify your Father which is in heaven. (Matt 5:16).

Probably the most significant single factor that allows Non Believers to have hope in Christ is the light displayed by those who are called by His name; therefore, let your light shine before others that God may be glorified. (Matt 5:14-16). Be a lighthouse shining upon the dark sea so that the lost may be found. Be a shining star, set aglow in the night, that someone may see the Light. Be a lightning bug, flitting to and fro, that someone sinking in sin will see glimmers of hope in darkness, and rise up rejoicing. Be a candle, flickering in every grim and dreary corner of the world that someone groping in darkness will be led unto the Light.

Let me be a candlestick.
Fire me up! Light the wick!
Set my heart and soul aflame burning bright in Jesus name.

Shine On!

I have learned in whatsoever state to be content. (Phil 4:11).

For many people, it is indeed extremely difficult to shine on no matter what the circumstances may be in life. With the light of His countenance shining upon us, however, we can for the most part learn in whatsoever state of mind to be content and shine on in the name of the Lord.

It is not enough, however, to learn how to stay contented unless we begin to practice dumping heavyweight afflictions by trustingly casting our cares upon Jesus. (1 Pet 5:7). Only then will we be able to view our concerns as lightweight afflictions, and keep on shining anyhow.

> When angry storm clouds gather
> As you put out to sea,
> Jesus will calm the tempest rage,
> So shine on faithfully.

Never Let Go Of the Light

Thy word is a lamp unto my feet, and a light unto my path. (Ps 119:105).

The truth is if you trustingly hold on to the light, you will never lose your way. Having said that; let it also be said that Jesus is the way, the truth and the life. (John 14:6). To place this in perspective, you can if you choose to do so, refuse to accept or ignore the Light, but doing so will allow no access into the Kingdom of God. Doing so, will keep you enslaved in captivity of the enemy, for only the truth will set you free. In the last instance, life without Jesus is night all of the time; therefore, if you have tasted of the Lord and found him to be good, then trust Him and continue to be blessed by holding on to the Light and never letting go of it. (Ps 34:8). Never let go of a good thing.

> Satan wants to rule your world
> And keep you lost in the night.
> No matter what his offer may be,
> Never let go of the Light.

Reflections of His Glory

You are the light of the world. A city that is set on a hill cannot be hid. (Matt 5:14).

It is a known fact that should the sun fail to shine upon the moon there would be no light in the darkness. Picture if you will, the night devoid of pale moonlight. Believers are like the moon and stars lighting up the night. The Light of the radiant Spirit of God shines gloriously upon us, and we are reflections of His glory revealed in us. If for any reason, we fail to position ourselves that His Light may shine upon us, then how will Non-Believers be drawn into the Light?

> Lord! Please keep us holy
> And blameless in thy sight,
> So that when you shine upon us,
> Others will see the Light.

God's Resources

For ye were sometimes darkness, but now are ye light in the Lord, so walk as children of light. (Eph 5:8).

The purpose of having received salvation is to remain deep-rooted in heavenly soil, and stay committed to walking within the pathway of Light. It is a sobering, if not scary thing to deliberately stray away from the Light when we have been chosen, for we have not chosen Him, but are chosen of Him and set apart as a peculiar people, and a chosen generation. (1 Pet 2:9).

God has chosen us, and ordained us to go and bring forth fruit. (John 15:16). How is this accomplished? By continuing to walk in the Light! Let it be strongly emphasized, however, the only way to live holy is to walk in the Spirit (Light), that we may not fulfill or satisfy the lust of the flesh.

> We are God's resources.
> We are Children of the Light.
> We have a purpose and Great Commission.
> We must rescue others from the night.

True Light

Then spoke Jesus again unto them saying, I am the light of the world. He that follows me shall not walk in darkness, but shall have the light of life. (John 8:12).

Make no mistake about it. It is of paramount importance that we follow the True Light. Jesus is absolutely and positively, "The Light" and the only true Light of the world. Many there are, including the devil himself, who deceivingly masquerade around as transformed Angels of Light. But the truth be told, they are false prophets, and that is why it is to your spiritual advantage to try every spirit whether they are of God. (1 John 4:1). After all, who will harm you if you follow all that is good?

> Many may appear to be
> True Angels of the Light,
> But wolves in sheep clothing,
> They are lurking in the night.

Let There Be Light!

Arise! Shine, for thy light has come! (Is 60:1).

Believers! Arise and shine, for the Light has come! Soldiers of the Cross! Arise! Shine! The Light has come! In every crack, crevice, and corner, let there be Light! Down in the valley and upon every mountaintop, let there be Light! As far as land can be seen, and across the mighty rolling sea, let there be Light! In every home, and while at work on the job, let there be Light! Everywhere you go, let there be Light, for the glory of the Lord has risen upon thee. What the world needs now is Light!

> As long as you are in the world
> Let your light so shine.
> The lost will surely follow you.
> To share the Light is so divine.

God is Like a Bow Wow! Right Now!

Greater love has no man than this; that a man lay down his life for his friends. (John 15:13).

Children too, experience a full range of emotions; let alone, undergoing gaping challenges. They fight illnesses! They hurt! They bleed, and many suffer mental, physical, and often sexual abuse at the hands of the not so innocent. Still, oddly enough, they find little to harp or complain about. So unlike us! Let's simply acknowledge that the age of innocence and dependency on others, allows them to remain less fearful, less suspicious of other's motives, and much more trusting in nature.

How important are children? As humbling as it may be, Christ pointed out that unless we ourselves become as children, we will not enter into the kingdom of heaven. Additionally, Jesus said, "suffer little children to come unto me," and forbid them not for of such is the kingdom of heaven." (Matt 19:14).

Were you to witness about the love of God to a child what would you say?

God is like a puppy that wags its friendly tail,
And always keeps us company as we walk down life's trail.
God is like a great big dog when trouble comes around.
He will attack your enemies and pin them to the ground.

God is like the instant love of a faithful, favorite pet.
The more you snuggle close to Him, the closer He will get.
They say a dog is man's best friend. He will protect you with His life.
Well! Jesus is that kind of friend who made that sacrifice. (John 3:16).

God Loves Animals Too

Of clean beasts, and of beasts that are not clean, and of fowls, and of everything that creeps upon the earth, There went in two, and two unto Noah in the ark, the male and the female, as God had commanded Noah. (Gen 7:8-9).

God told Noah to build an ark because there was a big flood coming. So Noah and his family, and all the animals got on the great big boat, and then it rained, and rained, and rained, until everybody and everything on earth was gone because of the great flood.

Birds have feathers to keep them warm.
Turtles have shells to shield them from harm.
Elephants can lift things with their trunks.
Phew! It stinks! Don't mess with those skunks.

Watch out now! Time to beware!
Please! Not too close to that bear!
A squirrel gathers a bunch of nuts.
The lion is the jungle king. He has a lot of guts.

Fish swim on the bottom of the ocean.
A jelly fish moves in slow motion.
The octopus has more legs than it needs.
An eel just slithers through sea weeds.

There were animals on Noah's Ark.
Betcha there was even a Shark!!!
God loves animals. He saved them too.
They were a part of Noah's crew.

Frogs leap and bees will sting.
How perfect God made everything.
How many more animals can you name?
Please do not repeat the same.

God Told Me

Be still and know that I am God. (Ps 46:10).

Even children are still enough at times to hear the voice of God.

I'm so glad God loves me.
My parents love me too.
Just like mom, and dad,
God tells me what to do.

He teaches my small fingers
How to shape the clay, and dough,
And then he guides my tiny feet,
Carefully, wherever they go.

He whispers in my childish ears,
That I should love everyone,
And it was God who told me
That Jesus is His Son.

Itty Bitty Me

But Jesus said to let the little children come unto Him, for so it is in Heaven. (Matt 19:14).

There is a great big God inside of itty bitty me,
And I am just as happy as any kid can be.
Jesus Christ is with me every single day,
When I am in school, at home, or out to play.

Sometimes I'm good. Sometimes I'm bad.
Please Sir, God, don't be mad.
Your Word will teach me right from wrong
And help me grow up big, and strong.

I'm just a little one, you see,
But Jesus lives inside of me.
So suffer little children to come,
And let the will of God be done.

Kid's Talk

Beloved, do not think it strange concerning the fiery trial which is to try you as though some strange thing happened to you. (1 Pet 4:12).

When those fiery trials leap out like flames to consume you, and the roaring lion is hot on your trail, God has your front and back because He is the Middle Man. Many people mistakenly believe that in order to stay ahead of the game, they must hurriedly scanter here and there, doing this and that, in order to keep up the pace in this rapidly moving world of today, but sometimes God has to slow us down so that we can remain in the race. Often we meet challenges that can potentially divert or defeat us, so we become unraveled and loose at the seams, and that is not all. Then we simply fall apart, little by little. The thorn pricks! The dog bites! The bee stings! Eventually, the dust will clear, and everything will settle down and fall back into place. Why? When the roaring lion is in hot pursuit, and you have finally arrived at your wit's end, is when a Friend who sticks closer than a brother will step in and restore things to calm. So Little Jack Horner, come out of that corner, a breakthrough is happening for you.

> Sometimes God slows down our pace.
> He refreshes us to remain in the race.
> From a galloping horse, to a slow crawling snail,
> We continue to move on down the trail.
>
> Life unravels like a big ball of yarn.
> Pluck a rose! Up pops a thorn!
> But when the dog bites, and the bee stings,
> Look Up! Prayer changes many things.
>
> A dog's bark is worse than its bite.
> Everything will be alright.
> So curl up and purr with a cat's meow,
> And praise the Lord anyhow.

When you tremble at the lion's roar,
Call on God like never before.
The real King of the Jungle is way up high,
And He will always hear your cry.

When the lion seeks to devour,
Remember God has claimed all power,
And when you arrive at your very wit's end,
You will discover that God is a Friend.

So don't sit around like little Jack Horner.
Your breakthrough is just around the corner.
So get you praise on, Smiley Face Style,
Your breakthrough has arrived, dear child.

Little Mountain Climber

Be ready in the morning and come up unto Mount Sinai, and present yourself there to me in the top of the mount, and no man shall come up with you. (Ex 34:2-3).

With patience, persistence and prayer, scale the heights, come what may, and God will meet you there.

A little boy set out to climb
And reach the mountain's peak.
He asked the Lord to strengthen him,
So he would not grow weak.

He had learned in Sunday School
That with patience, persistence and prayer,
He could climb life's mountain,
And God would meet him there.

Higher! Higher! Up! He climbed,
And as his feet began to slip,
He kept moving upward
With a strong and sturdy grip.

Suddenly! Without a warning,
Down came the rain!
Higher! Higher! Up! He climbed,
Not given to complain.

Darkness surrounded him,
His eyes could barely see.
He groped in hope! Rode out the storm,
And climbed on up determinedly.

Glory Hallelujah!
Much to his surprise,
Everywhere he looked,
There were bright, sunshiny skies.

Patience! Persistence! Prayer!
Thank God, he said," I didn't stop!"
God said," Welcome! Here am I.
"YOU MADE IT TO THE TOP!"

My Keeper

God has promised that He will never leave us or forsake us. (Heb 13:5).

Even as children, we are aware of a presence that is always with us. Yes! "Jesus does love us, for the Bible does indeed tell us so."

> God stays with me all through the night.
> He wakes me to the morning light.
> He walks beside me every day
> And even makes bad dogs go way.
>
> One day there was a bully at school.
> Things got hot! God kept me cool.
> I was as scared as I could be,
> But God made that old devil flee.
>
> There was a tough test, I had to pass.
> I studied real hard, and prayed in class.
> I aced the test. Slam dunked the exam,
> And Jesus is the great, I AM!
>
> God watches me! God keeps me! So when I tend to feel alone,
> I praise Him as the King of Kings who sits upon His throne.
> I can't help but brag on my very best Friend.
> I know I must be trouble, but God here I am again.

November

At the name of Jesus every knee shall bow. (Phil 2:10).

Newness of life is yours in Him.
Open your eyes. Don't let hope dim.
Victory is around the bend.
Everybody needs a friend.
Make Jesus your choice today.
Become a Believer. Do not delay.
Every knee shall bow and praise the King.
Rejoice! Give God your all and everything.

Many have eyes and see not, but as a Christian, God will open your eyes and allow you to see the truth, and your soul will be set free from the bondage of sin. There is no reason to lose hope, for the Lord will cause His children to triumph unto victory. His friendship is closer than that of a brother, but tomorrow, and not even the rest of this day is promised, so if you have not accepted Him, do so now, and seek Him while He may be found. There will come a time when time will be no more, and every knee must bow and honor Him as the King of Kings, and Lord of Lords. Continue to rejoice in Him, Saints of God, for all and everything that you have given to Him will be returned in fullest measure in the eternal life to come.

The Millennium

How shall we escape, if we neglect so great salvation? (Heb 2:3).

There are far more than 2000 reasons why we should move through the millennium with the Master. If you have not accepted Jesus as your Savior, time is not standing still. It is time to make that move.

According to its definition, the millennial period is defined as a thousand year period of holiness during which Christ will rule on earth. A hoped for period of serenity, prosperity and justice. So watch out! Satanic natives are restless.

Gratefully, those who bear the mark of the redeemed need not worry, especially since the fruit of their labor bears profound witness that they are among the reigning nation. There is another side to this however. In flipping the coin, it is devastating to think of those who have not received salvation, and bear the symbolic mark of destruction, for we are known by the fruit we bear, and are either saved, or unsaved.

> Move toward the Master.
> Join forces with the Holy Nation.
> How can anyone choose to ignore,
> Or turn away from salvation.

The Dark Shadow

Shun the appearance of evil. (1 Thess 5:22).

In going about daily rounds, know that the alluring, enchanting, dark shadow of passion is with you at all times and will continue to follow you wherever you may go, for when you would do good, evil is always present. (Rom 7:21).

Since the Devil is like a roaring lion stalking about and seeking to devour whomever he may, as outlined in (1 Pet. 5:8), absolutely no one is excluded from the dreaded foe's tempting grab bag of seemingly delicious goodies. Each day the table is set before us and we are enticed to feast upon the delicacies of an overwhelming abundance of enticingly tempting, and tantalizing assortments of forbidden fruit. Like the Pied Piper, Satan's magical enchantment is for real, and the stakes required in order to dance to his music is complete ownership of your soul.

By choice of free will, you are indeed able to resist the devil and he will flee. (James 4:7). Be forewarned however, that it is deemed necessary to put on the whole armor of God, that you may be able to stand against the wiles of the devil, for we wrestle not against flesh and blood, but the rulers of darkness and spiritual wickedness in high places. (Eph 6:11-17). The devil's greatest nightmare is that there will not be enough time to convince those who are unsaved to continue to waste golden moments in unrighteous living. Not enough time to race against the stopwatch of numbered days of the rest of our lives. Not enough time to attempt to steal souls away before it is too late for them to be capable of being redeemed. Simply stated, accept Jesus while time is on your side.

> Shun the appearance of evil
> No matter how it is dressed.
> Some day you will feast at the table,
> And be forever blessed.

The Heart of The Matter

And the rich man said, "I have many goods laid up for many years, take it easy, eat, drink, and be merry. But God said, Thou fool, this night thy soul shall be required of thee, then whose shall those things be which thou has provided? So is he that lays up treasure for himself and is not rich toward God. (Luke 12:16-21).

Most of us assume that hoarding riches increases financial security; however, that is not at all true. Moth eaten treasures are no good. Stolen possessions offer no security. Death terminates all earthly treasures. But given a choice, few things, if any, are as satisfying as spiritual security; that is, storing up treasures in the heavenly vault for safe keeping throughout eternity. If we are to benefit from heaven's stock market, we must become shareholders and invest while we are here on earth in order to reap the dividends of divine richness above.

A classic example of clinging on to prized possessions is found in a very good and prominent young ruler who lacked one essential quality which was giving to the poor. When Jesus asked him to sell all that he had that he might have treasure in heaven, he went away in sorrow. (Luke 18:18-25).

> Soon to be unearthed
> When we inherit heaven's treasure
> Are rare and priceless riches
> That no one on earth can measure.

He Is My Joy, And My Strength

Restore unto me the joy of salvation and uphold me with your free spirit, Dear Lord. (Ps 51:12).

Do not expect to move ahead in life if God is not the joy and strength of your life. Joy alone is getting to know God and acknowledging Him as the head of all that you are, all that you can be and all that you will be.

Try as we may, it is impossible to serve two masters at the same time. (Matt 6:24) so reads as follows: No man can serve two masters, for either he will hate the one, and love the other, or else he will hold to the one and despise the other. You cannot serve God and mammon; therefore, the big question to be asked is, of course, who is your Master?

The time has come to be ruthlessly honest. Tip the scales! If your desire to please man outweighs your need to serve God, think again, dear friend. Do you joy in man, or in Jesus? Are you weak in the world, or strong in the Lord?

> To worship and serve God only,
> One must daily sacrifice.
> But when you choose to do so,
> HE's the joy and strength of life.

Take Jesus as Prescribed

Behold, the Lord's hand is not shortened that it cannot save, neither His ear heavy that it cannot hear, but sin has come between God and man. (Is 59:1-2).

At the instruction of God, we are admonished that sin will separate us from Him; therefore, if we desire to partake of Him, we must wage the war against sinfulness.

And while it is true that we have all sinned and come short of the glory of God, as pointed out in (Rom 3:23), let us fear Him and depart from evil. This is not a "when in Rome, do as the Romans" type of thing here. Because others are sinning should not compel us to follow their lead, for doing so will only increase more ungodliness; therefore, we should be totally committed to drawing the line which separates us from sin.

Do we not unfit ourselves for the kingdom of God when we allow sin to run rampant and mar our spiritual countenances? No wonder Jesus said that if anything at all offends us, we should cut it off, for by doing so, we will escape eternal damnation. (Matt 18:8-10).

When you take Jesus as prescribed
Each and every single day,
All those sinful symptoms
Will disappear and fade away.

Spiritual Serenity

Only the pure in heart shall see God, for the wages of sin is death, but the gift of God is eternal life through Jesus Christ our Lord. (Rom 6:23).

One certain quality is evident in all believers, and that is spiritual serenity. Never having to worry about in which direction you are headed when your number is finally called. Of course, none but the righteous shall inherit the kingdom of God.

Now that it is known what is required in order to make heaven one's home, do not delay in seeking out salvation, for if you have not accepted Christ as your Personal Savior, it is highly recommended that you ask yourself, why not?

If you want a home eternal in the heavens should your earthly tabernacle dissolve, and it will, you must build your home in Jesus. There is no other way, save Jesus alone, and that is spiritual serenity. Earthliness is temporal but eternity is forever. One thing is for certain and that is, you will spend an eternity somewhere, one way or the other. So introduce yourself to God, and stake your claim right now!

> Be not deceived, dear friend,
> The Devil knows full well,
> Crossroads will lead to heaven,
> Or take you straight to hell.

A Sure Thing

Withhold not good from them to whom it is due when it is in the power of your hand to do it. Do not turn away your neighbor until tomorrow, for time is not yours to control. (Prov 3:28).

Here's hoping we will not cease to exist before we find the time to get around to it. Time is a terrible thing to waste. On a practical level, frittering away time is senseless. And while habits are not easily broken, there must be a heightened sense of awareness directed to the spirit of procrastination in order to eliminate it from our time banks.

There are far too many dead and buried dreams instead of live realities; too many unfinished projects instead of completed goals, and too many failures instead of final victories. Key issues to be properly addressed are as follows: Putting off for tomorrow what should be done today; stopping short of the goal midway, and failure to follow through with the end in sight all the way to the finish line. To make matters worse, as we muse, ponder and meditate; we foolishly believe that time is on our side, and there is always tomorrow to do charitable acts of kindness for others who are in need of our help today, right now.

It is always weakness to delay what is limited. To place this in perspective, we should not boast of tomorrow, but should say, if it is the Lord's will, we shall live and do this or that. So stop wasting time and be about God's business, and He will make it His business to take care of yours.

> Shun mystic voices
> That whisper, 'There's always tomorrow.'
> Death is marked on a time chart.
> Lost time, you cannot borrow.

Unimportant Things

But Martha was cumbered about much serving and came to Him and said: Lord do you not care that my sister, Mary, has left me to serve alone? Tell her to come and help me. And Jesus answered and said unto her: Martha you are careful and troubled about many things. (Luke 10:40-42).

Surprisingly, it is alarming how itty bitty things tend to pester, annoy and peck away at most of us, distracting us from focusing on what matters the most in a lifetime. Like worrisome, buzzing insects which playfully tease our emotions, we are bombarded by such tiny concerns. As a result, we find ourselves swatting away time by slapping away at insignificant incidents that aren't even worth the effort of our time, nor energy.

Let's not over indulge in small stuff happenings. Life is much too short. Time is far too valuable, and death is far too close. Of a certainty, Satan is a Con Artist and Jack of all Trades. Get with the program! The only thing that matters most of all is time to confess, repent and receive Jesus. Absolutely nothing else matters! To make it point blank and simple, Satan is aware that time to get to know God is indeed limited. His goal is to serve as a source of distraction without drawing undue attention to himself. What better way than making molehills into mountains.

Do not allow what is unimportant to consume your life away.

> Time is of the essence,
> So dispense with idle chatter.
> Most time consuming issues
> Really do not matter.

Wise Up!

If any of you lack wisdom, go to God for it. (James 1:5).

Failing to obtain wisdom may omit to be disastrous. If you of your own accord never seek after wisdom, your reasoning will, of course, be void of understanding, for only the Lord is the giver of wisdom and from His mouth come knowledge and understanding. (Prov. 2:6).

Nicodemus, a ruler of the Jews, lacked understanding until Jesus imparted unto him the following revelation: Except a man is born again, he cannot enter the kingdom of heaven, for that which is born of the flesh is flesh, and that which is born of the spirit is spirit. (John 3:1-6). So then, no matter how educated we are, or how scholarly we choose to become in a lifetime, there is no knowledge in the grave to which we are headed. Wisdom is the principal thing, therefore get wisdom, and with all your getting, get understanding. (Prov. 4:7).

While many are worldly wise, still they see through closed eyes. What is needed is seeing eyes and hearing ears for the Word of God.

> If we search for wisdom
> Like prospectors sought after gold,
> We will gain knowledge
> And solve mysteries untold.

Real Deal Non Fictional

Acknowledge Him in all your ways, and He shall direct your path. (Prov 3:6).

Each day the stage is set. Lights! Camera! Action! Every act is logged in as a live performance by the Recording Angel, and so are the "Days of Our Lives." There are no cuts for imperfection. Actually, from day to day, performances are real, and there are no fictional characters involved. Like Coke, "it's the real thing baby!"

You write your own script, and you are the star of each leading role, but to strike a responsive chord; however, you alone, must choose who will direct your performance each day. If you fail to ask God to keep the door of your lips, to search your soul and know your heart, to try you and know your thoughts, and see if there be any wicked ways in you according to His Word, and then don't ask Him to lead you in the way everlasting, your dramatization might be a total fiasco to the heavenly host of onlookers up above.

Unfortunately, we cannot fast forward, rewind, or relive past performances, but we can get our act together if we will surrender ourselves unto our Lord and Savior, Jesus Christ, and ask Him to direct us and teach us how to act like Him. Oscars don't last, but crowns do.

> Real life is not play acting, so if you want to steal the show,
> Get your act together before it's time to go.
>
> Every stage performance is flashed across heaven's screen,
> So get your act together before the final scene.
>
> If you want to earn a Heavenly Award,
> Please get your act together before you meet the Lord.

Prosperous

Whatever you do, will prosper. (Ps 1:3).

Frankly, if there is nothing to write home about, then something is wrong with your prosperity. The righteous will always prosper, for God is like a spindle that spins all straw into pure gold. With a Midas touch, the righteous flourish like healthy trees planted by an ever flowing river of living water. Their fruit is plentiful, and their leaves are vibrant, leafy green, and full of life.

A good case in point to remember here is that the ungodly are not so. So, if there is only straw in your barn, and the well is dry, and life is fruitless, and withered leaves are constantly falling down, and nothing seems to prosper anymore, perhaps it is wise to surmise that you need to flip on the switch that you may clearly see your way out of darkness and into the Light of prosperity. If you want the golden goose to lay golden eggs, you must first own one, and then it will begin to happen. Once you have claimed prosperity in Jesus, it is yours forever. It cannot be taken away by the enemy, for no weapon formed against you shall prosper. (Is 54:17) "No brag, just fact!"

> Sit on heaven's window sill
> That the glory of God may shine through,
> And the closed doors of prosperity,
> Will amazingly open up for you.

A Boomerang Thang

Be not deceived, God is not mocked, for whatsoever a man sows, he shall reap. (Gal 6:7).

The Golden Rule will always carry over. Do unto others as you would have them do unto you. (Matt 7:12). How profound and wise a true saying uttered from the lips of Jesus Himself. Really hits home, doesn't it? We've heard the stereotyped cliché, "What goes around comes around" more often than enough. But in essence, when the golden rule is deliberately ignored, is when it goes around and comes around, and goes around and comes around, over and over again. As a matter of fact, reaping is a 'boomerang thang.'

According to the Word, as pointed out in (Col. 3:25), wrongdoers shall receive for their wrongdoing, and pay close attention to this, there is no respect of persons. God has no favorites, so forget about an apple for the teacher.

Those who are in line with the divine purpose of sowing good seed will certainly reap in joy. The time has come to ask yourself, what kind of seeds are you sowing?

> Sin is like a boomerang. No matter what you do,
> All of your wrongdoing will come right back to you.
> One thing is for certain, and it will never fail,
> God's divine justice will always prevail.

Bonding Agent

For other foundation can no man lay than that is laid, which is Jesus Christ. (1Cor 3:11).

The word build is defined as constructing by assembling and joining parts or materials together for the sole purpose of establishing a solid foundation. As wise Master Builders, it is extremely important to remember that as we engage in the process of kingdom building and securing spiritual structures, there is only one bonding agent that is guaranteed to hold everything together. JESUS!

> When unto the Savior,
> Your spirit learns to yield,
> You will have all you need.
> The time has come to build.

Laying the Groundwork

As ye have therefore received Christ Jesus, the Lord; so walk ye in Him. Rooted and built up in Him and established in the faith. (Col 2:6-7).

Today, I want you to become aware of the fact that there is no way to lay the groundwork of a firm foundation unless you decide this day, to be rooted and grounded in the word of God. Doing so, takes the edge off of those underground and below the surface temptations as all of us are only too aware, that constantly attacks us in order to weaken our sainthood foundation by slowly chipping away at the base of Christian solidarity.

Remember Master Builders
As you labor long and hard,
Be sure that you are rooted,
And grounded in the Lord.

Build Upon a Rock Solid Foundation

Except the Lord build the house, they labor in vain that build it. (Ps 127:1).

How often in life have many attempted to build without a foundation? A classic example of such a time wasted endeavor is clearly outlined in (Gen 11:4-9).

Foolishly, the children of men attempted to build a city and also a tower whose top would reach unto heaven. Suddenly, however, the Lord appeared to see the city and tower in the making without His blessing. God, from the topmost place of power, immediately confounded their language resulting in a lack of communication among its builders and, of course, construction came to a screeching halt.

> Because the project was unblessed
> By God's almighty hand,
> The city and Tower of Babel
> Dissolved like grains of blowing sand.

No Base

But he that hears and does not, is like a man that without a foundation built a house upon the earth against which the stream did beat vehemently, and immediately it fell, and the ruin of that house was great. (Luke 6:49).

We should never forget to remember that the Word tells us we must continue to solidify our fellowship with Jesus Christ, not with mere words, but power packed action. Many more of us go through life hearing the Word, and not living it at all.

This much, I know, if you begin today to hear the Word, and then strive to obey it, tomorrow you will discover a deeper depth in the range of your spirit filled encounters with the Master.

> A house made without a base
> Built in vain upon the land;
> That house will be swept away.
> Only the Kingdom of God will stand.

You Gotta Have Roots!

Nevertheless the solid foundation of God stands, having this seal: The Lord knows those who are His. (2 Tim 2:19).

How good it is that we may be sure that once born again Christians realize that they can build their homes in Jesus, they amazingly begin to sprout roots that are deeply embedded into the healthy soil of a thriving relationship with Jesus Christ. Yes! You gotta have roots, and immovable roots shall not be uprooted!

> I shall not be moved!
> The stake is driven way down deep.
> My roots are bound in Jesus.
> I gave to Him, my soul to keep.

Finish What You Start

So the wall was finished in the twenty fifth day of the month, and fifty two days. (Neh 6:15).

Let us consider that in laying the groundwork on holy ground someone or something will, without fail, attempt to deter us from working on building up the Kingdom of God. There is a tendency at times to very easily grow impatient when obstacles or roadblocks get in the way during the process of kingdom building construction.

As scripture has it, we are told in (Neh 6:1-16), that there was a conspiracy going on against Nehemiah to stop him from completing the wall God had instructed him to build. But Nehemiah persistently stood his ground, and sent out messengers to tell his enemies that he was doing a great work for the Lord, and would not come down. He was confronted five times by the Tempter, but he in turn, stubbornly continued to build, and finished the wall unto its completion. What great work has been assigned you for completion? Finish the job!

> Many will come to discourage you.
> Keep on building! Don't come down.
> All who finish what they start
> Will some day wear a crown.

Who Is Head Of Your Household?

Choose this day, whom you will serve, but as for me and my house, we will serve the Lord. (Joshua 24:15).

Joshua was fully conscious of the fact that God was the center of his life, when he with holy boldness declared him and his entire household under the Lordship of His Heavenly Father.

Since Joshua decided to give the Lord free reign on that particular day, it stands to reason that his house was heavily insured and completely weather resistant to brave all and any harsh elements of a satanic atmosphere. How about your house? Have you completely surrendered yourself, and your house unto the Lord?

> If when trouble rises up
> Your house begins to fall,
> Perhaps your prop is leaning
> Against the wrong wall.

Become a Building Member

For Abraham looked for a city which had foundations; whose builder is God. (Heb 11:10).

We are all Masons. We are all Carpenters. We are all Builders. Each one of us may be sure that every single day, we are working on a building that will in time house our spiritual dwelling place upon entering everlasting eternity.

Absolutely nothing else but salvation, that supreme sacrificial gift of love, will positively ensure every saintly soul a permanent new abode in glory land.

> Keep working on the building.
> Don't stop sending up the timber.
> There's a city with foundations.
> Are you a Building Member?

Where Do You Run For Cover?

Whoever comes to the Lord and receives His word and obeys it, is likened unto a man which built a house; dug deep and laid the foundation on a rock, and when the flood arose, the stream beat vehemently upon that house, but could not shake it, for it was founded upon a rock. (Luke 6:47-48).

Satan will huff and puff, but he cannot blow your house down if, in fact, it is founded upon a rock and that rock is Jesus!

It cannot be too strongly emphasized that when the unrelenting Adversary incites an upheaval of violent storms and gusty winds, that your house will not fold if God has hold of it. The word is, Satan is mighty, but God is almighty! Is your home insured by All State, or God State?

> The storm unleashed its fury
> But throughout the weather beaten strain,
> The house remained unshakable;
> Anchored by an almighty chain.

Follow the Blueprint Special

For every house is built by some man; but he that built all things is God. (Heb 3:4)

Much of our trouble in life comes out of our failure to follow instructions, and this is why we fail so many times to be successful in building a secure relationship with the Lord.

Not without design does the Chief Architect reveal His 'Blueprint Special' as an instructional guideline to follow in building a rock solid foundation in our Lord and Savior, Jesus Christ.

Follow His Blueprint Special.
There is only one of a kind.
Only God can devise a plan
To create a wise building mind.

Not The Real Thing

Oh Lord, my strength, and my fortress; my refuge in the day of affliction. (Jer 16:19).

Some of us are questioning God concerning His directives. It is so when we fail to build according to His plan that our shoddy, imitation, and poorly designed, weak structured high rises, cave in and crumble at the slightest rumble of adversity.

What should remain constant is our willingness to build as directed in order to remain storm proof against all inclement weather conditions.

> Unless it bears the holy seal,
> 'Inspected by the king,'
> Our self-made place of refuge,
> It is not the real thing.

Build It God's Way

Thus did Noah, according to all that God had commanded him to do. (Gen 6:22).

As we study God's word in the 6th chapter of Genesis, we find that God instructed Noah to build an Ark in like manner; "Make an Ark of gopher wood, and make rooms in the Ark, and then pitch it within and without with pitch. The length of the Ark shall be 300 cubits, the breadth of it, 50 cubits, and the height of it 30 cubits. Add a window to the Ark, and in a cubit shall you finish it above, and set the door of the Ark in the side there of, with lower second and third stories as well."

Of course, the great flood came, and every living and breathing thing upon the face of the earth was destroyed. But the key issue to be addressed in this instance is that Noah was obedient unto the Master Builder.

> Yes! Noah built an Ark
> Just like God told him to,
> And the great flood happened.
> The wicked met their waterloo.

Embrace Tomorrow

God's compassions are new every morning. Great is His faithfulness. (Lam 3:22-23).

Yesterday is gone
Yes some things went wrong
The challenge fell apart
And you were left with a broken heart
But God mends broken hearts
God knew your test in times of despair
Ask his will for you
Lord guide me in what you want me to do
I will embrace tomorrow
I will look up to you
I will embrace tomorrow
For the dawn of a new day,
Victory is our goal
We must persevere on through
The thistles and the thorns
We will embrace tomorrow
It's across the river
Over the beautiful rainbow

~Daisy L. Barnett

Happy New Year

From the beginning of the year to the end, God's eyes are upon it. (Deut 11:12).

The old year is leaving fast
There's a lot of unfinished business of the past
I'm anticipating the New Year
With some questions of what to do about getting some positive answers
I've asked God for a new direction
In order to be more pleasing in my approach toward responsibility.
I've taken a long hard look at my unfinished business
And I realize that I need more answers than I have
So I'm putting some of the unfinished business
In a New Year's resolution to clean it up with God's direction

~Daisy L. Barnett

It's Worth the While

That you may walk worthy of the Lord, fully pleasing Him, being fruitful in every good work and increasing in the knowledge of God. (Col 1:10).

It's worth the while to accept
The task that nobody else will do
Just roll up your sleeves with
A willing mind ask God to carry you through
The road may be rough and rugged
With no friends in sight that you can see
But Jesus will pilot the way
No matter how rough the task may be
There's a rich reward at the end of the journey
And dividends of peace and love are far greater than money
It's worth the while to view a task well done
And to know that God rewards the obedient one

~Daisy L. Barnett

I've Had One Moment

Who is he that overcomes the world, but he who believes that Jesus is the Son of God? (1 John 5:5).

I've had one moment in time
That I have experienced true joy
Of ecstasy,
When I realized my dream of
Beating the challenge of time
To win, win, win
The game was really, really rough
But I realized I was running with the wind
And God heard me when I whispered
Lord let my challenge defend
Let me win, win, win

~Daisy Barnett

Love

Love one another as I have loved you. (John 13:34).

Judge not that ye be not judged
Quick judgment and disrespect
Breeds bad ill feelings and winners
Can become losers in the end result
Learn to bury the old,
Misjudged faults and mistakes
Instead of carrying them
In your mind and hip pocket for countless years
Prayerfully ask God to teach
You forgiveness as you would
That others forgive you
Let's pray for forgiveness
At the end of the day
For our trespasses as we
Work life's way.

~Daisy Barnett

December

Let us therefore come boldly unto the throne of grace that we may obtain mercy, and find grace to help in time of need. (Heb 4:16).

> **D**are to be bold. Holy bold!
> **E**ach Saint has a story that needs to be told.
> **C**ome! Eat of the Living Bread.
> **E**veryone should be spiritually fed.
> **M**editate upon His Word.
> **B**e sure the Gospel is preached and heard.
> **E**agerly spread and share the good news.
> **R**ally for Jesus! You can't lose.

God can and will empower you with holy boldness. Witness for Him. Who doesn't have a story to share about the goodness of God? Tell it! Daily eat of the Living Bread. You shall never hunger again. Think on His Word day and night. Your thoughts will be pure and lovely. Spread the Gospel wherever you go. Someone is waiting to hear the good news. Eagerly and excitedly rally for Jesus. There is so much to cheer about, and it is one campaign you will never lose.

Heads and Tails

The husband is the head of the wife, even as Christ is the head of the church, and He is the Savior of the body. (Eph 5:23).

After God said it was not good for man to be alone, he created woman, a spare rib special. (Gen 2:21 & 22). So woman was taken from man and became flesh of his flesh, and bone of his bones. Gen 2:23). And so, marriage happens. (Gen 2:24).

Holy matrimony! What a bond! But in order for marriage partners to successfully function at full throttle, the wife must reverence her husband as the head, and keep her tail in alignment with the body so that it will continuously move as one flesh. The husband, on the other hand, must love his wife as himself. He is the sauce that marinates his spare rib special. When this is done, everything else will be as it should be, for one body will operate in unison and harmony accordingly. He who finds a good wife finds a good thing. (Prov 18:22). Just remember it works both ways! Heads and tails!

> Rejoice with your companion
> As blessed joint heirs of life.
> Wife, love your husband,
> And husband, love your wife.
>
> Marriage is a sacred bond
> Sanctioned from above,
> A twofold, sharing privilege
> Deep-rooted in true love.
>
> The man is the Head
> And the woman is the Tail,
> They must move as one body,
> Or both of them will fail.
>
> So honor one another
> Until death do you so part,
> For marriage is a good thing.
> It's a matter of the heart.

It's all in the Word

In the resurrection therefore, when they shall rise, whose wife shall she be of them? For the seven had her to wife. (Mark 12:23).

We pay a high price for ignorance. Unthinkingly, the Sadducees who denied the resurrection dared to challenge Jesus and attempted to trip him up with a trick question. The Law of Moses allowed a man's brother to marry his wife if he died and left no seed. So the Sadducees mentioned seven brothers, the first of whom down to the very last, all died, left no seed, and all of whom were married to the same wife. Whose wife then, shall she be in the resurrection?

Jesus, tremendously thorough in His reply unleashed the Word of God. "Know you not the scriptures, neither the power of God? The dead don't marry, and are not given in marriage, but are like the angels in heaven." (Mark 12:24 & 25).

> The dead are not given in marriage,
> So cherish the spouse of your youth,
> For this is your earthly portion in life,
> And that is the gospel truth.

Maintaining a Healthy Marriage

A prudent and godly wife is from the Lord. (Prov 19:14).

Plaque buildup is a substance that clings and forms on teeth. Not only does it dull the natural shine of tooth enamel, but will eventually weaken and begin to destroy very healthy teeth.

A prudent wife is very cautious about marriage plaque. Since she is aware of the fact that it will also form, cling, and coat the surface of her marriage, she faithfully brushes away anything that might tend to dull the glow of matrimonial bliss. She never allows the sun to set upon any wrath between the two of them. (Eph 4:26).

Oftentimes, even faithful brushing cannot clean those hard to reach areas that serve as catchalls to entrap hidden things from view; therefore, she flosses with the Word of God in order to ensure that anything lurking between the cracks and crevices is completely removed. Wisdom has taught her that Satan will soundlessly drill holes in a marriage until the cavity becomes far too deep to be filled, or saved. Since a germ producing, diseased marriage is destined to decay, she does not wait until a dull throbbing, or aching sensation happens, nor does she wait until an unpleasant odor permeates the sweet breath of matrimony. Without fail, she never misses an appointment with the Marriage Dentist. She visits Him each day to ensure that all is well.

> Unless we take precaution,
> And brush harmful things away,
> Marriage plaque and bacteria
> Will buildup day to day.

Marriage Alamode

For this cause shall a man leave his father and mother, and shall be joined unto his wife, and they two shall be one flesh. (Eph 5:31).

When new relationships begin, love struck lovebirds shower one another with lots of cuddlesome affection, and plenty of undivided attention. That's great! After the vows, children, and years of togetherness; however, love begins to languish due to lack of passion. In order to continue to reap a reward unlike any you have ever before experienced, you must continue to fuel the sweetness of intimacy as often as you can. Why? Love begets love!

"You Don't Send Me Flowers Any More" and "Things Go Better with Love" are very popular songs that clearly call attention to the fact that we react to love when we are better loved. So go the extra mile, and above and beyond, and savor the flavor of romance to the height of ecstasy.

Marriage Alamode is one very special treat, with two straws, that any couple could ever dream up and share continuously. Apple pie is merely dessert, but when you add a scoop of ice cream on top, it is apple pie alamode. Serve it up! Enjoy!

> The flame of love will flicker out,
> So please, stoke up the fire!
> Love is always hungry,
> So feed its desire.

Black History

A Dream Comes True

And the Lord said, Arise, anoint him, for this is the one. (1 Sam 16:12).

Let liberty now reign.
Sea to sea! Shore to shore!
The world has witnessed a miraculous change,
And yet there is so much more.

From the top of every mountain
And down in the valley deep,
Equality has triumphed.
What a monumental leap.

"Not color, but content of character"
As Martin Luther King, once said,
Reveals the worth and destiny
Of those determined to move ahead.

So we pray, Barack Obama,
Be granted wisdom like Solomon.
It is the greatest gift required
For all that must be done.

Hands were laid upon him.
He was anointed for each task.
But he needs all Americans.
Did you not hear him ask?

A high flying flag upon a pole,
Or a cross upon a steeple
Is no good at all
Where there are divided people.

Our president cannot stand alone.
One cannot oversee the land.
Support from all is needed.
So let's walk hand in hand.

As He continues to sail across
A new, uncharted course,
We pray, he will move forward
With an able bodied force.

Only then will American voices
Blend into one powerful song.
God Bless America!
Keep us free, safe and strong!

Africa

Remove not the ancient landmark which thy fathers have set. (Prov 22:28).

One of the special marks of our ancestors, are footprints in the sand of time. We all want meaningful, down to the last detail history relating to our forefathers and descendants.

One of the most remarkable facts about heritage which in itself is a great thing, is there is no better way to claim it than to think back, relive, learn, and remember all the teachable things there are to discover about it.

Despite who we are, or from whence we came, it is never too late for us to reflect upon the past. So let us today examine our roots. It will bring out the very best in all of us. We honor Africa, the Motherland!

We salute with an upraised hand,
Africa! Motherland!
Gold, red, black and green
Proudly promenade on scene.

Africa with its jungles deep
Where wild animals crawl, and creep
Through a dense, thick growth of clinging vines,
And sparkling diamonds come from coal mines.

It's the second largest continent in the eastern hemisphere.
Africa, Africa, so very far away from here.
There is colorful, creative, art and much more than the eyes can see.
Africa! Africa! Come and go with me.

Long ago, Africans writhed in flames of slavery,
But through it all they left behind a glowing legacy.
Quiet! Listen! Hear the drumbeat! Ebony tribes with lively feet
Dance to the rhythm of beating drums. Feel the heat of the scorching sun!

Africa! Africa! What a thriving civilization.
Echoes of the past still resound throughout the nation.
Africa! Africa! Stand up and say it loud.
With Nia (purpose), and Imani (faith), we are Black and proud.

Chicken Moments

Whenever I am afraid, I will trust in you. (Ps 56:3).

When the raging tempest comes sweeping through your life,
How do you survive the storm, or free yourself from Satan's vice?
When we have Chicken Moments, here's what we're gonna do.
We will remember Vicki's message and simply follow through.

It's not for us to reason why, nor should we question, or doubt.
Relax in Him! Remain assured! Please! Don't chicken out!
What time we are fearful, or as frightened as a chicken,
We might lose some feathers, but Saints can take a 'lickin.'

Trust in Jesus! "Vicki said." There is no need for stressing.
Mount up! Continue to wing along and position yourself for the blessing."
News Channel 4 Anchor, Vicki Newton tells the news,
But in the pulpit, she's a Soldier in high stepping Gospel shoes.

Thanks for being our special guest.
You blessed us all on Women's Day.
If anyone should ask us, here's what we will say.
U DARN TOOTIN! WE LOVE VICKI NEWTON!

Dred Scott's Prayer

He has sent me to bind up the brokenhearted and to proclaim liberty to the captives. (Is 61:1).

Dred Scott was a slave who fought for his freedom all the way into the courtroom.

I believe there's hope for me. All I want is to be free.
From slavery's oppressed hand, unyoke me! Let me stand!
Must the chains of slavery shackle, bound and torment me?
Set me free to roam and trod. Give me freedom! Hear me God!

Does the hue of my dark skin count me less than other men?
Must our women, boys, and girls be captives in an un-free world?
Not me alone but others too, cry for freedom as I do.
We stand together on one accord. Wishing, wanting, freedom Lord.

Some born Black, and some born White, but whatever be my plight,
Like the wind unchained and free, loose the shackles binding me!
From my cradle to my grave, I choose not to remain a slave.
Let me live my own life free. That's the way it ought to be.

I watch the birds and view their flight, and how I wish somehow I might
Leave this cage and spread my wings and fly away to unchained things.
A world where I am free to do whatever makes daydreams come true.
A place that I can call my own, and be free to romp and roam!

Perhaps I may not live to see the day that we will be set free,
But I believe with all my heart, we will from slavery depart.
I too, proclaim sweet liberty, and pray the court will set me free.
Dear God! Please! Forget me not! This is the prayer of Dred Scott!

It Wasn't Nunna Me!

If we confess our sins, he is faithful and just to forgive us our sins, and to cleanse us from all unrighteousness. (1 John 1:9).

Paul Lawrence Dunbar, a very young and famous, renowned poet, was gifted in the art of dialect poetry. Dis and dat, and hunny chile, was superbly written to a dialect beat that still captures the hearts of poetry lovers the world wide.

I honor the memory of Selena Clemmons, my elementary, English Teacher at Dunbar Elementary School, who believed in me, critiqued all of the poetry I had written up to age 14, and put together a poetry recital for me at the school. It was an unforgettable experience, I will forever cherish. The following poem is from that recital that took place many years ago.

Dat was you I seen las nite.
It wasn't nunna me!
I saw you wit my own good site.
It wasn't nunna me!

I saw you when you kissed dat gal.
It wasn't nunna me!
You kan't fool me. Um yo pal.
It wasn't nunna me!

I was hidin hind dat tree.
It wasn't nunna me!
Ain't I got two eyes ta see?
It wasn't nunna me!

Can spot yo profile miles away.
It wasn't nunna me!
Dat was you, I saw, I say.
It wasn't nunna me!

Cmon now! Admit the truth!
It wasn't nunna me!
I spect I gotta git some proof.
It wasn't nunna me!

Glory Be! I do declare.
"A hit dog sho will holler."
Tell me now, can you deny
Dat lipstick on yo collar?

Jimmie Jon

Behold, I send you forth as sheep in the midst of wolves. Be ye therefore wise as serpents, and harmless as doves. (Matt 10:16).

Jimmie Jon, a sho nuf, deep in the heart of south, down home country boy, was privileged to earn a scholarship to the big fancy university way up North. Mama; however, forewarned Jimmie Jon of the fact that he would be subjected to ridicule, made to feel like a misfit, and a fish out of water, but Jimmie Jon was determined to head on up North anyhow, and we must also be willing to go forth as sheep among wolves no matter how anyone may attempt to deter us from our Christian duties.

> Pleese! Jimmie Jon! Don't give me no lip!
> I don't wanna hear no mo about dat skolarship.
> Pleese! Jimmie Jon! Son! Don't go way to dat skool.
> You got some book learnin and ain't nobody's fool.
>
> Evybody up dat way has a big sootcase,
> And I can harly wate to see yo beet red face.
> Cause when you walk throo town wit yo clothes tyed to a stick,
> Daze gonna point and laugh, and chuckle demselves sick.
>
> And chile when you saloot dem wit yo southern drawl,
> Den tip yo hat and say, "Howdy do! Yall!"
> Daze gonna make you fill like a fish wit out a fin.
> I warn you now, Jimmie Jon, son, you won't have one frien.
>
> Dase so prim and proper! Ware all dem fancee clothes.
> Dey strut around with heads held high, and a turned up nose.
> Jimmie Jon, don't ware yo hare all slicked down on both sides,
> And held in place with possum greese dat smells like sumptin died.

Honey! You don't wanna be around dem city slickers.
I can already hear dare loud and funnie snickers.
Cause Jimmie Jon, Darlin, when it's time fa lunch,
I've got an erry feelin chile, dat the hole bunch, ...

When you commence to eatin and pull out dat hoe cake,
Dase gonna laugh at you, fa sho. O my goodness sake!
I win't up North with Peggie Sue to a big fine sto.
Tell you what! Jimmie Jon. I won't go no mo.

Peggie pushed a button on some kind of elevata.
I thawt for sho at any time dat I wood meet my Maker.
My bellie tossed and turned like it was inside out,
And once I stepped outta it, I squeeled out wit a shout.

The air out dare smells funnie too. Sumpthin called pollootion,
And folks is locked up hind dem bars in dem dare instiootions.
So pleese, Jimmie Jon! Son! Don't leeve yo home.
You is just a country boy, and here's ware you belong.

M. J.

For as in Adam all die, even so in Christ all shall be made alive. (I Cor 15:22).

We fantasized, as Mike mesmerized, and shared his unique, unequalled gift.
Fan's shouts and cheers, down through the years, gave the music world a lift.
He was uncommonly electrifying, and surely there is no denying, with tidal waves of ecstasy
He rocked our world when he unfurled such live, raw energy.

Michael danced to the beat. He moon walked with his feet, and cast an enchanted spell.
He lit up the dance floor. We begged for more, as he set ablaze, a star studded trail.
Hit after hit! Song after song! M.J. skyrocketed steady and strong. He was an awesome icon.
Gifted, prolific and terrific! In his span of time, he left little undone.

The music world is no longer the same because Michael Jackson came, and there's only one M.J.
Alive and real, he felt the thrill, and moved in a phenomenal way.
For every idol, there lurks a rival in hot pursuit somewhere out there,
But Michael Jackson's magnetic attraction classified him as unusually rare.

He reclaimed his childhood and few understood that he had never been there.
Gossip picking bones and casting stones from glass houses is so unfair.
Such a generous soul could not resist becoming a philanthropist. Mike loved humankind.
For those in need, he planted a seed, and left it growing and blooming behind.

The King of Pop will remain at the top, and a glowing legacy will long outlast
Fading memories, of 'used to be(s), who cast dim shadows from their past.
Fingers pointed mockingly at a famed celebrity. It is so easy to criticize.
But when Mike entertained, the whole world gained. He won prize, after prize, after prize.

Modern Moses

Follow peace with all men, and holiness, without which no man shall see the Lord. (Heb 12:14)

A Baptist preacher arrived on the scene.
Boldly he proclaimed his dream.
Dr. Martin Luther King!
He vowed to let freedom ring.

Strong desired, as God so willed,
He fought to see his dream fulfilled.
Injustice and inequality,
Surely was not meant to be.

He loved his children, and his wife,
But still, he made the sacrifice.
King was a peculiar man.
He proceeded on with God's plan.

A courageous spirit braved the danger.
A calm demeanor soothed all anger
As he led us fearlessly,
King Marched on triumphantly.

Longevity, King counted dear.
Untimely death hovered near.
So little time, a dream undone,
He fought on to overcome.

King envisioned the Promised Land
After which an assassin's hand
Felled him on the balcony
While in Memphis Tennessee.

King fought well nonviolent fights.
He turned the tide for Civil Rights.
His dream lives on though shadow cast.
"Thank God Almighty! Free at last!"

Salute to Oprah!

To whom much is given, much more is required. (Luke 12:48).

Oprah Winfrey! What a woman!
She is multitalented and endowed with skill.
She commands an audience.
Oprah knows how to appeal.

It is not her wealth or fortune
That sets her from so many apart,
But love begets love,
And love comes from the heart.

Of course, Oprah tops the chart
For world-wide popularity,
But countless people have been blessed.
Oprah gives so generously.

For years, the number one host
Of her own televised talk show,
And then, Oprah decided,
It was time to challenge the radio.

Congratulations! Movie star!
Entrepreneur! Millionaire!
What a woman of achievement.
Emulate her if you dare.

There are thorns among life's roses.
Some prick the heart to bleed.
Oprah Winfrey reaches out
And touches lives where there's a need.

Who knows what else she will do,
Or what else may lie in store.
A Girl School in Africa,
And yet, there's so much more.

Oprah Winfrey's Book Club,
Cookbooks! The O Magazine!
How can one help but kneel.
Salute a reigning queen!

If bold enough to take a risk
And in one's authentic self believe,
The sky is the limit! Go for it!
Oprah does! Believe! Achieve!

To whom much is given,
Much more is required.
There are countless people
She has mentored and inspired.

All has not been easy
For the Shining Star we've come to know.
Persistent! Passion driven!
Oprah! Way to go!

Few of us will ever walk
Star studded Halls of Fame.
A lady of distinction!
OPRAH WINFREY is her name.

Scott Joplin's Gift

Take therefore the talent from him and give it unto him which hath ten talents. (Matt 25:28).

You have only begun to realize the splendor of a life changing encounter when you finally discover, and step up to claim your God given gifts, and then maximize them to the greatest possible degree. The best of you will not emerge if you are prone to equate and compare your gifts, or talents with some greater, multi talented super star. You are who you are, so use what God has given you, and amazingly, your gifts will make room for you. (Prov 18:16).

There is a very sad footnote to the Parable of the Talents as mentioned in (Matt 25:28). The one with only one talent failed to use it, so it was taken away and given to another.

In what ways are you gifted? Everybody has something special God has given them. And even if it is only one talent, use it, or lose it!

> He was the Father of Ragtime Music.
> Scott Joplin is His name.
> He played and wrote music.
> Scott loved to entertain.
>
> He was young, Black and gifted,
> And he composed numerous tunes.
> He performed in honkytonks, and bars,
> And even in laidback saloons.
>
> We salute Scott Joplin!
> Music was his bag.
> He composed a very popular song.
> It is titled "Maple Leaf Rag."

Scott's fingers ruled the keyboard
Like a magical musician.
He colored the world of music.
Long live his Ragtime compositions.

He wrote songs! Operas! Ballet!
He loved music so very much.
With an upbeat, staccato style,
He rang out the Maestro touch.

A native of Saint Louis, Missouri,
His talent earned him much acclaim.
His gift to the world is music.
Scott Joplin! Remember that name!

Unforgettable Rosa Parks

I will praise thee, for I am fearfully and wonderfully made. (Ps 139:14).

With a tired body, and aching feet,
She boarded the bus, and took her seat.
Rosa decided today was the day
That no one on earth would stand in her way.

No more you know the rules for the colored and black.
No more give up your seat and stand in the back.
No more signs and dividing lines on the bus.
No more restrictions for folk like us.

Fixed eyes were positioned with a cold stare,
But Rosa Parks seemed not to care.
She feared not a lonely cell,
Nor confinement locked in jail.

A courageous woman remained in her seat.
She refused to surrender unto defeat.
With a proud, uplifted head,
"I won't give up my seat!" She said.

"Don't look at me as though I'm strange.
The time has come to make a change.
I will pay the price! I will bear the pain!
Today is the day! Let freedom reign!

I too am fearfully, wondrously made.
Christ died for all! The debt is paid!
Until all are treated equally,
There is no such thing as liberty!"

We can sit anywhere today.
Rosa Parks began the way.
A fiery, young teacher ignited her sparks!
Unforgettable Rosa Parks!

Neva's Cake

Every good gift and every perfect gift is from above, and comes down from the Father of lights, with whom there is no variation or shadow of turning. (James 1:17).

Heard you placed an order for a special treat.
Who would not enjoy something good to eat?
So here it is Neva! Your wish is God's command.
Sweets for the sweet, delivered hand to hand.

It's not the traditional birthday cake like you had in mind,
But it's the sweetest delicacy of a lasting kind.
Even when life is bitter, God can make it sweet.
He stirs in all ingredients to make your cake complete.

It is served, hot from the oven, to warm up your life.
So go ahead Neva, have a hearty slice.
Oh! Taste and see that God is good. Dig in! Enjoy! Eat!
Satisfy your soul. Gobble up your treat.

There is a good reason for you to jump and shout.
The candles on this birthday cake never will burn out.
The glow will keep on shining to give your heart delight.
God is always with you. Jesus is the Light!

So here's a cake designed for you, with your name written on it.
All of God's blessings and well wishes are upon it.
And to top it off, He's the icing on the cake.
God spreads Himself all over you, simply for your sake.

Birthdays come and go, and with each passing year,
We cherish special times with those we count as dear,
So when another birthday rolls around again,
Eat this cake and celebrate with a happy grin.

God has richly blessed a wonderful young mother, my friend, and Piano Teacher, Neva Finnie, with the good and perfect gift of music. Continue raising an army of musicians!

We Love you Neva! Your students, Jewel, Danielle, and Mariah

Old Fashioned Mama

Who can find a virtuous woman, for her price is far above rubies? (Prov 31:10)

Give me an old fashioned mama
Who loves and understands
That it takes a firm, yet gentle,
And strong, upbringing hand.

An upright, Christian Mama
Will save all of her boys and girls,
For "the hand that rocks the cradle,
Surely rules the world."

Give me an old fashioned mama,
Who never fails, to pray.
She keeps her children within view,
And never looks away.

A mama knows her child's voice.
The sound is like none other.
She listens with a hearing ear.
Now that's a real mother.

An old fashioned mama
Gave us chores to do,
And would double back and check
To be sure, we followed through.

She taught her daughters to be women.
She taught her sons, to be 'real' men.
Yes! An old fashioned mama!
Please! Bring her back again!

Real Mothers Matter

The rod and rebuke give wisdom, but a child left to himself brings shame to his mother. (Prov 29:15). Foolishness is bound in the heart of a child, but the rod of correction shall drive it far from him. (Prov 22:15).

It was Madam C. Walker who introduced the press and curl.
She created sleek, sassy, and stunning styles to glamorize a "Sista Girl.'
Now there is modern day hair styling to make the hair behave.
You may choose perms, braids, freeze it, wrap it, or cold wave.

Things have changed through the years. Remember matching gloves and hats?
Ladies of today might say; 'Away! No more of that!'
But as can be seen, it is notable to mention,
That it still is, up until now, a time honored tradition.

Some cock their hats to one side; turn brims down, or whatever.
Others may sport ribbons, or add a pretty bow, or feather.
Nothing spells out woman like an old fashioned hat,
And a sweet scented handkerchief. Honey! Fancy that!
Some things never change at all, like a real mother.
So cherish her while you can, for you will never have another.
When 'Down Home' mothers warn you once, don't think about it twice.
Wise with wisdom and experience, they offer sage advice.

Real mothers raise their children, and train them the upright way.
They may wander from the Word, but will not stay astray.
Real mothers matter! This is not a tale or fable.
Children are true products of hands that rock the cradle.

When God Made Mama

Her children rise up and call her blessed. (Prov 31:28).

When God made you, Mama, he designed a Gem of Art.
All the love that you could hold He poured into your heart.
Gems are rich and priceless, and nothing can compare.
We only have ONE mother who is blessed, unique and rare

Down throughout the passing years, come what may! Whatever!
You are the full strength, super glue that bonds us all together.
When God made you, Mama, He made you gentle and strong.
He made you soft enough to comfort us, and gently lead us along.

He made you tough enough to discipline and put us in our place;
And quick enough to wipe a smirk off of a childish, pouting face.
When God made you, Mama, he threw away the mold.
Now we can testify. Yes! Let it be told.

In today's modern world where things are all 'up tight',
Thank God for a mother who raised her children to do what's right.
When God made you mama, No! Meant no! One time!
Not only that, you taught us that life doesn't turn on a dime.

Life turns on Jesus! You taught us to seek Him, trust and pray.
A God fearing, old fashioned mama made us what we are today.
When God made you, Mama, a thriving mother of ten,
He has kept you all these years, and He will do it again.

Happy Birthday! Mama!
Be it sunshine or rain, laughter, or tears.
No wonder ADDIE PAULINA ELY
God blessed you into ninety years.

Poem requested by daughter, Annie McCloud

An Every Day Christmas

For there is born to you this day in the city of David a Savior, who is Christ the Lord! (Luke 2:11).

Christmas comes but once a year bringing tidings of good cheer.
Families gather by the fire. Spirits soar higher, and higher.

Christmas trees are set aglow. Shoppers scurry to and fro.
Christmas presents are under the tree. Santa! Please! Don't forget me!

We celebrate the Christ Child blessing, and thank God for the turkey and dressing.
On Christmas day, we lend a hand to promote good will throughout the land.

Why is it that the Yuletide Season reminds us that there is a reason
To give to those who are in need, or do a Good Samaritan deed?

If God waited on Christmas to bless, we would suffer great distress,
But faithfully His blessings flow from up above, to down below.

If you are healthy, strong, and able and there is food upon your table,
Your Christmas may be merry and bright, but the homeless are outside tonight.

No "Silent Night!" No "Joy to the World" when there are starving boys and girls.
No Christmas presents under the tree where there is only poverty.

No "Hark the Herald, Angels Sing!" No "Silver Bells" to merrily ring,
Unless we live in such a way that Christmas will be every day.

We celebrate the Savior's birth. Merry Christmas! "Peace on earth!"
The love we share each Christmas Day should never fade or pass away.

No Christmas

Worthy is the Lamb that was slain to receive power and riches, and wisdom, and strength, and honor, and glory and blessing. (Rev 5:12).

And so it was long ago, one day in Bethlehem,
A virgin, known as Mary, birthed the great I AM.

Beckoned by the shining star, the Wise Men sought the way.
Rejoicing when they found Him, they worshipped Him that day.

Destined to the weighted cross to bear it all in agony,
A little Babe named Jesus was born to set all sinners free.

No! There would be no Christmas had not God so willed
His son, a ransom for many by whose stripes, we are healed.

Ring out the Yuletide joyous news. Praise God with a mighty shout.
The sacrificial Lamb of God is what Christmas is all about.

The Christmas Story

And so it was that while they were there, the days were accomplished that she should be delivered. And she brought forth her first born son, and wrapped him in swaddling clothes, and laid him in a manger because there was no room in the inn. (Luke 2:6-7).

Take the time to reveal the true meaning of Christmas with your children, and they will share it with their children also. Listen to a mother's response to her little son in the following Christmas Poem.

Mommy dear, I must insist that you listen to my list.
Christmas time is almost here. It's my favorite time of year.
I want a Wilson basketball, a pup that answers when I call.
I want a floating rubber duck, and a big 'you dump it' truck.

I want an electric Choo Choo train, a jet propelled airplane,
Some candy, puzzles, a radio, and Mr. "T" with eyes that glow.
I want a baseball mitt and bat, a Bronco Buster cowboy hat, and also a colored T.V.
Guess that should be enough for me.

Gee! I love Santa Clause. He can have all my applause.
Can we put up the Christmas tree? November is not too soon for me.
Santa has a lot of toys for all good little girls and boys.
I know that I have been real good. So hurry Santa if you would.

Well! Thank the Lord for Santa Clause, but let us take some time to pause
And talk about the real reason, we celebrate the Yuletide season.
Long ago in Bethlehem, there was born a little Lamb.
Baby Jesus was destined to be a sacrifice for you, and me.

Sacrifice?

Yes! Sometimes we are not so good. Don't always act like we should,
So God sent His precious Son to earth to get the job done.
The Christ Child grew into a man, and carried out His Father's plan.
Christ died and washed us clean of sin. The blood of Christ redeems all men.

Redeems?

Yes! God loves us so, He gave His son. Jesus paid the price for everyone,
And that is why God will forgive. Eternal life is ours to live.
We all do things we should not do, but Jesus died for me and you.
No one else could take His place. His gift unto the world is grace.

Grace?

Yes! Baby Jesus, Lord and King, was born to change everything.
Had He not hung upon the cross, son, our souls would be lost.
I love to sniff pine trees and holly, and welcome Saint Nick, all fat and jolly.
But I just had to make things clear why Christmas day brings us cheer.

The little boy bowed his head thinking the little Lamb still dead.
But mom in a joyful way shared the meaning of Easter Day.
In his Letter to Santa, Attention! Dear Lord! Her son enclosed a homemade card.
It simply stated "How happy I am that God gave us that Little Lamb."

Unlike Santa

And the Child grew, and waxed strong in spirit, filled with wisdom, and the grace of God was upon Him. (Luke 2:40). As children eagerly anticipate the coming of Christmas, tell them about the Jesus Child who became the Savior of humankind. By and by, they will come to understand the true meaning of Christmas.

Jesus doesn't ride on a sleigh,
But a cloud from heaven rode Him away.
Unlike Santa, there are no reindeer
To bring to us, Christmas cheer.

Jesus may not give away one toy,
But He will fill your heart with joy.
Unlike Santa, He doesn't carry a sack,
But the weight of the cross was upon his back.

God is so good, and it gets even better.
Praying is faster than writing a letter.
Unlike Santa, He doesn't live at the North Pole.
Jesus builds His home inside of your soul.

Year round there are presents under the tree,
Gift wrapped in love, for you, and for me.
Unlike Santa, be it so understood,
Only God knows who's been bad or good.

ME

Then God said, Let us make man in our image. (Gen 1:26).

I will speak out in this world.
I have a voice of my own.
I am aware of individuality.
I will express myself!
My opinions matter to me.

I will magnify my existence.
I have a soul of my own.
I am conscious of my being.
I am a free spirit!
I learn to grow by all I am seeing.

I will accept a challenge.
I have guts of my own.
Win or lose, fail not to try.
Away with comfort zones!
Always a winner Am I.

I will trust in God.
I have a choice of my own.
I was fashioned by His mold.
I am a Child of God!
What a wondrous creation to behold.

I will educate myself.
I have a mind of my own.
Brain power gives me wisdom.
I will dare to risk! Live to dream,
For I have a vision.

I will reach out to others.
I have a need of my own.
Without love, we die.
To love myself is to be loved.
Lord! Who am I?

Shirts and Skirts

How fair and how pleasant art thou, oh love, for delights. (Song of Solomon 7:6).

Understand that "flowers that bloom too early are fair gain for a late frost." Teen pregnancy is at an all time high. One sweet moment of short lived ecstasy may very well lead to a lifetime of long term despondency. Who wouldn't love a beautiful, bouncing, brand spanking new baby? The big question asked, more often than not though, is how do I know it's mine? Gotcha! DNA! Still, there are more and more unmarried, and single parents, and abortions continue to happen.

Naturally, sex is an enjoyable, undeniable pleasure, and some too young mothers, are fortunate enough to marry or have the willing financial support of the father. But then too, there are countless other teens left holding the short end of the stick, and having to wing it all alone after the child is born. Of course, babies are so easy to love, but very expensive to care for, especially when you are the sole provider. Sadly stated, knees will buckle under the weight when you are left to shoulder the load of responsibility all by yourself. Sure, some have parents who will assist them, but before you decide to grow up and take the plunge, "don't step into muddy waters without your boots." You may have to wade through troubled waters all by your lonesome.

> While life is young and tender,
> And unripe fruit clings to the vine,
> Enjoy those youthful, carefree days
> While life is good, and all seems fine.

The Bags We Drag!

Lay aside every weight and run on! Heb. 12:1

Feeling marooned and isolated on a desolate island of loneliness?
At wits end, are you sinking deeper down into distress?

Attempting to downsize your problems, but find they tend to enlarge?
Time out! Big question! Are you the Boss in Charge?

Are you constantly drifting afloat on an endless sea of unrest?
Try as you may, are you failing to pass, test after test, after test?

Perhaps the time has come for you to learn how to pack.
How many bags are you dragging around as you move on down life's track?

Are you walking around in a crazed daze? Are you trying to find your way out of a maze?
When there is too much baggage on board, it rings up a price you cannot afford.

There is no quick fix to numb your pain. Working 'your plan' will drive you insane.
Controlling the reins will make your head throb. So why not turn it over to God?

Weighted down with baggage? Is there too much on your plate?
How often do you struggle to carry around dead weight?

When your mind and body is under satanic attack;
The way to look is up while lying flat on your back.

As troubles continue to unwind, carry bags, drop them, and leave them behind.
You're not meant to shoulder such heavy demands, so drop it, Bag Lady, right into God's hands.

In the flowing mainstream of life, almighty God will suffice.
Whatever you need for your day to day trip, the Lord will provide. He shall equip.

Is there a piece of your puzzle missing? Still searching around and haven't found it?
Perhaps it's far too complex, for you to wrap your head around it.

Here is what you need to do! God has a grab bag of goodies for you.
Call Him by name! He will cease your stressing. Reach in the bag and claim your blessing!

There are too many gifts in lay-a-way. Show up! Pick up yours today.
God's storehouse is open and free, and ready and waiting for you and me.

Don't be a Bag Lady! Learn to pack light! Dump it on Jesus! He's joy, strength, and might!
Demonstrate spiritual exaltation and rise above each situation.

Call him up, Bag Lady, today! He'll lighten your load right away.
One thing is for certain, don't get it twisted! Jesus' phone number is never unlisted.

Turn That Music Down

And after the earthquake, a fire; but the Lord was not in the fire, and after the fire, a still small voice. (1 Kings 19:11-13).

The Lord was not in the strong wind, nor an earthquake, or the fire, but Elijah heard a still, small voice, and it was God. God will bring about a wonderful peacefulness to our lives if we will simply turn down the volume and listen to the silent hush. Music is therapeutic in that it is soothing to the soul when played softly, but blasting music too loudly, drowns out everything around us, and tunes everybody out. We can't hear God and no one else, including the emergency vehicle rapidly coming up alongside of us.

Turn that music down!
Quit driving around with your head a bobbing.
Later on, you will wonder why
Your poor head is still a throbbing.

Hard rock softens and weakens the soul,
And loud music numbs the ear.
By the time you are all grown up,
You won't be able to hear.

Hull Offerings

Remember now your Creator in the days of your youth, before the difficult days come, and the years draw near, when you say," I have no pleasure in them." (Eccl 12:1).

It is so wonderful to be young, but to seek out Jesus early on in life is even more wonderful. Youthfulness is a part of lifetime many regret leaving behind, but youth, like anything else, though "a thing of beauty" is not a joy forever, but whatever we do for Christ is.

The abovementioned scripture reminds us that unavoidable woes are sure to come. How are we to understand this? With our choices, come consequences. Serve the Lord with the strength of your youth, and you will be more than glad that you did.

Golden years are not given to all because death does not discriminate. It claims the young, as well as the old, so don't squeeze all the juice out of the lemon and offer God the hull. Give Him your best years, and should you happen to grow old, He will never leave you, nor forsake you. (Heb 13:5).

> Sunlight is pleasing to the eyes,
> And bright, sunshiny, cloudless skies
> Beckon youthful, joyous cheer.
> Enjoy yourself while you are here.
>
> Lean not unto your own ways
> Nor in vain live out your days.
> Do not rely upon your sight,
> Or trust your own will, and might.
>
> Oh! Youthful soul drawn to folly,
> Do not spend all lifetime jolly,
> For dark days are sure to come,
> And you'll be judged for all that's done.

Anchors Away, Full Speed Ahead!

And if I go and prepare a place for you, I will come again, and receive you unto myself, that where I am, there you may be also. (John 14:3).

"I heard the Master calling me. His voice was tender, kind, and sweet.
So how could I not answer Him, and kneel down at His feet?
This is **John Jennings**, Lord! Hello! I'm phoning home!
Come and take me to the King who sits upon the royal throne."

"My earthly tabernacle, Lord, is weary, worn, and weak.
Nonnie calling! Beam me up! Hear me as I speak!
I know my friends, and loved ones will miss me very much.
But earth can in no way compare with heaven's healing touch."

"Oh! Yes! My house is in order! I am moving very slow,
But my ticket is punched! I'm already packed! I'm set, and ready to go!
So let not your heart be troubled! How could I not choose to bask in heavenly ecstasy?
Such an offer, I could not refuse."

"I saw the nail-prints in His hands, His wounded side, and thorn pricked head!
I saw the King of Glory! He has risen! He's not dead!"
Jesus said, "Fear not! **John**. I AM the resurrection and Life!
Come! Partake of heaven, **Nonnie**. Join me today in paradise!"

"Launch out into the deep! Let's cross over to the other side!"
"It was such a proposition that could not be denied!"
"Then I saw 'Jacob's Ladder; as I climbed each rung, higher, higher!
I heard the angels singing up above in heaven's choir."

"Step by step, my feet felt light and then my soul began to tingle.
I saw a mansion RESERVED FOR ME! I shouted and hung out my shingle."
"While seek ye the living among those who are dead?"
"I shall rise, alive in Jesus! Anchors Away, Full Speed Ahead!"

In loving memory of Dr. John Henry "Nonnie" Jennings

Came aboard, August 16, 1921, Anchors away, May 20, 2013

Born an Angel

It was Job who tore his clothes, shaved his head, and fell down upon the ground and worshiped God. And it was Job who said, "Naked, I came into the world and naked will I depart." And it was Job who penned the words in the midst of his grief, "The Lord gave, and the Lord has taken away. Blessed be the name of the Lord." (Job 1:20-*21).*

My son, **Kevin** and his wife, **Jennifer**, shared some astounding news in the latter part of 2008. Quadruplets were on their way! It was later revealed that the gender of the quads was an even split of two boys, and two girls! I chose spiritual names for the quads known as Babies A.B.C. and D. **Amazingly Awesome! Completely Blessed! Heavenly Chosen! And Totally Divine!** As with multiples, problems did arise, and the slow growth of Baby D, one of the little girls, caused great concern for us all. It was discovered that both baby girls had what appeared to be a bowel obstruction, and Saints everywhere joined in and petitioned the Lord in prayer for the 'Quad Squad.' Additionally, Jennifer was very swiftly running out of storage room for four babies, so surgery was performed and isn't it just like God to make adequate room in a crowed space for four little ones! And while the doctor never dimmed our hopefulness, his truthfulness prepared us for a decision that would eventually have to be made concerning Baby D. The other three were steadily growing and gaining required weight, but not Baby D. She weighed one pound, and when she gained an ounce more, we jumped for joy. Consequently, God made the decision Himself. On Thursday, April 9, 2009, a visit to the doctor revealed that there was no longer a heartbeat for Baby D. On Good Friday, April 10, 2009, Logan Quinn, Landon John, and Leila Ruth were delivered alive along with Ella Faith, who was born an angel and rebirthed into eternity. Baby D miraculously hung in there long enough for her two brothers and sister to reach the point of being able to be viable and exist outside of the womb. Amazingly, according to the doctor's time chart, she stood her ground. When I beheld her angelic form, I thanked God for her presence however brief, and the purpose for which she had served, and I know that He always knows what is best. Like the spiritual name I gave her, she is indeed **Totally Divine.** The birth of the Quads was televised on Multitude of Multiples, which premiered on August 30, 2009, on TLC. Logan, Landon, and Leila are healthy, blessed, and are now 5 years old. They also share their lives with their big brother, **Taylor**, and big sister, **Ava Camille**, and of course, mom and dad.

> Someone to love, God loaned us. It was only for a while.
> How we were drawn to her. She was our tiniest, fourfold child.
> She was nowhere near as big as her sister, and two brothers,
> But we continued to plead her case, and we encouraged one another.
>
> Our precious, little **Ella Faith**, she kept us on our knees.
> Dear Lord! Let her gain more weight. A few more pounds, if you so please.
> Then Jennifer ran out of room, but God provided more space.
> Through surgery God blessed her and enlarged her storage space.

A safe arrival due date was thirty weeks plus.
Isn't it amazing how the Lord blessed us?
When God deemed it safe enough for **Ella Faith** to fly away,
Logan, **Landon**, and **Leila**, He kept from harm's way.

God blessed us with the 'Quad Squad' and He took one away
On April 10, 2009! Good Friday! What a glorious day!
We trusted God all the way. He gave us all but one.
Ella Faith stood her ground until God said, "Well done!"

Faith must be exercised, so God put it to a test.
He healed our dearest **Ella Faith** as only He knows best.
God in His infinite wisdom chose to claim her as His own.
She was born an angel. We will meet her at the throne.

In loving memory of our granddaughter and born again angel, **Ella Faith Tabb. Good Friday, April 10, 2009.** The sun arose in our hearts at the thought of your presence, and the sun set in our hearts, as an unforgettable memory of your absence.

Much love! Grandparents, Papa & Beba, (Bobby & Jewel Tabb) & Nonnie & Mimi, (John & Norma Jennings)

'CC' Phone Home

When you pass through the waters, I will be with you; and through the rivers, they shall not overflow you. (Is 43:2).

There was a very popular extraterrestrial movie that was featured years ago. It was called E.T. E.T. was not a human being. He came down to earth from another planet. As time passed by, he fell ill, and earthly medicine could not cure him. Those who had grown to love him stood by helplessly because there was nothing they could do. E.T., however, knew exactly what to do. Undoubtedly, he cried out. E.T. Phone home! E.T. Phone home! E.T. Phone Home!

'CC' and so are we, are not from this planet. Earth is not our home. All of us, and I quote," are heavenly beings having an earthly experience." Just like E.T., 'CC's health began to fail. But when he got the news that there was nothing earthly doctors could do; a stranger in a foreign land simply followed through. He looked up unto Jesus, sitting on the heavenly throne, and with all his might he cried out. 'CC' Phone home! 'CC' Phone home! 'CC' Phone home!

It has been said, one life to live, is not a dress rehearsal.
We cannot back track time, for it is irreversible.
So then, it is wise to choose this day who you will serve.
Death is but a step away as we round life's curve.

Just keep on living! You will find this to be true.
We serve a God who will never say; "Sorry! There's nothing I can do!"
Sadly, we all know that separation is always painful,
But every time a Saint goes home heaven is more gainful.

Heaven becomes more valuable to each of us, day by day.
All our friends and loved ones keep heading up that way.
If you are acquainted with the Master of the sea,
You will pass through death unto life eternally.

Clyde Clark led many roles within his journey throughout life;
A father, father-in-law, worker, grandfather, friend, and he adored, Evelyna, his wife.
'CC' was a man who showed so many different sides.
He was humorous, he was serious, and so full of life was Clyde.

But underline this in your mind he felt no greater pride
Than when he joined in membership, and served the Lord, at New Northside.
As Clyde grew in grace, he came to understand
That he could put it all into his Savior's hands.

Suddenly! A violent storm came sweeping through Clyde's life.
It swiftly swept him out to sea. It seemed that nothing could suffice.
But even when the doctors said, "I'm sorry! We can't help!"
Clyde knew that God could intervene, undergird, and overstep.

As the time drew nearer for him to venture home,
He leaned on his church family, for he was not alone.
He anchored himself in Jesus, for in his heart, he knew
That God would never say to him," Sorry! There's nothing I can do!"

The storm increased in its intensity. The skies were dark and dreary.
The outer man was fading fast, and his soul grew weary,
But the inner man kept flourishing. God gave Clyde dying grace.
We heard it in his voice, and then, we saw it on his face.

'CC' just kept on trusting God all throughout those stormy days,
And he continued to look up toward heaven with a steady gaze.
God heard his child cry out! "Oh! Lord! Deliver me!"
So He stepped into the water, and walked upon life's troubled sea.

In such a gentle, godly way, as only Clyde could understand,
God spoke unto the raging sea, and it obeyed His command.
Then the storm subsided and ceased unto God's will.
The storm passed on over. "Peace! Peace! Be still!"

The grim skies overhead changed from gray to blue
And heavenly, radiant beams of light came shining right on through.
Transition is complete. Clyde moved on up higher.
Goodbye! Male Chorus! Hello! Angelic Choir!

Passing through death unto life is a very happy ending story.
Clyde Clark has been inducted into the Hall of Glory.
In the year of Our Lord, March 23rd, 2011,
God's Soldier claimed his inheritance, and citizenship in heaven.

In loving memory of Clyde Clark, Sunrise: July 12, 1943, Sunset: March 23, 2011

Daddy

You have not received the Spirit of bondage again to fear. But you have received the Spirit of adoption; whereby we cry, Abba! Father! (Romans 8:15).

God is my Heavenly Father, for He adopted me, and not me only, but all of us. Because He did, we can cry Abba! Father! And He will hear us. I am also grateful for the earthly father God blessed me with. The following poem honors his memory.

I am so proud and very glad
That **Alton Phelps** is my dad.
Although He is no longer here,
Precious memories are so dear.

Daddy was gentle. Daddy was strong!
I followed him, and tagged along.
I sat by the window and watched for his car.
He was my hero! My superstar!

Whenever he said, "Daddy's girl,"
It always brightened up my world.
I would run to him, and sit on his knee,
And listen while he read to me.

He never backed up because he was small.
Daddy was short, but walked real tall.
Dad was always number one.
Somehow he always got things done.

He was the boss and breadwinner.
He always thanked God for our dinner.
When big brother and I played in the street,
Little Al would walk his beat.

He kept us safe and under control.
Some might call it Father Patrol.
He could fix anything around the house.
He took good care of his kids and his spouse.

Fathers have a weakness for curls.
They love bows, lace, and their little girls.
At sixteen, I landed my very first date.
My anxious daddy could hardly wait.

Dad checked him out, and gave him the eye.
He treated my boyfriend like he was a spy.
With a broad grin, and fatherly smile,
Years later, he walked me down the aisle.

Right after, Dad called the groom aside.
"Be good to my daughter! Take care of your bride!"
God made Alton Phelps, and then, He threw away the mold.
My Daddy was lots of love to grab hold.

In loving memory of my daddy, Alton Phelps

Sunrise: June 10-1917, Sunset: July 31, 1972

Enjoy Yourself to the Height!

But I would not have you to be ignorant concerning those which are asleep, and that you sorrow not, even as others which have no hope. For if we believe that Jesus died and arose again, even so them also which sleep in Jesus will God bring with Him. (1 Thess 4:13-14).

It should come as no surprise that God still speaks to us through dreams. I dreamt that mama was walking along. Suddenly she fell to the ground and began to crawl. Not too long afterward, Mama told me that she was beginning to have visions of loved ones who had passed away. Mama had been cancer free about fifteen years. It returned in her early eighties. The very last words my Mother said to me as I was leaving for a very brief trip to California was "Enjoy yourself to the height!" I left town on Monday, and Mama joined the angels that Wednesday.

I recited the following poem at Mama's Home going Celebration. Family members mentioned in the poem include my mama, Luella Hawkins Phelps, daddy, Alton, Phelps, my only sibling & big brother, Ordell Phelps, my granddaddy, Albert Phelps, known as Papa Son, and me, Willie Jewel Phelps Tabb, fondly called sister.

It was on October first, nineteen-fifteen, a precious, beautiful baby girl arrived on the scene.
A gift from God above, and all gift wrapped too, our mama, Luella Hawkins, made her debut.
Papa Larry and Mama Lenora were proud. They welcomed her to the Hawkins' crowd.
She was fancy and frilly with bows, and curls such as becomes cute baby girls.

Marshall Texas was mama's home, but southern natives tend to roam.
Her husband, Alton, could not wait to move his family to the Show me state.
So with her son, Ordell, by the hand, and daughter, Willie Jewel, on her hip,
From Texas to Saint Louis, Missouri, Luella boarded the train for the trip.

The year was nineteen forty-five, and things really came alive.
2949 Easton; two tiny rooms, but everything was tidy with Luella's mops and brooms.
Mama's religious upbringing gave her roots and kept her spiritually strong.
She joined Trinity Mount Carmel Baptist Church. It was where she would always belong.

Whatever the situation, Luella never shirked.
Times were hard. She found a job, rolled up her sleeves and worked.
Cleanliness is next to God. Mama labored as a maid.
She pitched in and helped her husband, and somehow the bills were paid.

Who kept Ordell and Sister? Of course, it was Papa Son.
Granddaddy took good care of us until the day was done.
In nineteen fifty five, mama claimed her dream,
We moved into a six room house at 3003A Magazine.

It was raggedy, huge, and drafty, but none of us seemed to care.
One thing was for certain, there was plenty good room there.
Then in nineteen fifty-nine, Mama landed a winner.
We moved to 2905A North Vandeventer.

King Alton ruled his castle, and Queen Luella graced her throne.
We had never lived in such a swanky, modern home.
Mom was the best role model her kids could ever follow,
And she prayed her three grandchildren would know a better tomorrow.

Luella had a special gift granted from above.
She shared and cared for others. Dear Mama was pure love!
She was a Child of the King. No pretense! Her love was real,
And she was always calling folks. "It's Luella! How you feel?"

Mama lived a God-fearing life. Each day she counted dear.
Precious, golden memories will always hover near.
Now our beloved Mama is in a very special place.
We know she jumped and shouted when she met God, face to face.

"Lord, whatever I fail to ask, please Sir, don't fail to give,"
Were mama's words of wisdom and hand me downs to help us live.
She is dwelling in her mansion now where all is sweet and bright.
Mama! Big Mama! How we'll miss you! Enjoy yourself to the height!

Until we meet again, all my love, Sister

In loving memory of my mother, Luella Hawkins Phelps

Sunrise: October 1, 1915, Sunset: January 13, 1999

Forever My Elder

Let the elders that rule well be counted worthy of double honor, especially they who labor in the word and doctrine. (1 Tim 5:17).

Have you ever experienced the role of a Pastor, Bishop, or Elder's wife? When church is out, the Bishop is still in. So then, there are going to be days when it is of no use whatsoever to throw up your hands and say, time out! Give him a break! And while it is true that he is indeed your husband, there is one big catch. He is also married to the church. Not only did he receive his calling, but you too, First Lady. Now that is a challenge! Of course, all of life is none too soon for living it best and serving God in order to advance His purpose of kingdom building; however, even the leader of the flock must pear down, and steal away by the still waters every so often just to restore the soul fit for constant duty, and you too.

> Well! I'm not given to silence like a church house mouse.
> Here's a little poem for you, from your loving spouse.
> Sometimes things are trying dear, but I do understand.
> The role of an Elder's wife is yours to command.
>
> I guess it must have all been written in God's Plan.
> I love you as my Elder, my husband, and my man.
> Sometimes I'm given to complain with wifely idle chatter.
> I worry when you agonize over churchy matters.
>
> When duty calls for the Lord, the family is forsaken.
> Elder, **David Wilkins**, upholds the vows he's taken.
> Every day, in every way, your love for God grows wider.
> You're a devoted Elder, a wonderful husband, a loving father, and great provider.
>
> As presiding Elder and Presiding Elder of the St. Louis District; years add up to ten.
> If I had to make another choice, I would choose you again.
> For those who truly love the Lord, all things work out good.
> Dear, I would not change you, though sometimes, I wish I could.

In loving memory of Elder **David Wilkins**, husband of Cousin, **Edwena Wilkins**

How Far is that Light?

In my Father's house are many mansions. (John 14:2-3).

As my blind grandfather was making his heavenly transition upward to be caught up with the Lord, he asked his daughter-in-law at his bedside, "Lou! How far is that light?

How reassuring and comforting it is to know that while walking through the valley of the shadow of death, granddaddy, as he was fondly called, feared no evil, for the Light was with him. Granddaddy was the only grandparent I was privileged to know in my lifetime. He could not read, nor write, but attentively listened to the spoken words of God, understood, believed, and received salvation early on in his lifetime. Often betimes, I would awaken to hear him praising the Lord with a soul stirring hymn. His favorite grace at the dinner table was always "In my Father's house are many mansions." Like the well loved, down home spiritual, "Plenty Good Room in My Father's Kingdom," granddaddy knew that one day he would be heavenly blessed to choose his seat and sit down.

On October 17, 1976, God prepared a place for **Albert Phelps**, and came and received him unto Himself.

> When at last to venture
> Deep into the moonless night,
> The sun will rise in Jesus.
> Behold! He is the Light

Missing you! Love, Sister

I Cannot Promise You

Bear one another's burdens, and so fulfill the law of Christ. (Gal 6:2)

When we live in the spirit, we also walk in the spirit, and so we weep with those who weep, and moan with those who mourn. Comforting one another is what we as Fellow Believers are expected to do.

I cannot promise you that I can wipe away each tear,
But I can promise you that God is always near.
He shares in your sorrow, and He feels your grief and pain.
The loss of your dear daughter is surely heaven's gain.

I cannot promise you when the sky is overcast
Just when the storm will end, but I know it will not last.
For when the Lord speaks, He commands as He so wills,
And everything obeys Him. "Peace! Peace! Be still!"

I cannot promise you that you will not sadly miss
The child you held in your arms and greeted with a kiss.
But I can promise you that she is safe and warm.
She was ushered by the angels into her Keeper's arms.

I cannot promise you when the hurt will ease away.
But I can promise you that I will not forget to pray.
God Himself has promised to answer every prayer,
And will allow no burden beyond what we can bear.

I cannot promise you when heaven will unfold.
But I can promise you that there will be joy untold.
God in all His glory will ascend from up on high
And we will be reunited with our loved ones by and by.

In loving memory, of Charles and Juanita Tipton's precious daughter, **Monette Renee Tipton**

Sunrise, December 6, 1958, Sunset, June 1, 2004.

Laura's Love

Verily, verily, I say unto you, he that hears my word, and believes on Him that sent me has everlasting life, and shall not come into condemnation, but is passed from death unto life. (John 5:24).

Mine were the arms that held you when you were very small.
I cradled and protected you. Yes! I did it all!
Mine were the lips that kissed you before you fell asleep.
I taught you how to pray, and asked the Lord, your soul to keep.

Mine were the eyes that watched you when you went out to play.
You never left my sight whether night, or day.
Mine were the hands that touched yours when you needed help.
These same hands supported you when you took your first step.

Mine were the ears that heard your very first cry,
And as you grew, I listened to you, as the years passed by.
Mine was the heart that loved you more than you will ever know.
Yet I knew the day would come when I would have to go.

Oh! How the good Lord blessed me with longevity.
I witnessed generations added to the family tree.
Every mother's wish is to live and see her children grown.
What love for me in my lifetime, I have shared and known.

Although you may have lost me, I am heaven's gain.
So God's arms now will comfort you when tears fall like rain.
Eternal life has beckoned me unto the closing of my day.
Carry on and trust the Lord, for I have gone away.

The precious lips of Jesus will kiss your hurt away.
Remember when I did that? It was way back, many a day.
My time for earthly things, and such, is over, done, and through.
His eye beholds the sparrow, and He'll keep on watching you.

When you are feeling helpless, God will help you stand.
You can always count on Him to lend a helping hand.
God's ears will always hear you, so don't forget to pray.
My heart belongs to Jesus now; I'm absent, yet present with Him this day.

To all of my dear children, and my grandchildren too,
Smile when you think of me. Do not feel sad or blue.
I know that you will miss me, but I am high above.
A gift, I leave behind for you. Open it! It's **Laura's** love.

May the love I leave for you comfort you each day,
And live on in the hearts of loved ones dear, I pray.
No need to say goodbye, but I will say goodnight.
Come morning, we will meet again in the presence of the Light.

In loving memory of **Laura King** (2007)

'Movin Marvin'

Even a child is known by his deeds, whether what he does is pure, and right. (Prov. 20:11)

Marvin Anthony Winston, an eleven year old at the time, was diagnosed with a terminal form of cancer. He rarely, if ever complained about his weighted cross. Marvin simply trusted and depended on God to see him through it all. **'Movin Marvin'** as he was fondly called by his NYA Football team mates, skillfully maneuvered out on the football field, but his spiritual moves and ways of combating illness was, on a very large scale, absolutely amazing to all who came to know him, love him, and support the Winston family throughout the season of Marvin's cross bearing days. He consistently remained radiant, warm, and humorous. Marvin composed a song about his life, what it meant to him, and that his soul was set free.

After a courageous battle, at the innocent and tender age of 14 years, his soul was indeed set free, and on the wings of glory, the angels transported him safely as God received him unto Himself. Home at last! Marvin's Home going was celebrated on Thanksgiving Day, in the year of our Lord, 1984. As an NYA parent, I shall never fail to honor the memory of such an unforgettable, brave, young soldier of the cross.

The following poem was composed and shared with Marvin in 1982.

> I love snowy winters with sheets of scarlet white.
> I love the shining stars and moon off set against the night.
> I love the warmth of sunshine with its golden hue,
> But most of all **Marvin**, I love, I love, guess who?
>
> I love the heat of summer and the chill of cold ice cream.
> I love the flowing oceans and the rolling streams.
> I love the scented freshness of early morning dew.
> But most of all, **Marvin**, I love, I love, guess who?
>
> I love the scenic view of valleys, hills and plains.
> I love the sound of music and the splitter splash of rain.
> I love to play with children, and to myself be true.
> But most of all **Marvin**, I love, I love, guess who?

I love the way you move about even when you're tired.
I love your courage, and trusting faith that keeps us all inspired.
I love your will of iron, and belief to walk on through.
But most of all **Marvin**, I love, I love, guess who?

I love you, Marvin Winston! Yes! Indeed I do!
I love your shy, sweet, spirit and the little devil too.
We love you so much **Marvin**, but you know that it is true,
There is no greater love than the love God has for you.

In loving memory of Marvin Anthony Winston, May 1970-November 1984

My Young Hero

Greater love hath no man than this; that a man lay down his life for his friends. (John 15:13).

A very dear friend of mine's son, who was only a teenager at that time, was visiting a friend's home when suddenly, without warning, a fire ignited and raged uncontrollably. Surely, **Rose White's** son, **Chris**, could have very easily escaped from harm's way had he not decided to reenter the burning house in a courageous attempt to save some children who were helplessly trapped inside. But **Christopher** was moved with a compassionate spirit to do whatever possible to help those children to safety. What great and unselfish love was shown by such a young, Hero. It wasn't the fire that claimed his life, but God Himself.

Whenever we see his twin brother, **Paul**, we amazingly see Chris mirrored in his reflection. My daughter, Eva Marie, composed the following poem to honor his memory.

> There was not enough time
> To tell you how I feel.
> **Christopher**, dear friend of mine,
> My love for you is real.
>
> You tried your best to save those kids
> And rescue them from the fire.
> Not even thinking of your own life,
> You braved it all, as flames rose higher.
>
> We did not want to let you go,
> But it is very plain to see
> That God had a plan for you,
> And it was meant to be.
>
> **Chris**, it won't be very long
> Before we all must go,
> So keep a place up there for me.
> My brave, sweet, young, Hero!

Love always, your childhood friend, Eva Marie

Present!

So we are always confident, knowing that while we are at home in the body we are absent from the Lord. (2 Cor 5:6).

Remember how during school days the teacher would call the roll, and ask us to raise our hands to show that we were present? Well, God calls the roll in much the same manner, and when he does so, those who are absent from Him in the body become present when they respond to His beckoned call.

> I was so busily involved
> When an angel whispered in my ear,
> Call your friend, Omega,
> She is much in need of cheer.
>
> So I stopped what I was doing.
> I grabbed some paper, and a pen,
> And felt the Spirit of the Lord.
> My soul stirred deep down within.
>
> When you lose someone you love
> What words are there to say?
> Just know that when you read this
> Someone thought of you today.
>
> God has keys to many doors,
> And one unlocks eternity.
> Your sister is present with the Lord!
> What better company could there be?

In loving memory of your precious sister, **Gladys Webb**, now present with the Lord.

Recycled

As we have borne the image of the earthly, we shall also bear the image of the heavenly. (I Cor 15:49).

It was September 21, 1993, while gainfully employed on the job that I received some astounding news. With my stomach tied in knots, I immediately rushed to the hospital to be at my big brother's side. There was a 50/50 chance of survival, but I attempted to remain calm and reassuring. Mama said little, but with her head held high, straight posture, and warm smile, she was a very strong pillar of support to her son's wife, his son, me, and all who had come to encourage us, and possibly witness a miracle in the making. It happened! The double lung transplant was successful and Ordell recovered, returned to work at American Airlines, continued to serve as a Deacon at his church home, and walked around without the assistance of any oxygen. With a spirit of gratitude and thanksgiving, Dell cheerfully referred to himself as a recycled man who was reborn on September 21, 1993.

Years passed on by, and after many blessed, cancer free years, mama's breast cancer returned, and as Dell and I were in the doctor's office deeply concerned about mama's failing health, he quietly informed me of the fact that his borrowed lungs were finally beginning to reject their new owner. It is understandable that tears settled in my eyes, but be it fully understood that it is verifiable in scripture that God knows how much we can bear. Mama's courageous battle with cancer did not prevent her from praying for her son who was fighting his own battle yet again. Nor did it stop her from praying for each and every one of us. Mama was gloriously transformed into the angelic host on January 13, 1999. Soon after mama departed, once again, my brother resumed using the oxygen tank. Once again, like with my mom, God tapped me on the shoulder. I dreamed that Dell was leaning on crutches before a flowing fountain. All of a sudden, when I looked again, he was happily running around without the assistance of crutches, or oxygen. Then I saw a white building, and Ordell looked at me and said, "Sister! I'm going to see daddy!" When I awoke from the dream I thought to myself, "Daddy passed away, July 31, 1972." On Sunday, November 19, 2000, Dell's beeper sounded off, and a second attempt was made to recycle him yet again, but God said, "Enough is enough!" So it came as no surprise to me when the angels transported my only sibling to glory land on November 21, 2000. I honored my brother's memory with the following poem, 'A Conversation with God' at his Home going Service.

"Hello God! It's me! Here I am again!
My beeper sounded for surgery. I'm so glad, YOU are my Friend.
I felt your presence ever near that very first time around.
YOU blessed me through my first transplant. What an anchor in YOU, I found."

"Hello back! I hear you my child, and please know, Ordell,
Although you must go through again, all will work out well.
As a double lung recipient, I added years onto your life,
And with that new leased energy, you faithfully served with vigor and spice.

You made a difference at church, at home, and everywhere you went.
The extra years tacked on have all been well spent.
As a Co-worker, you touched lives of those you worked with on the job.
They marveled at the miracle of a recycled man of God.

What a caring husband, loving father, wonderful son, and brother too.
You were voted favorite uncle of the entire family crew.
And while your little sister was always a worrisome little brat,
She could always count on you to show up at the drop of a hat!

There was never time enough to relax or occupy a perch,
For you were gainfully employed at Trinity Mount Carmel Baptist Church.
Let not your heart be troubled to be caught up in the air.
I will sustain you! Come! Let me take you there!

Don't worry about your loved ones. You must leave them behind.
Soon they will join you as time continues to unwind.
Of course, you will be dearly missed, but I can fill the void.
Heaven heals all earthly grief. Ordell, I AM the Lord!

Your daddy's waiting for you, granddaddy, and mama too,
And through the shadowed valley of death, I will accompany you.
So come now unto me, dear child. Lay your head upon my breast.
Well done! Faithful Servant! Come on home, and rest!"

In loving memory, of my brother, Ordell Phelps

Sunrise: December 11, 1943, Sunset: November 21, 2000

Roses Are Forever

I am the resurrection, and the life, he who believes in me, though he may die, he shall live. (John 11:25-26).

Once there was a thriving rose.
Suddenly! Came the onset of night, and bitter frost,
And then the earthly flower drooped, and lowered its head,
And folded its petals as though it were dead, and so it seemed all hope was lost.

Amazingly! All at once!
There appeared an all-consuming glorious light.
It shone upon the withered rose, and gave it warmth,
And tender care all throughout the night.

Morning came, and the wilted flower
Proudly raised up its head,
For those who are asleep in Christ
Awake and are not dead.

What a wondrous celebration,
And victorious resurrection to behold
When reborn, heavenly flowers commandingly unfold
At just a touch of the Gardener's hand in that celestial forever land.

Bloom on! Annie Mildred,
For a brand new day is dawning.
Goodnight! Oh! Precious Rose of God!
We will meet you in the morning.

In loving memory of Mrs. Annie Mildred Outlaw Bush
Sunrise: July 7, 1922, Sunset: January 16, 1998

That's When I'll Think of Lou

Happy is the man who finds wisdom, and the man who gains understanding. (Prov 3:13).

Life's chief values and character are often handed down to us by grandparents. There is a saying that goes as follows: If you want to know what's down the road, ask someone who is coming back. Been there! Done that!

Most African Americans have had, or will have someone in their lifetime called Babe, Nana, Ma Dear, G.G., or Big Mama. My son, Kevin, chose to honor the memory of his grandmother, fondly called Big Mama, with the following poem.

> When darkness falls from Heaven's Eye;
> When I hear my new born baby's cry;
> When my Savior and Lord descends from on high;
> That's When I'll Think of Lou!
>
> When rain falls from up above;
> When my spirit rises like a dove;
> When I'm full of lots of love;
> That's When I'll Think of Lou!
>
> When I read the Master's Word,
> In meditation, a voice is heard.
> "Stay strong! He is worthy in whom you serve!"
> That's When I'll Think of Lou!
>
> When hearts are lifted, and fear is gone;
> When voices praise with Heaven's Song;
> When all is right! And nothing is wrong!
> That's When I'll Think of Lou!
>
> When children laugh with joyous glee;
> When leaves fall softly from a tree;
> When my own son sits upon my knee;
> That's When I'll Think of Lou!

When I'm sad, and I'm feeling down;
When my lip drags upon the ground;
But I wear a smile, instead of a frown;
That's When I'll Think of Lou!

When darkness looms in the dead of night;
When demons shriek, and roar with fright;
With His blood, I stand fearless, whatever the plight;
That's When I'll Think of Lou!

When I grow older, and my life is spent;
Whether I'm rich, or have not one cent;
I'll thank the Lord for His grace to repent.
That's When I'll Think of Lou!

Big Mama! Thank you for the wisdom and precious memories!
        Love, Your grandson, Kevin

In loving memory of Luella Hawkins Phelps, October 1, 1915-January 13, 1999

Tour of Duty Ended

I have fought a good fight. (2 Tim.4:7).

I saw every wound and battle scar that you sustained during the war.
You stood your ground and fought well. The enemy did not prevail.
Although you were under attack, not even once did you look back.
You pressed on with marching feet. A soldier of God does not retreat.

When you were cold, I kept you warm. I sheltered you throughout the storm.
Wearing the whole armor of God, shielded you on enemy sod.
When you hungered, I was your bread, and so your famished soul was fed.
When you thirsted, I gave you water. It was no illusion.
When you bled, it was My Blood that gave you a transfusion.

Now the time has finally come. The war is over! The day is done!
These orders are too good to miss. Come! Partake of heaven's bliss.
No more hardship, stress or strain. No more illness. No more pain.
No! This is not a furlough thing. Curtis! Salute the reigning King!

Lay down your trumpet, sword and shield, and come on off the battlefield.
You have claimed the victory. So now inherit eternity.
Move on up to higher ground. Soldier! You are heaven bound.
Active duty, time served! Depart the earthly scene. Tour of duty ended! Receive your DD214!

Your house is in order, so soldier time to go.
Your earthly eyes have dimmed, and your footsteps have grown slow.
Yes! Tour of duty ended! Weep not for those around the throne.
Just another soldier made his journey home.

In loving memory of Curtis Bush Senior
Sunrise December 13, 1920, Sunset November 29, 2008